Martin Buber's Journey to Presence

The Abrahamic Dialogues Series
David B. Burrell, series editor

Donald Moore, *Martin Buber: Prophet of Religious Secularism*

James L. Heft, ed., *Beyond Violence: Religious Sources of Social Transformation in Judaism, Christianity, and Islam*

Rusmir Mahmutćehajić, *Learning from Bosnia: Approaching Tradition*

Rusmir Mahmutćehajić, *The Mosque: The Heart of Submission*

Alain Marchadour and David Neuhaus, *The Land, the Bible, and History: Toward the Land That I Will Show You*

James L. Heft, ed., *Passing on the Faith: Transforming Traditions for the Next Generation of Jews, Christians, and Muslims*

Rusmir Mahmutćehajić, *On Love: In the Muslim Tradition*

Martin Buber's Journey to Presence

Phil Huston

Fordham University Press
New York   2007

The Abrahamic Dialogues Series, No. 7
ISSN 1548–4130

Library of Congress Cataloging-in-Publication Data

  Huston, Phil.
    Martin Buber's journey to presence / Phil Huston.—1st ed.
      p.   cm.—(The Abrahamic dialogues series, ISSN 1548-
  4130 ; no. 7)
    Includes bibliographical references.
    ISBN-13: 978-0-8232-2739-6 (cloth : alk. paper)
    ISBN-10: 0-8232-2739-1 (cloth : alk. paper)
    1. Buber, Martin, 1878–1965.   2. Presence of God.   3. God
  (Judaism)   I. Title.
  B3213.B84H87   2007
  181'.06—dc22
                                                    2007014121

Printed in the United States of America
09   08   07   5   4   3   2   1
First edition

Contents

Acknowledgments

I wish to record my sincere gratitude to the late Dr. Gerald Hanratty, University College Dublin, for his help in the preparation of this work. His advice and careful correction of drafts were invaluable. I also wish to thank Dr. Brendan Purcell for his very helpful comments.

I visited the Martin Buber Archives in the Jewish National and University Library while on a trip to Jerusalem in 1999. I was delighted to meet the Director of the Archives, Ms. Margot Cohn, who was Buber's personal secretary from 1957 until his death in 1965. I have since addressed many requests for archival material to Ms. Cohn and am indebted to her for her pleasant and efficient replies.

On my journey to an appreciation of Buber's philosophy, I have been fortunate to meet other philosophers who shared my passion and were very encouraging. In particular, I wish to express my gratitude to Dr. Donald Moore, Fordham University; the late Dr. Daniel Murphy of Trinity College Dublin; and Dr. Marie Neiers.

Finally, my deepest gratitude is to my family: Brian, Ian, Paul, and Anne and friends Irene Fitzpatrick, Bill Mathews, Marian McCluskey, and Des O'Grady for their presence on the journey and their unfailing encouragement and support.

Introduction

This work began with a question: What is meant by Buber's statement in *I and Thou* that the one thing needful is full acceptance of presence? Having studied *I and Thou* I then examined the "Religion as Presence" Lectures, which Buber gave in 1922, before *I and Thou* was published. These lectures, which are not widely known, form the basis for *I and Thou*. In particular they develop an understanding of presence that leads to an appreciation of God as Presence. This understanding of presence is the key to *I and Thou*. But they are also very critical of Buber's own previous writings. The first three lectures, one could say, look backward and correct Buber's previous views, sometimes explicitly but mostly implicitly. The remaining five lectures look forward to *I and Thou*. Buber's previous philosophical work was *Daniel: Dialogues on Realization*, which was published in 1913. I decided this was the text that had to be examined in order to understand and come to a judgment on Buber's mature philosophy. This work was influenced by Buber's intellectual and existential journey from childhood to 1913. Buber's journey is a movement from absence to presence. More precisely, it is a movement toward an appreciation of the paradox of the absence in presence. Buber pointed to this paradox when he wrote: "I have always guarded myself against the simplification practised by the 'dialectical theology' that God is Wholly Other. One may only so name Him when in the same breath one knows and confesses that he is the not-other, the here, the now, the mine."[1] Buber's desire for an Eternal Thou begins with the overwhelming experience of a Thou who became (almost permanently) absent to him: the absence of his mother from the time he was three years old. The experience of absence is also evident in Buber's comment on his early years in university, when he lived "without Judaism, without humanity, and without the presence of the divine."[2]

A significant turning point in Buber's journey was his reading of the testament of Rabbi Israel Baal-Shem—the *Zevaat Ribesh*.[3] Buber later commented on this experience:

> The primally Jewish opened to me, flowering to newly conscious expression in the darkness of exile: man's being created in the image of God I grasped as deed, as becoming, as task. And this primally Jewish reality was a primal human reality, the content of human religiousness. Judasim as religiousness, as "piety," as *Hasidut* opened to me there.[4]

Buber added that he accepted this document of Rabbi Baal-Shem in the spirit of Hasidic enthusiasm. He described himself as a result of this experience as a Polish Jew.[5] Buber attempted to bring his study of Hasidism, of Christian mysticism, and of Taoism together in his first philosophical text. Schaeder writes, "In *Daniel* we have the adumbration of an East-West synthesis and the unexpressed implication of the mediating role of Judaism between the Orient and the Occident."[6]

My aim is to arrive at an understanding of Buber's concept of God in 1913 when *Daniel* was first published. This is prior to his "conversion" or transformation during the period of the First World War. It is well known that after the war Buber began to develop his understanding of the "I–Thou" and "I–It" relations. In *I and Thou* his concept of God is that of the Eternal Thou who is always present to us.

Presence is a controversial topic among philosophers today. Ralph Harper writes: "In the past, presence was a religious and personal theme above all, not a theme for philosophy. But today, at a time when presence is dogmatically denied by some philosophers and literary critics, there is a wealth of example and speculation to draw on. This is, therefore, the right time to write seriously about presence."[7]

George Steiner begins his book *Real Presences* by writing:

> We speak still of 'sunrise' and 'sunset.' We do so as if the Copernican model of the solar system had not replaced, ineradicably, the Ptolemaic. Vacant metaphors, eroded figures of speech, inhabit our vocabulary and grammar. They are caught, tenaciously,

in the scaffolding and recesses of our common parlance; there they rattle about like old rags or ghosts in the attic.

This is the reason why rational men and women, particularly in the scientific and technological realities of the west, still refer to 'God'. This is why the postulate of the existence of God persists in so many unconsidered turns of phrase and allusion. No plausible reflection or belief underwrites His presence. Nor does any intelligible evidence. Where God clings to our culture, to our routines of discourse, He is a phantom of grammar, a fossil embedded in the childhood of rational speech. So Nietzsche (and many after him).

This essay argues the reverse.[8]

Buber also argues the reverse. But his early writings could represent the other side of the argument. In these, Buber focuses on his quest for unity and fails to appreciate presence, either self-presence or the presence of another being, human or divine. Derrida may be quoted as the chief proponent of the postmodern critique of the metaphysics of presence. He argues that Nietzsche as well as Heidegger and Freud worked within the inherited concepts of metaphysics.[9] According to Derrida, these concepts are the center and ground of the history of metaphysics:

> The history of metaphysics, like the history of the West, is the history of these metaphors and metonymies. Its matrix . . . is the determination of Being as *presence* in all senses of this word. It could be shown that all the names related to fundamentals, to principles, or to the center have always designated an invariable presence—*eidos, arche, telos, energeia, ousia* (essence, existence, substance, subject) *aletheia*, transcendentality, consciousness, God, man, and so forth.[10]

Derrida argues that the history of metaphysics is dominated by a "presumption of and orientation towards an absolute *logos*."[11] The history of philosophy has assumed an "eternal, creative subjectivity, the source of all truth and being, the absolute *logos*, the ultimate presence. The presence of an absolute *logos* is not only presumed, it constitutes the ultimate object of desire."[12] Morelli recognizes that Derrida aims to expose an "exigent, powerful, systematic, and irrepressible desire for such a signified [an absolute transcendent presence]" as corrupting the history of philosophy.[13] Martin Buber, I believe, was motivated by such a desire. I will argue that it was the absence of presence that corrupted his early philosophy. Buber's search is for a presence that will not let him down, that will not be a "mis-encounter"—i.e., for a presence "by means of which we are told that nevertheless there is meaning."[14]

In tracing Buber's movement from a failure to appreciate presence to the wonderful exploration of presence in *I and Thou* I will follow a particular line of inquiry that needs to be defined more exactly. When asked what was the core of his life's work, Buber answered:

> If I myself should designate something as the "central portion of my life work," then it could not be anything individual, but only the one basic insight that has led me not only to the study of the Bible, as to the study of Hasidism, but also to an independent philosophical presentation: that the I-Thou relation to God and the I-Thou relation to one's fellow man are at bottom related to each other. This being related to each other is—if I may retain the expression—the central portion of the dialogical reality that has ever more disclosed itself to me.[15]

Some confusion exists in explorations of Buber's writings on his position on the transcendence and immanence of God. For example, Grete Schaeder writes: "The titanic features we find in *Daniel* are compensated for by Buber's remarkable naiveté. His mystical experience is meant to realise God, but it fails to see that this is the path that leads to the deification of man, which was the prevalent view in his day."[16]

However, Friedman, writing of Buber's attempt to reach Kantian "reality" in his pre-dialogical philosophy of realization, claims: "Buber found this reality through perceiving that in addition to man's orienting function he also possesses a 'realizing' function which brings him into real contact with God, with other men, and with nature."[17] Friedman's mention of this "real contact" suggests that Buber was already writing of confrontation, relation, and presence in *Daniel: Dialogues on Realization.* However, it is clear from the early German text, though not from Friedman's English translation of this text, that identification of oneself as the divine rather than relation with the divine is primary in *Daniel.* I will draw the reader's attention in particular to the apposite sentence "This I is the unconditioned," which was omitted from the English translation.

Paul Mendes-Flohr writes: "A full discussion of the pre-dialogue Buber's conception of God is a desideratum. Whatever conception he may have had, it was definitely not theistic; there is even evidence that he was a non-believer."[18] This work is a contribution to this discussion.

I begin with an account of Buber's childhood. Following this, there is a consideration of Buber's early writings in which there is a denial of the presence of God but an acceptance of Nietzsche's concept of a "becoming God." An examination of Buber's essay on Jacob Boehme is central here as Boehme continued to exercise a great influence on Buber's writings. Buber's early mystical phase included the publication of a number of articles, addresses, and books on Hasidism, Judaism, Taoism, and ecstatic experiences. I will consider a number of the relevant texts. The examination of the concept of God in *Daniel* represents the major part of the work. Having reached a conclusion on the concept of God, in a final chapter I will turn to a brief consideration of Buber's "Religion as Presence" Lectures. Attention will be drawn to the points on which Buber disagrees with his previous understanding of God and His presence.

This work is a contribution that I hope will enable a deeper appreciation of Buber's mature writings on the presence of the Eternal Thou. The clarification of Buber's early concept of God will establish a position against which his more mature understanding may be contrasted and as a result the latter will become more distinct. Acceptance of God as the Eternal Thou is as important today as it was in 1945 when Buber wrote:

"And it would seem to me, indeed, that in this hour of history the crucial thing is not to possess a fixed doctrine, but rather to recognize eternal reality and out of its depth to be able to face the reality of the present."[19]

NOTES

1. Martin Buber, "Replies to my Critics," in *The Philosophy of Martin Buber*, ed. P. A. Schilpp and M. Friedman (La Salle, Ill.: Open Court, 1967), 712.

2. Martin Buber, "My Way to Hasidism," in *Hasidism and Modern Man* (Atlantic Highlands, N.J.: Humanities Press, 1988) 49.

3. Ibid., 51. An alternative spelling is *Tzava'at HaRibesh*.

4. Ibid., 51.

5. Martin Buber, foreword to *For the Sake of Heaven* (New York: Harper & Row, 1966), xii.

6. Grete Schaeder, *The Hebrew Humanism of Martin Buber*, trans. Noah J. Jacobs (Detroit: Wayne State University Press, 1973) 121.

7. Ralph Harper, *On Presence, Variations and Reflections* (Philadelphia: Trinity Press, 1991), ix.

8. George Steiner, *Real Presences* (Chicago: University of Chicago Press, 1989), 3.

9. Jacques Derrida, "Structure, Sign, and Play in the Discourse of the Human Sciences," in *Writing and Difference*, trans. Alan Bass (London: Routledge & Kegan Paul, 1978), 281.

10. Ibid., 279–80.

11. Elizabeth Murray Morelli, "Oversight of Insight and the Critique of the Metaphysics of Presence," in *Method: Journal of Lonergan Studies*, 18 (2000): 8. I wish to thank Des O'Grady, S.J., for drawing this article to my attention.

12. Ibid.

13. Ibid., 8.

14. Martin Buber, *Between Man and Man* (New York: Collier, 1965), 14.

15. Martin Buber, Answer given in discussion; see Sydney Rome and Beatrice Rome, *Philosophical Interrogations* (New York: Holt, Rinehart & Winston, 1964), 99–100.

16. Schaeder, *The Hebrew Humanism of Martin Buber*, 24.

17. Maurice Friedman, *Martin Buber: The Life of Dialogue* (Chicago: University of Chicago Press, 1956), 34.

18. Paul Mendes-Flohr, *From Mysticism to Dialogue: Martin Buber's Transformation of German Social Thought* (Detroit: Wayne State University Press, 1989) 165, n321.

19. Buber, 'Foreword' to *For the Sake of Heaven*, xiii.

Martin Buber's Journey to Presence

1. Childhood

Early Childhood and Family

Martin Buber was born on 8 February 1878 in Vienna. His parents, Carl Buber (1848–1935) and Elise (née Wurgast), lived in a house over the Danube. Martin was the only child of their marriage. He recalls that as a small child he enjoyed watching the Danube canal under the house with a feeling of certainty that nothing could happen to him. However, the separation of his parents when he was three years old "broke up" the home of his childhood.[1]

His mother left the family home without leaving a trace;[2] Buber's daughter informs us that she had in fact eloped with her lover.[3] Young Martin was brought to live in the home of his wealthy paternal grand-parents on their large estate near Lvov (Lemberg), then the capital city of the Austrian "crownland," Galicia.[4] Buber lived here with his grand-parents until he was fourteen, although he began visiting his father's estate for the summer each year from about his ninth year.[5] His father, Carl, remarried, and when fourteen, Buber moved to live in his father's townhouse. His relationship with his stepmother was distant.[6] Two daughters were born to Carl and his second wife: Nelly (1886–1972),[7] who was only eight years younger than Martin, and Irene.[8] When he returned to live in his father's house at the age of fourteen, Martin must have had some experience of family life with his half-sisters. Nelly in particular remembered his birthday each year and wrote a warm letter for his fiftieth birthday expressing how little they knew about each other, but how his writings influenced her life.[9] In this letter, Nelly also speaks of the love and tenderness of Carl, their father, for Martin. His son was Carl's favorite topic of conversation, according to Nelly, and he delighted in any news of him and his family.

Very little is written about Buber's mother. Her maiden name is simply given in a caption with her photograph in Friedman's biography of Buber.[10] Through correspondence with Margot Cohn, Director of the Martin Buber Archives in Jerusalem, I have discovered that when Elise Buber remarried, her married name was Elise Brick.[11] In this second marriage, Elise had two daughters, Sonia and Lilly, and a son, Nicholas. Elise was in contact with Martin through six letters, written in German gothic, or black-letter, handwriting, dating from 1909 to 1914.[12] In these, she invites Martin to his half-brother's wedding. Although it appears that Buber did not attend the wedding, he wrote offering his congratulations. His mother wrote that she was very happy that the wedding brought them closer, and she expressed the wish to very soon personally get to know and love him and his family. According to his "Autobiographical Fragments," Buber met his mother thirty years after he was told that she would not return, in about 1912.[13] In 1913, Elise Brick wrote from Meran, a health resort on the Italian border, where she brought her daughter Lilly for health reasons, and mentioned that she looked forward to seeing him again in Berlin. In 1914, Buber's mother invited him and his wife Paula to the wedding of his half-sister Sonia on 23 March. Sonia wrote warm friendly letters to Martin in French, four of which are in the Archives. These letters show her delight in photographs that he sent of his two children, Rafael and Eva. Sonia mentions her legal studies and also invites him to her wedding.

BUBER'S GRANDPARENTS

Adele and Salomon Buber were described by Martin, their beloved grandson, as "both people of high rank, noble persons in the exact sense of the term and, in a special manner, suited to and supplementing each other."[14] They were not inclined toward openness or intimacy in their conversations and did not explain or talk to the young child about his parents. "Of what had taken place between my parents, nothing, of course, was spoken in my presence; but I suspect that it was also hardly ever a subject of discussion between them, except in practical and unavoidable connection. The child itself expected to see its mother again soon; but no question passed its lips."[15]

The reticence that Buber experienced as a child continued in his relationship with his own granddaughters, who lived with him and his wife, when their parents, Buber's son Rafael and his wife, were divorced. Although they lived with Buber from the late 1920s, it was only after Paula died in 1958 that Buber spoke seriously about the reason they grew up in his house. At that time, Buber was surprised that one of his granddaughters, Judith, explained that she had a very good relationship with her mother. He commented that his own mother had never been a mother to him. Judith pointed out that her case was significantly different to his because her mother never gave up her children willingly, as Buber's mother had done. However, the actions of Buber's mother's had led to his parents' divorce, and as a result, Judith assumed, she had few rights.[16]

The disappearance of his mother had a depressing effect on Martin who, Friedman reports, bore signs of mourning and bereavement throughout his childhood. Ernst Simon has described his personality as being characterized by pathos.[17] In a letter to his friend Franz Rosenzweig concerning the use of a Psalm at the commencement of a course of lectures, Buber said: "For me, the psalms have always kept that sense of physical intimacy they had in my childhood (a motherless childhood, but one spent dreaming of my living but inaccessibly remote mother): 'You have put friend and neighbour far from me'" (Psalm 88:19).[18]

Something inside the lonely little boy waiting to see his mother again was crushed on the day that he realised that his mother would not return. The crucial event for the understanding of Buber's intellectual quest happened in his fourth year. Buber describes it in his autobiographical fragments, published in 1967, as follows:

> The house in which my grandparents lived had a great rectangular inner courtyard surrounded by a wooden balcony extending to the roof on which one could walk around the building at each floor. Here I stood once in my fourth year with a girl several years older, the daughter of a neighbour, to whose care my grandmother had entrusted me. We both leaned on the railing. I cannot remember that I spoke of my mother to my older comrade. But I hear still how the big girl said to me: "No, she will never come back." I know that I remained silent, but also that I cherished no doubt of the truth of the spoken words. It remained fixed in me; from year to year it cleaved ever more to my heart, but after more

than ten years I had begun to perceive it as something that concerned not only me, but all men. Later I once made up the word "*Vergegnung*"—"mismeeting" or "miscounter"—to designate the failure of a real meeting between men. When after another twenty years I again saw my mother, who had come from a distance to visit me, my wife, and my children, I could not gaze into her still astonishingly beautiful eyes without hearing from somewhere the word "*Vergegnung*" as a word spoken to me. I suspect that all that I have learned about the genuine meeting in the course of my life had its first origin in that hour on the balcony.[19]

Buber explained to Aubrey Hodes: "I wanted to see my mother. And the impossibility of this gave me an infinite sense of deprivation and loss. Do you understand? Something had broken down."[20] Grete Schaeder writes that "Buber was convinced that his personal 'trauma' was intimately bound up with the creative center of his being."[21] Schaeder, who became a friend of Buber during the years 1961–65, was aware that he was always sensitive to the "sparks of interrelationships and was never so insulated against them that his trauma would fail to be aroused in an encounter."[22]

Buber's grandmother Adele (née Wizer) was the daughter of the wealthy owner of a paper factory in Sasov, a small Galician town. Buber writes that among the Jews in this town the reading of "alien" literature was proscribed. Indeed, for the girls, the reading of all literature with the exception of edifying popular books was regarded as "unseemly."[23] However, when fifteen years of age, Adele kept secretly in a storehouse copies of Schiller's periodical *Die Horen*; Jean Paul's book on education, *Levana*; and many other German books that she had read. She continued this habit of concentrated reading after her marriage to Salomon Buber in her seventeenth year. She brought up her two sons, Carl (Buber's father) and Rafael (Buber's uncle) and Buber himself with a "respect for the authentic word that cannot be paraphrased."[24] Buber still had her copy of Jean Paul's *Levana* in 1961.[25] Paul's contemporary, Schiller, also influenced some of Buber's early writings. The influence of Schiller we will discover in some of his early writings.

Adele Buber looked after the business affairs of her husband; each day she would record income and expenditures. Buber noticed that she would record not only passages that had become important to her from her readings, but also her own comments as part of a dialogue with the great classical authors. He also noticed that she seemed to listen when meditating. It was unmistakable as well, to even the small child, that when she addressed people, she focused her full attention on them.[26]

Buber writes that his grandfather was a true philologist, a "lover of the word," but his grandmother's love for the genuine word was a more important influence because this love was so direct and so devoted.[27] Schaeder comments that Buber was impressed "by her pithy and splendid command of German which she guarded like a treasure." Adele Buber's easy familiarity with classical German, Schaeder writes, was reflected in her speech.[28]

Adele and Salomon Buber tried to keep in contact with their grandson during his student days and his early married life. At times, however, their efforts were not quite appreciated by Martin. He wrote in December 1899 that he always received complaints when what he needed was encouragement. In this letter, he said that he had a great deal of hard work, some of which was as a result of his election as secretary of the Zionist Association in Berlin. He commented that he was always asked about his grandfather when he met Zionists.[29] In some letters, Adele Buber addressed Martin as "Infinitely beloved Grandson," expressed delight at receiving a photograph of his children, and inquired as to whether he was in debt again. She also kept her grandson informed on the lives of his two half-sisters.[30] Gordon mentions that it was Adele who managed to mend a rift that had arisen between Martin and his family, as they seemed to have been unhappy that he married Paula, who had converted from Catholicism to Judaism.[31] In 1905, Adele treated Buber, Paula, and their two children to a year-long vacation in Italy. In the last published letter from Adele, she addresses Martin and Paula as "My infinitely dear ones" and writes that a reunion with them is the "summit of my wishes." When Adele Buber died in 1911, Buber attended her funeral.

Buber's grandfather was a great landowner, a corn merchant, an owner of phosphate mines, and at least one oil field in the East Carpathians.[32] He was a leading member of the Jewish community, a director of two banks, and a member of the town's chamber of commerce. Free from the daily running of his business interests, Salomon Buber devoted himself to scholarship and the study of the Torah. Although self-taught, "he was a genuine philologist who is to be thanked for the first,

and today still the authoritative, critical edition of a special class of Hebrew literature: the Midrashim—a unique mixture of interpretation of
the bible, wise sayings, and rich saga," wrote Buber in 1963.[33] In a letter to his grandfather to congratulate him on his seventy-third birthday,
Buber wrote: "When I think of his dear face, I have trouble fighting
back the tears—tears of warmest reverence. . . . The unflagging and
undivided quality of your creative work has often guided me back to
myself from the bad path of incoherence. . . . You are a close and inspiring example."[34] Salomon Buber died in 1906.

Aubrey Hodes reports from his conversations with Buber that the
atmosphere in his grandparents' home was one of piety and learning,
with a strong emphasis on the Jewish tradition. However, his grandparents were also familiar with the works of Kant and Goethe. Buber
grew up reading the prose and poetry of Heine, Schiller, and other German authors, as well as studying the Bible and the Talmud.[35] It was a
wealthy household in terms of affluence and learning.

CARL BUBER

Buber portrays the influence of his father on his intellectual development as of a different kind to that of his grandparents. Rather than being
an intellectual influence, it was his father's relation to nature, and to
other people, and his ability as an "elemental storyteller" that impressed the young Martin.[36] All these paternal influences are visible in
Buber's philosophical writings and his own recounting of the Hasidic
tales. On visits to his father's estate, the serious young boy observed
the interaction of his father with his horses and his enlightened attitude
to agriculture. He remembers that his father carried a packing case of
breeding eggs of a type of hen, foreign to that part of Europe, on his
knees during the long train journey from the International Exhibition in
Paris (1889). Accompanying his father as he drove through the fields,
the growing boy learned something that he had not learned from any of
the many authors that he read: "This wholly unsentimental and wholly
unromantic man was concerned about genuine human contact with nature, an active and responsible contact."[37]

In his father's relations with the labourers and tenants on the estate,
Martin noticed solicitude in the sense of active responsibility. Carl
Buber was concerned with the upbringing and schooling of the labour-
ers' children and with their health: "all that was not derived from any

principles. It was solicitude not in the ordinary, but in the personal sense, in the sense of active responsible contact that could rise here to full reciprocity."[38] In the town of Lemberg, where Carl Buber's house overlooked the Parliament Square, he had a personal concern for the people and was opposed to "sightless charity." In his old age, when elected to the "bread commission,"he attempted to ascertain the wants and necessities of each family.[39]

When Buber was eleven, he loved to visit a favorite dapple-gray horse in his grandparents' stables. Unobserved, he would stroke the neck of this horse, which he describes as a deeply stirring experience: "I must say that what I experienced in touch with the animal was the Other, the immense otherness of the Other, which, however, did not remain strange like the otherness of the ox and the ram, but rather let me draw near and touch it."[40] He felt that the horse "placed itself elementally in the relation of *Thou* and *Thou* with me."[41]

On one occasion, however, when Martin was conscious of enjoying the experience and failed to be totally present to the horse, he felt as if the horse noticed the difference. At the time, the sensitive boy considered himself judged when the animal failed to respond. Later, he no longer supposed that the horse had noticed the shift in his attitude.

EDUCATION

Until he was ten years of age, Buber was educated in his grandparents' home. "I received private tutoring, chiefly in languages, both because of my own inclination and talents and because for my grandmother a language-centered humanism was the royal road to education." German was the spoken language in his grandparents' house, but Polish was spoken in the street and in the school Martin would attend. Yiddish was the language of the Jewish quarter, and Hebrew was the language of the synagogue. As well as acquiring knowledge of these languages, Martin studied French. This enabled him to help his grandfather understand French phrases used in commentaries on Hebrew texts. Buber also learned Latin and Greek. Friedman comments that his favorite language as a child was Greek, a thorough reading of Plato being the foundation of his philosophical education.[42] Buber had a gift for languages, later adding Italian, English, Dutch, and Spanish to his repertory.

Buber also noted the different ways in which speakers and listeners appropriated the meanings of words:

The multiplicity of human languages, their wonderful variety in which the white light of human speech at once fragmented and preserved itself, was already at the time of my boyhood a problem that instructed me ever anew. In instructing me it also again and again disquieted me. I followed time after time an individual word or even structure of words from one language to another, found it there again and yet had time after time to give up something there as lost that apparently only existed in a single one of all the languages. That was not merely "nuances of meaning": I devised for myself two-language conversations between a German and a Frenchman, later between a Hebrew and an ancient Roman and came ever again, half in play and yet at times with a beating heart, to feel the tension between what was heard by the one and what was heard by the other, from his thinking in another language. That had a deep influence on me and has issued in a long life into ever-clearer insight.[43]

"The problem of the One and the Many—the need of a dialogic relationship" as Schaeder points out, was beginning to disturb him.[44] The questions and problems of the future translator were also becoming clear. Along the difficult path that led from helping his grandfather to his famous translation of the Bible, "he was guided by a deep fidelity to the precise inner truth that dwells in the living word."[45] In his insight into the tension between the two sides of a dialogue, the emergence of Buber's concern with experiencing the other side of a relation may be found. This is also present in a memory of a descent to the edge of a meadow (probably after a walk on a mountain), when he stood in the twilight. He pressed his walking stick against the trunk of an oak tree, "then I felt in twofold fashion my contact with being: here, where I held the stick, and there, where it touched the bark. Apparently only where I was, I nonetheless found myself there too where I found the tree."[46]

SCHOOL

Between the ages of ten and eighteen, Buber attended "Franz Josef's Gymnasium." This was a school not only attended mostly by Polish children, but also by a small Jewish minority. The atmosphere, Buber remarks, was one of mutual tolerance without mutual understanding.

There was no perceptible animosity toward the Jewish children, and the teachers were tolerant. However, Buber found the obligatory participation in morning prayers more hurtful than any act of intolerance. While the Christian children were praying, the Jewish children had to stand: "Compulsory guests, having to participate as a thing in a sacral event in which no dram of my person could or would take part, and this for eight long years morning after morning: that stamped itself upon the life substance of the boy."[47] Buber admits that no attempt was ever made to convert any of the Jewish pupils, but he grounds his antipathy to all missionary activity on this experience.

It is with some surprise then that one reads Buber's statement in a conversation with Aubrey Hodes: "I would like to convert you to Judaism."[48] When Hodes expressed his astonishment, Buber explained: "When I say Judaism I mean the kind of Judaism I believe in, which I call Hebrew humanism." This assertion of Buber's encompasses the decisive role of the Bible and the aim of transforming both the inner and outer life of the whole person and community in the light of the eternal values.[49] Buber's philosophy is concerned with each person being responsible, becoming truly human, and these goals are attainable through the forging of genuine relationships between people in social action rather than through the rigid observance of rules.

The problem of personal responsibility arises from an experience that Buber had at school prior to his twelfth birthday.[50] It was a wet autumn, and the pupils were obliged because of the weather to remain in the classroom rather than entertain themselves in the schoolyard. Two of the boys began acting as mimics to entertain the others. After a while, the game took on an unmistakably sexual character. "Now the faces of the two looked, I imagined, as souls in the pains of hell, about which some of my fellow pupils knew enough to report to me in the tone of experts." The other boys looked on at the cruelly forced movements, but did not discuss them among themselves. A few weeks later, the school director called the young Buber to his office. He was received with the director's customary gentle friendliness and asked what he knew of the activities of the two boys. Buber screamed, "I know nothing." Then the director spoke gently: "We know you well, you are a good child, you will help us." Buber felt like saying, "Help? Help whom?" Instead, he remained silent. He writes that "a great weeping as never before overcame me, and I was led away almost unconscious." Later, when he remembered the last look of the director, it was that of a frightened rather than a relaxed or gentle person. He was kept at home for a few days and then returned to school. The bench occupied by the two mimics remained empty for the remainder of the school year.[51]

The beginning of Buber's advocacy of personal responsibility rather than obedience to authority is evident in his response to the concrete situation. Was he to betray the two boys or obey the teacher? Buber comments on this situation: "The long series of experiences that taught me to understand the problematic relationship between maxim and situation, and thereby disclosed to me the nature of the true norm that commands not our obedience but ourselves, had begun with this convulsion of my childhood.'[52]

The serious emotional disturbance that Buber experienced at the time of the incident in his school was to be repeated later. It can be understood as a manifestation of the lasting sense of loneliness and insecurity experienced by him as a result of his mother's absence. Schaeder writes that this elemental insecurity expressed itself with terrifying vehemence when the child felt the force of powers that were beyond his understanding.[53] In "The Way of Man according to the Teachings of Hasidism," Buber argues that "a man should realise that conflict-situations between himself and others are nothing but the effects of conflict-situations in his own soul; then he should try to overcome this inner-conflict, so that afterwards he may go out to his fellow-man and enter into new, transformed relationships with them."[54] Perhaps the conflict in Buber's soul was too elemental to be resolved satisfactorily. In the process of his philosophical writing, however, a journey can be traced in which he attempted to work toward an understanding and acceptance of the cause and nature of these very personal conflicts.

PHILOSOPHERS

In *Between Man and Man*, in the context of a discussion of the philosophy of Pascal and Kant, Buber recalls an experience he had when fourteen:

> A necessity I could not understand swept over me: I had to try again and again to imagine the edge of space, or its edgelessness, time with a beginning and an end or a time without beginning or end, and both were equally impossible, equally hopeless—yet there seemed to be only the choice between the one or the other

absurdity. Under an irresistible compulsion I reeled from one to the other, at times so closely threatened with the danger of madness that I seriously thought of avoiding it by suicide. Salvation came to the fifteen-year-old boy in a book, Kant's *Prolegomena to Any Future Metaphysics*, which I dared to read although its first sentence told me that it was not intended for the use of pupils but for future teachers.[55]

Later, in his "Autobiographical Fragments," Buber added that at the age of fourteen it was the question of time that oppressed him in a far more tormenting fashion than the question of space. In order to take the matter seriously, he had to transpose himself either to the beginning of time or to the end of time:

> Thus I came to feel the former like a blow in the neck or the latter like a rap against the forehead—no, there is no beginning and no end! Or I had to let myself be thrown into this or that bottomless abyss, into infinity, and now everything whirled. It happened thus time after time. Mathematical or physical formulae could not help me; what was at stake was the reality of the world in which one had to live and which had taken on the face of the absurd and the uncanny.[56]

The question of time was the disturbing question at the end of the nineteenth century and the beginning of the twentieth century. It was Kant, however, who exercised an initial calming effect on the young Buber. It was in Kant's *Prolegomena to any Future Metaphysics* that Buber found that he no longer had to ask the question. He learned that space and time are "formal conditions of our sensory faculty" and "not real properties that adhere to the things in themselves." As the question was unanswerable by its nature, Buber felt liberated from it: "Time was not a sentence hanging over me; it was mine, for it was 'ours.'"[57]

In *Between Man and Man*, Buber expresses a further insight that he derived from his reading of Kant—that eternal being was distinct from the categories of the finite and the infinite that were deployed in discussions of space and time: "At that time I began to gain an inkling of the existence of eternity as something quite different from the infinite, just as it is something quite different from the finite, and of the possibility of a connexion between me, a man, and the eternal."[58] The possibility of this connection is the linchpin of Buber's later understanding of the

I-Thou relation between God and each human being. How is it possible to understand the presence of each partner in this relation? What is the understanding of time at the point of the *meeting*?

However, before Buber moved to a more mature understanding of time, another philosopher excited him and even transported him into a state of sublime intoxication. It was a long time before he escaped from this intoxication. Two years after the encounter with Kant, in his seventeenth year, Nietzsche's *Thus Spake Zarathustra* took possession of him. The effect of this book, he remarks, was similar to an invasion that deprived him of his freedom. Buber writes that Nietzsche himself wished "the basic conception" of this book to be understood as an interpretation of time. This "interpretation as 'eternal return of the same,' that is, as an infinite sequence of finite periods of time, which are like one another in all things so that the end phase of the period goes over into its own beginning." "This is no teaching at all," continues the mature Buber, "but the utterance of an ecstatically lived-through possibility of thought played over with ever new variations."[59]

Nietzsche had a great influence on Buber for a long time; he portrays this influence as "a negative seduction," though he writes that as a seventeen-year-old he did not and could not accept this interpretation of time. However, despite the impact of Kant, he was not able to ask the questions that could have led to an insight into the reality of the world: "But if time is only a form in which we perceive, where *are* 'we'? Are we not in the timeless? Are we not in eternity?" This is not the circular eternity of Nietzsche, but something that is incomprehensible in itself: "that which sends forth time out of itself and sets us in that relationship to it that we call existence. To him who recognizes this, the reality of the world no longer shows an absurd and uncanny face: because eternity is. That the entrance to this way long remained closed to me is to be traced to a certain, not insignificant, extent to that fascination by 'Zarathustra.'"[60] As we shall see, there is a significant Nietzschean influence in Buber's early writings.

DEATH AND LIFE

Another important event happened when Buber was seventeen. Although this event affected Buber very deeply, it is not included in his "Autobiographical Fragments." It is included, though not explicitly as

an autobiographical note, in Buber's *Daniel: Dialogues on Realization.*[61] In the fifth dialogue, the importance of which I will discuss later,
Daniel responds to his friend Lukas on the subject of unity and the relation of life and death:

> Let me tell you an event out of my youth. I was seventeen years
> old when a man died whom I had loved. Death laid itself about
> my neck like a lasso. It seized me as the Christian God seizes a
> sinner who must atone in God's place. That there was dying in
> the world had become my sin for which I had to do penance. Be-
> cause of my isolation I could take no sleep and because of my
> disgust with living I could tolerate no nourishment; I believed this
> happened as a penance. My family, strengthened by friends and
> physicians, regarded me fussily and helplessly as a changeling.
> Only my father met me with a calm, collected glance that was so
> strong that he reached my heart, inaccessible to all other percep-
> tions. It was also this man, silent but united with the future, who
> soon came to the special decision through which I was saved: he
> sent me all alone into a secluded mountain place. I believe that
> the great time that I lived through there will return once more in
> the images of my dying hour.[62]

In his introduction to *Daniel,* Friedman, who had received suggestions
from Buber, does not directly mention that this event was an autobiographical one. However, in a later discussion of *Daniel,* in his biography of Buber, Friedman states that "what he describes is the response
that Buber himself had at the age of seventeen to the death of an uncle
who was killed by a fall from a horse while the horrified boy looked
on."[63] I conclude that the experience related to the death of Rafael, who
was the only brother of Buber's father.

RELIGION

In his "Autobiographical Fragments," Buber mentions very little regarding his religious education or the significance of his early Jewish
upbringing. His grandparents were intellectually engaged in their Jewish heritage, and the atmosphere in the home was one of piety and
learning.[64] He comments that although his grandfather did not trouble
himself about Judaism, it nevertheless dwelled in him.[65] So long as the

boy lived with his grandfather, he reports that "his roots were firm," although he had many questions and doubts.

When he was still a boy, another event gave rise to a distinct personal response. This time, it was not an event in Buber's own life, as in the case of the mimicry of his classmates, but a reaction to a particular narrative in the Bible. A step in the movement toward the insecure position that he was later willing to embrace can be traced to his rebellion against the concept of a vengeful God. He was appalled by the story of Saul being rejected as king because he did not follow God's command and kill Agag, King of the Amalekites. Hodes reports Buber's comment on the story:

> The scene in which Agag approached Samuel and was "hewed in pieces before the Lord" filled me with fear and trembling every time I read it. . . . Even many years later, when I had to translate this passage into German, I found it difficult to put down these words from the Scriptures. I could not believe in a God who punished Saul because he had refused to kill his opponent.[66]

Later, Buber met a Jew whom he already knew to be from that observant tradition that had its source in the man's relationship to God. He told this man how it horrified him as a boy when he read or remembered the incident in which the heathen king approached Samuel with these words on his lips: "Surely the bitterness of death is past" before being hewn to pieces. Buber said to his companion: "I have never been able to believe that this is a message of God. I do not believe it." The face of the other man became angry; he was silent and then almost threateningly asked what Buber believed. Buber replied: "I believe . . . that Samuel has misunderstood God." Buber continued: "But now something happened the like of which I have rarely seen before or since in this my long life. The angry countenance opposite me became transformed, as if a hand had passed over it soothing it. It lightened, cleared, was now turned toward me bright and clear. 'Well,' said the man with a positively gentle tender clarity, 'I think so too.'"[67]

Buber was aware that an interpretation of God's will can be subject to some misunderstanding: "What is involved here is not ultimately the fact that this or that form of biblical historical narrative has misunderstood God; what is involved is the fact that in the work of throats and pens out of which the text of the Old Testament has arisen, misunderstanding has again and again attached itself to understanding, the manufactured has been mixed with the received."[68] Buber continues by stating a point that is crucial to him: "We have no objective criterion for the distinction; we have only faith—when we have it."[69] Buber began to question accepted wisdom as a boy and later learned to trust his own understanding while being aware of its limitations and fragility. Buber experienced "the inescapable tension between the words of God and the words of man" when he translated or interpreted a biblical text.[70]

When living with his grandparents, Buber had been an observant Jew, but his practice of religious customs such as the wearing of phylacteries during morning prayers ceased around the age of fourteen.[71] As a boy, he experienced some events associated with religion with a marked intensity. He remembered an experience of his fourteenth year on the eve of the Day of Atonement in which he felt that his whole body was as important as a sacrificial animal. He experienced the day, he recalls "with an intensity not equalled since." He also recalls his giving offence in the Lemberg [Reform] "temple" when he gave an actual physical demonstration of the difference between *we bow down* and *we prostrate ourselves*. This offence took place, he explains, when his father "took him away" from his grandfather: "the latter used to take me with him into his *klaus*, where he, the *enlightened one*, prayed exclusively among Hasidim—from a prayerbook full of *kavvonot*."[72]

By the time of his *bar mitzvah* ceremony on 8 February 1891, Buber was not observing the ritual of the synagogue. He chose to speak on Schiller's "The Words of Faith" rather than on the usual pentateuchal weekly text.[73] Throughout his life, Buber would occupy the lonely narrow ridge, being unwilling to conform to a specific creed or to accept any particular label. In explaining his position as the occupant of the narrow ridge, Buber wrote that "he did not rest on the broad upland of a system that includes a series of sure statements about the absolute, but on a rocky ridge between the gulfs where there is no sureness of expressible knowledge but the certainty of meeting what remains, undisclosed."[74]

Another memory from Buber's youth was of great importance later. During the summers spent on his father's estate in Bukovina, his father would sometimes take him to visit the nearby village of Sadagora.[75] This village was the seat of a dynasty of Hasidic *zaddikim*. *Hesed* is a Hebrew word that means "loving-kindness." The Hasid is a person who goes out into the world with loving-kindness. The *zaddik* was the righteous, proven man, a Hasidic rabbi or *rebbe*, the leader of a community.

The boy watched the Hasidim swaying and chanting in ecstasy around the leader.

Buber writes that the Jewish movement was called "*Hasidut*—a word that can be translated into English still far less than the Latin *pietas* that corresponds to it; its meaning might most easily be rendered through a verbal paraphrase: to love the world in God."[76] However, he reports that the high faith of the first Hasidim or the fervent devotion that honoured in the *zaddik* the perfected man was no longer present in the community: "Rather the present day Hasidim turn to the *zaddik* above all as the mediator through whose intercession they hope to attain the satisfaction of their needs."[77]

As a child observing the Hasidic crowd, he realised that "as a child realises such things, not as thought, but as image and feeling—that the world needs the perfected man and that the perfected man is none other than the true helper."[78] Buber compared the *zaddik* with the headman of the province whose power rested on habitual compulsion and with the Rabbi in the orthodox synagogue in Lemberg who though an honest and God-fearing man was an employee of the "directorship of the cult." In the *zaddik* and the Hasidim, he found "debased yet uninjured, the living double kernel of humanity: genuine *community* and genuine *leadership*." The child found that the showy palace of the *rebbe* repelled him, and the prayer house of the Hasidim with its enraptured worshippers seemed strange. "But when I saw the *rebbe* striding through the rows of the waiting, I felt, 'leader,' and when I saw the Hasidim dance with the Torah, I felt 'community.' At that time there rose in me a presentiment of the fact that common reverence and common joy of soul are the foundations of genuine human community."[79]

Later during adolescence, this early presentiment began to slip into the unconscious. He was now spending the summers in a different province and nearly forgot the Hasidic impressions of his childhood. After many years, however, he visited a newly inherited family estate in the area of Czortkov. Here resided a collateral line of the same dynasty of *zaddikim* as at Sadagora. This time, though, his experience was different; his impressions were paler and more fleeting: "That might be caused by the fact that meanwhile I had been seized by the fermenting intellectuality which is often characteristic of the decisive years of youth and which puts an end to the natural seeing and experiencing of the child. Through this intellectuality I had become alienated from the Hasidim; it robbed me of my native affinity with their being."[80] He found that he now looked down on Hasidism "from the heights of a rational man."

However, at that time Buber heard the name "that would mean the most precious discovery" for him many years later: the name "Besht." This word represents the initial letters of the name "Baal Shem Tov" (Master of the Good Name) and designates the founder of Hasidism, Rabbi Israel ben Eliezer (1700–60). This man was a poor teacher of small children in Tluste. One night, as legend has it, he had a dream that the time had come for him to go forth to men. Buber was deeply moved when he read the testament of the Baal Shem Tov in a small book called *Zevaat Ribesh.* As result of this experience, he spent five years [1904–9] among the Hasidim gathering Hasidic lore and literature.

Soon after Buber left his grandparents' house, "the whirl of the age" took hold of him. Later, Buber wrote of the state that he was in at this time:

> Until my twentieth year, and in small measure even beyond then, my spirit was in steady and multiple movement, in an alternation of tension and release, determined by manifold influences, taking ever new shape, but without center and without growing substance: it was really the "*Olam-ha-Tohu,*" the "World of Confusion," the mythical dwelling place of wandering souls. Here I lived—in versatile fullness of spirit, but without Judaism, without humanity, and without the presence of the divine.[81]

On reflection, Buber sees his intellectual journey as one moving from this apparent absence to an understanding of the presence of the divine.

RETURN TO VIENNA

Martin Buber returned to his native city, Vienna, to begin his university studies in 1896, when he was eighteen.[82] The prevailing cultural climate was neo-Romanticism, particularly in the form of lyric poetry and the lyrical dialogue of novels and plays. Viennese culture was a unique mix of south German, Jewish, and Slavic influences. Kohn mentions that Vienna was the center of cultural contact with Scandinavian and Romantic literature, and here these influences took on a warm, more feminine nature.

The ability of the city to attract and assimilate foreign elements was also evident in its treatment of Jews who came from the east, Grete Schaeder argues.[83] Only the situation of the Jews in fifteenth-century Spain equalled the position of eminence attained by the assimilated Jewish population of Vienna during this time. The Jewish population was prominent in the artistic world and made significant contributions to all the intellectual disciplines.

However, Vienna also harboured threatening undercurrents that were evident in a nationalistic pan-German and petite-bourgeois anti-Semitism.[84] This was the city of Karl Lueger, who became mayor of Vienna, and owed his popularity to anti-Semitism.[85] The growing threat may be seen in the event of the unveiling of a monument to Abraham a Sancta Clara in August 1910. Lueger had initiated the financing of this monument to the greatly revered court preacher of the seventeenth century. It was situated at Kreenhainstetten, which was the birthplace of Abraham a Sancta Clara. This small village was near Messkirch, the birthplace of Martin Heidegger, who witnessed the ceremony. The Catholic antimodernists of southern Germany had adopted the preacher as their role model. Safranski explains that "in the writings of the famous Augustine monk it was easy to find strong words against pleasure-seeking and depraved urban life, against spiritual pride that no longer bowed to the revealed teachings of the Church, against the love of extravagance of the wealthy, but also against the so-called cupidity of 'money-lending Jews.'"[86]

For many Viennese intellectuals, the importance of religion and politics had been superseded by art. Carl Schorske points out that "By the 1890s the heroes of the upper middle class were no longer political leaders, but actors, artists and critics. . . . The life of art became a substitute for the life of action. Indeed . . . art became almost a religion, the source of meaning and the food for the soul."[87] Writing of Buber, Hans Fischer-Barnicol claims that "The well-to-do student of philosophy and of the history of art and literature loved the playful elegance, the sublime pathos of the new-romantic sensibility and aesthetic . . . the urbane spirit of the coffeehouse intelligence. Soon he became the friend of the poets, Hofmannsthal, Beer-Hofmann, Schnitzler . . . and, in fact, appeared to want to become 'only' a poet, a member of the literati."[88]

In the poetry of Hugo von Hofmannsthal, Buber discerned the "charming seduction" that gripped many of the young people of artistic inclinations in turn-of-the-century Vienna: "here first was the primordial gold of speech poured into the laps of heirs who had taken no pains to earn it."[89] "Let the heir be a squanderer," Hofmannsthal wrote in his *Lebenslied*. Buber purchased the pamphlet in which this poem was published and read it in a park in Vienna. As a result of the reading, he wrote: "A shudder (not of enjoyment, but truly a 'holy shudder') overcame me: this verse there had been written only a short time ago."[90] He understood that "the German language was not only brought to its full spokenness in this city; it also brought into being ever new poetry." Associated with this artistic life was a wonderful ease: "the nonchalance of the heir," who in Hofmannsthal's words "squandered the treasures of antiquity" enchanted Buber's heart; later, he could recognize that it penetrated into his reading and writing.[91]

In his first year at university, Buber studied literature, the history of art, and philosophy. The lectures during this year did not have a decisive effect on him. However, the method of regulated yet free exchange between teacher and students in the seminars impressed him greatly. The master at times took part in these seminars with a rare humility, as if he also were learning something new. This shared experience of texts and the practice of question and answer disclosed to Buber the "true actuality of the spirit, as a 'between.'"[92] Later, Buber argues that the relation in education is one of pure dialogue.[93] Again and again, Buber returns to the reality *between* two or more people, a reality that is repeatedly reconstituted when people meet, as in the seminar, in a sphere that is common to them, but that extends beyond the special sphere of each.[94]

It was the Imperial Theater, the *Burgtheater*, that affected Buber most strongly in this first year. From a place in the highest gallery, Buber distinguished between the genuine speaking of the words of the play and the reciting of the words: "Then along with the genuine spokenness of speech, dialogical speech or even monological (in so far as the monologue was just an addressing of one's own person as a fellow-man and no recitation), this whole world, mysteriously built out of surprise and law, was shattered for me—until after some moments it arose anew with the return of the over-against."[95] Here, one can appreciate the actor treating the speech as an object, an "It" in Buber's later terminology. The genuine speech held real meaning for Buber. We may discern an echo of his grandmother's real address to a person in this account, but there is also a seed of Buber's later appreciation of "the shudder of the now" in which one realizes that it is oneself who is addressed at the present moment. Buber received from the theater what he called a great instruction: "in the books that I had read the signs were indicated; here first did they become the sounds that were meant."[96] Subsequently, Buber was more aware of this difference in everyday conversations. He mentions a conversation overheard at an inn in which he says he perceived the "spokenness" of speech, "sound becoming 'Each-Other.'"[97]

It was especially through the spoken word that Buber came to the kernel of the question, "What is man?" In "Replies to my Critics," he states that "nothing helps me so much to understand man and his existence as does speech. . . ."[98] He draws attention to the ability of speech to disclose the unique, particularly speech "in its living context, in the context of genuine conversation, of genuine poetry, of genuine prayer and of genuine philosophy." Buber gave attention to each of these areas during his life. However, it was not until he discovered Hasidic speech that Buber truly found the immediacy that was to ground his philosophical writings on dialogue.

PAULA WINKLER

In the summer semester of 1899 at the University of Zurich, Buber met Paula Winkler whom he later married. The relationship continued until her death, in Venice in 1958, when they were on the way home from a seminar in America. Buber himself died seven years later on 13 June 1965. Paula was a Bavarian Catholic who later converted to Judaism and was a year older than Martin when they met. In 1901, she wrote an article for *Die Welt*, entitled, "Confessions of a Philozionist." In this article, she explained that as a young girl, her mother had lived close to a Jewish settlement and often spoke warmly of her impressions. Paula also mentioned the wonderful intensity of Buber's voice as he spoke at the Third Zionist Congress in Basel in 1899, and of the manner in which this address evoked the tremendous longing of a whole people.[99]

Paula was described by her teacher as a "wild elfin creature, tough, brilliant, reckless" and as "uncannily clever and strong-willed."[100] In 1901, Theodor Herzl, the founder of modern political Zionism, spoke of her great talent as a writer and published some of her writings. Her first book, *Die unechten Kinder Adams* (*The Inauthentic Children of Adam*), was published in 1912 under her pseudonym of George Munk.

She was a significant and independent German storyteller who subsequently published three further books and other writings.[101] In fact, Paula wrote some of the legends in Buber's collection of stories that was published as *The Legend of the Baal-Shem*.[102]

From their letters in the early years of their relationship, Schaeder concludes that Paula was the stronger and more mature personality when they met. She argues that:

> It is of tremendous importance that Buber, while still so young, met a woman who was his equal, indeed his superior, in poetic talent and articulateness, and who understood his achievement so completely and spurred him on. But their communion introduced a rather dangerous measure of poetry into ordinary life, an elevated mood which could scarcely stand up to the exigencies and misunderstandings of everyday reality.[103]

Commenting on this crucial meeting in Buber's life, Friedman notes that if it "did not entirely remove the inner division that his mother's disappearance had brought about, it nonetheless made possible a life of trust in which Buber found again the strength to go forth to meet the unique and unforeseeable person or situation as his Thou."[104] Furthermore, Friedman claims that the existential trust that underlies *I and Thou* and all of Buber's mature works would have been unthinkable without this relationship to Paula: "In this sense we have before us in full reality a philosopher whose thinking did not emerge from his individual being but from the 'between' which he knew first and foremost in his marriage."[105]

Rafael Buber, Paula and Martin's son, was born on 9 July 1900, and their daughter Eva was born the following year on 3 July. Rafael's relationship with his father was full of tension.[106] He and his sister were tutored in their home in Heppenheim when they were young. Rafael went to high school when he was twelve years of age and found it difficult. During the First World War, he left school and enlisted in the Austrian army at the age of seventeen.[107] Later, he spent some time in Vienna training in mechanical engineering, especially in agricultural machinery. Rafael married the writer Margarete Buber-Neumann and fathered two daughters, Barbara in 1921 and Judith in 1924. The couple divorced in 1928. Rafael remarried and settled for a time in a kibbutz in Israel. At the time of their son's divorce, Buber and Paula became guardians of their two young granddaughters.[108] The two girls lived with their grandparents for the remainder of their childhood, though they had some contact with both of their parents.

Eva Buber was not sent to school as a child.[109] When she was eighteen, she attended a gardening school and wanted to continue her studies in this area, but her parents were against it, thinking that she should stay at home where she was needed. In 1925, she married the poet and literary historian, Ludwig Strauss. They had two sons, Emanuel and Micha. In 1953, Ludwig died and Eva remarried. She worked in a home for disturbed children in Jerusalem.[110] Eva remarks in an interview that when she was about sixteen years of age, her father read to her the first draft of *I and Thou* and that it influenced her entire life. "I always tried to live in light of the book's message."[111] By 1953, Martin and Paula had five great-grandchildren. As Buber wrote in a letter in 1953: "Thus together with the hard fate and the enchanting little joys, all this may be called something like a clan."[112]

CONCLUSION

At the beginning of his "Autobiographical Fragments," Buber explains that he is not giving a comprehensive account of his personal life, but solely "rendering an account of some moments that my backward glance lets rise to the surface. Moments that have exercised a decisive influence on the nature and direction of my thinking."[113] Some of these fragments were composed in an earlier phase of Buber's life, and some were written when Buber was in his eighties, as part of his contribution to the series *Philosophen des 20. Jahrhunderts.*[114] His backward glance over a long life highlights those experiences of mis-meetings and meetings that addressed him in a personal manner and had a significant influence on his journey through life.

This realization of the importance of encounters with others indicates a shift from the position of the youthful Buber who, as I mentioned, identified with the psalm that laments "You have put friend and neighbour far from me" (Psalm 88:29). He writes that if he had been asked in his early youth whether he preferred to have dealings only with human beings or only with books, his answer would certainly have been in favor of books. As he got older, this changed:

Not that I have had so much better experiences with human beings than with books; on the contrary, purely delightful books even now come my way more often than purely delightful human beings. But the many bad experiences with human beings have nourished the meadow of my life as the noblest book could not do, and the good experiences have made the earth into a garden for me.[115]

His early identification with Psalm 88 is thus only part of the story; he later wrote to Rosenzweig: "Once, after I had no longer occupied myself with them (the psalms) for many long, bad years, while walking in the mountains, after having scaled a ridge that in memory seems absolutely incredible, they '[delivered] my feet from stumbling' [Psalm 116:8] came over me not like a prayer but like a—report (that is still not the right word but you will certainly understand). At that time the 116th [Psalm] dawned on me; now almost all the others flow out of it."[116] This psalm addresses and thanks God, and commits oneself to walk in His presence in the land of the living. Buber does not turn away from "the clattering highway"[117] as he calls it, but strives to establish a place for the divine presence in the world. I will now proceed to discuss the next steps of Buber's journey, where the awareness that the goal is to walk "the clattering highway" in the presence of God is temporarily eclipsed.

2. THE BECOMING GOD

INTRODUCTION

In the winter semester 1899–1900, Buber studied in Berlin at the Royal Friedrich Wilhelm University and enrolled for courses on the General History of Philosophy and Philosophical Exercises under Professor Wilhelm Dilthey and Nineteenth-Century Philosophy and Sociology under Georg Simmel. Both of these professors made a profound impression on Buber.[1] Paul Mendes-Flohr has demonstrated Simmel's influence on Buber's thought, and I will later discuss part of this influence, that is, the distinction between religion and religiosity that is an element in Buber's journey toward presence.

Buber's essay, "Über Jakob Boehme," will enable us to appreciate his early position regarding the presence of God. First though, an introduction to Dilthey and the concept of *Erlebnis* is essential.

WILHELM DILTHEY

As a student of Dilthey in Berlin, Buber became interested in the Mystics of the Renaissance, Reformation, and post-Reformation periods.[2] He was above all interested in Boehme, about whom he wrote one of his first published essays in 1901. Benz remarks that it was Dilthey who emphasized the continuity of the tradition between the German mystics of the Middle Ages and German idealist philosophy.[3] Dilthey's interest in Boehme led Buber to also study Cusanus, Paracelsus, Weigel, and to a lesser degree, the Pietists such as Zinzendorf.[4] A contemporary of Zinzendorf in the eighteenth century, Rabbi Israel ben Eliezer, known as the Baal-Shem-Tov (Master of the Good Name) was one of the founders of Hasidism.[5] It was reading the Baal-Shem-Tov's testament that led Buber to study Hasidism.[6]

Buber wrote later of Wilhelm Dilthey as "my teacher" and names him as the founder of the history of philosophical anthropology.[7] Dilthey's wavering attitude toward Nietzsche, which encompassed enthusiasm and distaste at different times, may have attracted Buber.[8] Buber's essay on Nietzsche, "A Word on Nietzsche and Life-Values," conveys a similar ambivalence, as when he writes of Nietzsche: "He appears to us as the crystallisation of our own tragedy and we learn to love him as a near and distant friend, the suffering friend who like us needs bread and medicine, the creating friend, who always has a finished world to give away."[9]

Dilthey had a lasting influence on Buber's understanding of philosophy. In a lecture that Dilthey frequently delivered from 1898 in his university courses, one may appreciate the spirit of that time, and the view of philosophy that Dilthey presented to his students.[10] Presentation of the main points of this lecture, in which Dilthey is critical of Nietzsche, will enable us to appreciate Dilthey's characteristic themes. The main elements underlying his method in human studies will also be outlined. This brief consideration of Dilthey's thought will bring into focus some of the questions posed by Dilthey to Buber.

Dilthey commences his lecture by saying that he wants to offer his students more than academic philosophy. He states that the correct philosophic stance can only be established on the basis of the present, and the most basic feature of the contemporary philosophical climate was a world-immanent realism. This standpoint is vividly portrayed in the following lines from Goethe's *Faust*:

> Well do I know the sphere of earth and men.
> The view beyond is barred to mortal ken;
> A fool! Who thither turns his blinking eyes
> And dreams he'll find his like above the skies.
> Let him stand fast and look around on earth;
> Not mute is this world to a man of worth.

Since Goethe's diagnosis (1808–32), Dilthey contends, the progress of science has buttressed the claims of this world-immanent realism. He then reviews the philosophical and scientific progress since the seventeenth century and remarks: "Fill yourself completely with this realism, this worldliness of interest, this dominance of science over life!"

Buber was concerned at this period with the decline of the spiritual and aesthetic aspects of personal and communal life as a result of the rise of bourgeois civilization.[11] This decline was due, Buber argued, to the acceptance of the phenomenal world as the single and ultimate reality. The claim that the sensibly perceived world was the only reality leads to the view that the world is a collection of phenomena with no underlying unity.

According to Dilthey, however, this "worldliness of interest" does not satisfy the human desire to understand existence or the quest for the "ground of the world."[12] "But when, today, we ask what is the final goal of action for the individual or for mankind, the deep contradiction which pervades our time emerges. We face the enigma of the origin of things, the value of our existence, the ultimate value of our actions, no wiser than a Greek in the Ionic or Italian colonies or an Arab at the time of Averroes."[13] He claims that surrounded by the rapid progress of the sciences, people are even more at a loss for an answer to this question than at any earlier period. Dilthey identifies three causes of this deprivation. First, the presuppositions, which lay at the foundations of the religious faith and philosophic convictions of former centuries, have been progressively dissolved by the sciences. It is merely the appearance of something unknown that is the reality experienced by our senses. Second, this destruction has been aided by the greatest achievement of philosophy in the last century, that is, the analysis of consciousness and knowledge. Third, through historical comparison, one finds the relativity of all historical convictions: "Historical consciousness increasingly proves the relativity of every metaphysical or religious doctrine which has emerged in the course of the Ages. Something tragic seems to lie in man's striving for knowledge, a contradiction between will and capacity."

There are times in the course of history, claims Dilthey, in which all firm presuppositions about the value of life and the goals of action are questioned. He also argues that there is increasing skepticism through the ages regarding the presuppositions of thought and action. Out of this discord between the sovereignty of scientific thought and the inability of the spirit to understand itself and its significance in the universe comes the final and most characteristic feature of the spirit at the end of the nineteenth century and its philosophy:

> The grim pride and pessimism of a Byron, Leopardi or Nietzsche presupposes the domination of the scientific spirit over the earth. But, at the same time, the emptiness of consciousness asserts itself in them because all yardsticks have gone, everything firm has become shaky; an unrestricted freedom to make assumptions, and playing with unlimited possibilities allow the spirit to enjoy its sovereignty and at the same time inflict the pain of a lack of content. This pain of emptiness, this consciousness of the anarchy in all deeper convictions, this uncertainty about the values and goals of life, have called forth the different attempts in poetry and fiction, to answer the questions about the value and goal of our existence.[14]

Positivism and neo-Kantianism dominate the sciences and the universities.[15] In the pervading skepticism, metaphysics in the traditional mold comes to an end. The philosophy of life becomes a dominant power again through Schopenhauer, Richard Wagner, Nietzsche, Tolstoy, Ruskin, and Maeterlinck.[16] These all influenced the young—not least because of the range of their literary and artistic outreach—"for the problems of poetry are the problems of life." However, they are similar to the metaphysicians because they too want to grasp something ultimate and unconditional, but their means are inadequate. Each speaks of himself and interprets what he sees of life outside himself from his individual perspective. Their mistake is that each takes "his own corner for the whole world."[17]

Dilthey then criticizes the efforts of these authors. Of Nietzsche he writes: "Man as a creator of culture is, for him first, the artist, then the scientific consciousness and, finally, because he despairs of that mission too, the philosopher who creates and sets values. . . . The philosopher's job is to heighten men's feeling of the positive value of life and thus to reform them."[18] However, Dilthey argues, Thrasymachus and Critias, Spinoza and Hobbes, Feuerbach and Stirner had already expressed acceptance of the will and its power so strongly that history had no need of Nietzsche. What was required of Nietzsche was to express what is valuable in all the varied forms that the will to live produces, but his works give no answer on this point. Furthermore, according to Dilthey:

[Nietzsche] remains a complete amateur in the use of historical facts for the understanding of functional connections within a culture; at the same time he has isolated the individual because of his original starting-point, namely the cult of genius and great men. He has divorced the purpose of the individual from the development of a culture; for to him great men are not merely the moving forces but also the essential achievements of the historical process. So the individual, divorced from the functional contexts of a culture, becomes devoid of content; formally he loses the relation to something progressive and firm. Yet the most significant feature of the real morality of the modern age lies in the transfer of interest to this. Acceptance of life is now a personal immersion either in the eternity of knowledge and artistic apprehension or in the progress of culture itself.[19]

What human nature requires in order to achieve its full reality and power and the full richness of human existence is historical consciousness: "The totality of human nature is only to be found in history; the individual can only become conscious of it and enjoy it when he assembles the minds of the past within himself."[20] Only when all the forms of life have been grasped is it possible to see the "generally valid in the relative, a firm future in the past, greater esteem for the individual through historical consciousness and so recognize reality as the yardstick for progress into the future; this we can then link with clear goals for the future."[21]

The idea of the totality of human nature only being found in history affected Buber's early philosophy; the notion of finding "the generally valid in the relative" and learning to respect the truth that emerges in each worldview forms the lesson of history that Buber later took from Dilthey. The fundamental idea of Dilthey's worldview was incorporated into Buber's approach to the philosophical question of the human person. This idea, Dilthey wrote:

... is that no one, so far, has based his philosophizing on the full, unmutilated whole of experience, and so, on the whole fullness of reality. Speculation is certainly abstract. . . . But empiricism is no less so. It bases itself on mutilated experience, distorted from the outset by an atomistic theoretical view of mental life . . . no complete human being can be confined within this experience.[22]

Dilthey argues that humanity only becomes the subject matter of human studies when "we experience human states, give expressions to them and understand these expressions."[23] This correlation of life, expression, and understanding includes gestures, facial expressions, words, and artistic creations that reveal their author's deeper meaning and lasting objectifications of the mind in social structures where a common human nature is manifest. Self-knowledge is gained only through the circuitous route of understanding, but this is only possible if what is experienced is projected into the expressions of our own and others' lives.[24]

The presupposition is that the knowing subject shares with other human beings common, fundamental features, which Dilthey calls the categories of life. He can thus write:

> Understanding is a re-discovery of the I in the Thou: the mind rediscovers itself at ever higher levels of complex involvement: this identity of the mind in the I and the Thou, in every subject of a community, in every system of a culture and finally, in the totality of mind and universal history, makes successful co-operation between different processes in the human studies possible.[25]

However, having discussed the formation of different worldviews as a response to the enigma of life, Dilthey ends a discussion on objective idealism by asking:

> Is this world-ground reason or will? If we define it as thought will is still necessary for anything to originate. If we think of it as will purposive thought is pre-supposed. But will and thought cannot be reduced to each other. Here logical thought about the world-ground comes to an end; all that remains is the reflection of its vitality in mysticism. If one thinks of the world-ground as a person the metaphor requires that it should have concrete, limiting characteristics. But if one applies the idea of the infinite all its characteristics vanish and only the inexhaustible and incomprehensible—the darkness of mysticism—remain. If it is conscious, the contrast between subject and object applies to it but, if it is unconscious, we cannot comprehend how out of itself it could produce consciousness, which is something higher; once more we are faced by something incomprehensible. We cannot think how world unity can give rise to multiplicity, the eternal to change;

logically this is incomprehensible. The relationship of being and thought, of extension and thinking, does not become more comprehensible through the magic word identity. So these metaphysical systems, too, leave only a frame of mind and a world-view behind them.[26]

It was precisely to these problems that Buber first addressed himself in 1900. Beginning with his essay on Jacob Boehme, Buber struggled with these questions for many years. Dilthey died in the Tyrol on 30 September 1911. Martin Buber was the young student who helped his widow to prepare the funeral arrangements.[27]

Erlebnis

Dilthey's epistemology differs from those of the Empiricists and Kant. He remarks that no "real blood flows in the veins of the knowing subject constructed by Locke, Hume and Kant; it is only the diluted juice of reason, a mere process of thought."[28] His own historical and psychological studies of man led him to explain cognition in terms of the powers of man as a willing, feeling, and imagining being. In order to distinguish his own understanding of experience from that which focused exclusively on sense data, Dilthey availed himself of the German-language distinction of Erlebnis from Erfahrung, which are both translated as experience. It is a distinction that will greatly influence Buber. Dilthey argued that Erlebnis, the word that he used to convey the sense of the subjective, personal, inner experience of human beings, is the capacity to know the nonlogical, dynamic events of the human spirit.[29] An Erlebnis is a state or condition viewed subjectively: "an event by which one is affected." In this sense, Rickman remarks, we speak of "going through an experience" or "something having been quite an experience."[30] On the other hand, Erfahrung, according to Rickman, has the sense of "the actual observation of facts or events, considered as a source of knowledge."[31]

Dilthey did not claim that Erlebnis provided a noumenal or "higher" form of knowledge; however, some of his followers who adopted this distinction took this step. They celebrated Erlebnis as a "uniquely graced epistemological faculty—akin to what Rudolf Otto would later call a sensus numinus—quickening one's apprehension of a sacred reality."[32] This understanding of Erlebnis and his interpretation of Boehme's symbolization of the manifestation of God's presence in the world led Buber to make further exaggerated claims. Buber subsequently develops an aversion to uttering the word *Erlebnis*.[33] As this concept played a significant part in Buber's philosophical development and is crucial for the understanding of presence, it is necessary to examine it further.

Surprisingly, the noun *Erlebnis* became common only in the 1870s.[34] It first appeared in one of Hegel's letters, but it enters general usage at the same time as it begins to be used in biographical writing. *Erlebnis* is formed from the verb *erleben*, and the meaning of this word, Gadamer remarks, must be analyzed in order to determine why the new word was formed:

> Erleben means primarily "to be still alive when something happens." Thus the word suggests the immediacy with which something real is grasped—unlike something which one presumes to know but which is unattested by one's own experience, whether because it is taken over from others or comes from hearsay, or whether it is inferred, surmised, or imagined. What is experienced is always what one has experienced oneself.[35]

However, the form *das Erlebte* is used to mean the permanent content of what is experienced. Gadamer writes that this content is like "a yield or result that achieves permanence, weight, and significance from out of the transience of experiencing."[36] Both of these meanings lie behind *Erlebnis*: "the immediacy, which precedes all interpretation, reworking, and communication, and merely offers a starting point for interpretation—material to be shaped—and its discovered yield, its lasting result."[37] It was in biographical literature that the word took root. The essential element of biography is the attempt to understand the works from the life. This involves mediating between the two meanings of the word and seeing the two meanings as a productive union: "something becomes an 'experience' not only insofar as it is experienced, but insofar as its being experienced makes a special impression that gives it lasting importance."[38] Gadamer notes that Dilthey's title, *Das Erlebnis und die Dichtung* (Experience and Poetry), succinctly expresses the association.

The word *Erlebnis* encapsulates the criticism of Enlightenment rationalism that stemmed from Rousseau's emphasis on the concept of life (*Leben*).[39] Gadamer claims that it was probably Rousseau's influence on German classicism that introduced the criterion of *Erlebtsein* (being experienced) and thus made possible the formation of the word *Erlebnis*.[40] However, this concept of life also forms the metaphysical background for German speculative idealism. Against the abstractness of understanding and the particularity of perception or representation, Gadamer points out that this concept implies a connection with totality, with infinity:

> Schleiermacher's appeal to living feeling against the cold rationalism of the Enlightenment, Schiller's call for aesthetic freedom against mechanistic society, Hegel's contrast between life (later, spirit) and "positivity," were the forerunners of the protest against modern industrial society, which at the beginning of our century caused the words *Erlebnis* and *Erleben* to become almost sacred clarion calls. The rebellion of the *Jugend Bewegung* (Youth Movement) against bourgeois culture and its institutions was inspired by these ideas, the influence of Friedrich Nietzsche and Henri Bergson played its part, but also a "spiritual movement" like that around Stefan George and, not least, the seismographical accuracy with which the philosophy of Georg Simmel reacted to these events, are all part of the same thing. The life philosophy of our own day follows on its romantic predecessors. The rejection of the mechanization of life in contemporary mass society makes the word seem so self-evident that its conceptual implications remain totally hidden.[41]

This confluence of influences, with the exception of that of Bergson, contributed to Buber's understanding of *Erlebnis*.[42] He will critique many of these influences in his later philosophical writings. Furthermore, remembering that Dilthey was Schleiermacher's biographer, Gadamer writes that although the word *Erlebnis* is not found in Schleiermacher, there are many synonyms,[43] which cover the range of meaning of the word, and the pantheistic background is always clearly in evidence: "Every act, as an element of life, remains connected with an infinity of life that manifests itself in it. Everything finite is an expression, a representation of the infinite."[44] In the connection of each *Erlebnis* with an infinity of life, Buber finds the experience of the overcoming of individuation. In each of these moments, the fullest possible response of the person leads to the realization of the unity of all things that is the meaning of life. Buber later responds to a suggestion that the concept of meeting arose out of the concept of *Erlebnis*: "In reality it arose, on the road of my thinking, out of the criticism of the concept of *Erlebnis*, to which I adhered in my youth, hence, out of a radical self-correction."[45]

Kohn remarks that the new generation at the turn of the century found the mechanization and specialization of science to be cold, lifeless, and unfruitful.[46] Buber found an intellectual home in a group called the *Neue Gemeinschaft* (New Community) during his time in Berlin, from 1899 to1901. The New Community, founded by brothers Heinrich and Julius Hart, adopted Nietzsche's Dionysian *Weltanschauung*.[47] A joyful, pantheistic, and naturalistic mood was its inspiration.[48] The concept of *Erlebnis* was adopted by this fraternity as a *sensus numinus* that gave access to a transcendent reality.[49] They held that as each *Erlebnis* is unique, if each individual person responds with his unique personality, then the *Erlebnis* (residing in the "I" of the person) and the corresponding moment of the eternal flux would be realized as one. This oneness liberates man from his individuated status and "engenders a noumenal-cum-sacred consciousness."[50] Buber adopted this understanding, as we shall see when we examine *Daniel*. In a lecture that Buber gave while associated with the New Community, *Alte und neue Gemeinschaft*,[51] he argues that the ideal is to extend these moments to the everyday and to enrich "all of life (*das Leben*) with a new meaning derived from the experience of the 'endless unity of becoming.'"[52] The group would be guided by the personal revelation of each individual rather than by dogma or creed of faith.[53] Buber then writes that he and some others want to live the ideal in their everyday lives.[54] The New Community has committed itself to this ideal through which a life would be established in which creative energy would glow and throb, existence would then become a work of art, "a new kind of art which creates from the sum of everything an integrated totality, and renders each day a divine sacrament."[55]

Buber writes of the shared *Erlebnis* that unites the individuals in the group. He quotes Gustav Landauer on this crucial *Erlebnis*, which, when individuals are differentiated thoroughly, they nevertheless find in their deepest selves this ancient and universal community with humanity and the cosmos.[56] Landauer, who became one of Buber's closest friends, was a leader of this New Community while Buber was associated with it. It may have been Landauer, who was eight years older than Buber, who encouraged him to switch his university studies from science and the history of art to Christian mysticism.[57] Landauer himself published the first modern edition of Meister Eckhart's writings in 1903.[58] Buber's interest in mysticism was in tune with the reaction of his generation to the rationalism and materialism of the Enlightenment. The new mysticism of this generation was not tied to any doctrine resting on a cognitive basis.[59] It was, according to Nietzsche, an ecstasy, based on a skepticism and a longing "that was not rooted in faith: *'je suis mystique et je ne crois a rien'*—as Flaubert expressed it in an oft-quoted dictum."[60] Crucial to an understanding of the variety of mysticism before the First World War, which influenced the arts, literature, and philosophical discourse of this generation of central Europe, is the influence of Fritz Mauthner.[61] Landauer was a close friend of Mauthner's and introduced him to Buber. Buber wrote to Mauthner on 24 April 1906 requesting him to contribute to the series of social-psychological studies that he edited, *Die Gesellschaft*.[62] Buber encourages Mauthner to consider a contribution to the series by writing: "*sie braucht Sie, braucht Sie mehr als irgend einen Anderen*" (it needs you, needs you more than everyone else).[63]

Mauthner (1849–1923) made a significant contribution to the formulation of the philosophical issues discussed by those interested in the New Mysticism.[64] However, this mysticism was not necessarily focused on God.[65] Mauthner explicitly developed an atheistic, or what he called a "godless," mysticism. A forerunner of modern linguistic philosophy, Mauthner questioned whether language was a suitable tool for gaining and expressing genuine knowledge, especially of the world in its totality. Landauer summarized Mauthner's argument in his study, *Skepsis und Mystik*: "Language, the intellect, cannot serve to bring the world closer to us, to transform the world in us. As a speechless part of nature, however, man transforms himself into everything, because he is contiguous with everything. Here begins mysticism."[66]

Mauthner fascinated his contemporaries, one of whom was Wittgenstein, with his conception of mysticism, particularly the mystic's difficulty in attempting to articulate the experience. Mauthner argued that "as soon as we really have something to say, we are forced to be silent." Note the similarity of this statement to Wittgenstein's at the end of the *Tractatus*: "What we cannot speak about we must pass over in silence."[67] Buber concerns himself with this inadequacy of language in his introduction to *Ecstatic Confessions*.[68] At a later stage, Buber acknowledged that from 1900 he was influenced by the German mystical tradition from Meister Eckhart to Angelus Silesius.[69]

During the years that Buber was associated with this community, he not only delivered the lecture, *"Alte und neue Gemeinschaft,"* but he also lectured on Boehme.[70] The lecture on Boehme probably formed the basis for the published essay "Über Jakob Boehme."[71]

BOEHME'S SYNTHESIS: A NEW SYMBOLIC FORM

Jacob Boehme (1575–1624) was born at Altseidenberg in Silesia.[72] His parents were only able to afford the usual religious schooling for him, together with some instruction in reading and writing.[73] He was a quiet, introspective youth who had a certain visionary tendency; he experienced highly personal visions that assumed for him the character of outwardness and reality. As Jacob was not suitable for agricultural work, he was apprenticed to a shoemaker. He spent several years wandering before settling as a shoemaker at a neighbouring town, Görlitz, in 1599. He was happily married with four sons and achieved a degree of prosperity. In 1600, he had a profound experience in which he saw the sun reflected on a burnished pewter dish with such splendour that it seemed to him that he could now look into the principles and deepest foundations of things. This experience opened for Boehme the process of God's self-manifestation through all things.[74] However, he did not record his experience until a second revelation in 1610 encouraged him to write on the meaning of his experience. This he did in his first book, *Morgenröthe im Aufgang*, published in 1612. He was then commanded to cease writing by the town council under the persuasion of the new Lutheran pastor. He obeyed until 1619, when a third renewal of the experience and the encouragement of some learned friends persuaded him to break his silence. He then wrote about his mystical illumination in a number of works, including *Vom dreifachen Leben der Menschen* (1620), *De Signatura Rerum* (1622), *Von der Gnaden-Wahl* (1623), and *Mysterium Magnum* (1623).[75]

Boehme lived at the last fruitful period of the Renaissance and in his writings created a synthesis of the underlying implications of the major streams of esoteric religious speculation.[76] This synthesis created the symbolizations through which the elements of a "magico-mystical philosophy" later passed to the Romantics and Idealists. Walsh argues that the main purpose behind the various spiritual impulses united by Boehme was "the recovery of a substantive experience of God's presence, and their common approach was a search for divinity in the more massive and indubitable realities of the immanent world. They believed with Giordano Bruno in the 'God in things.'"[77]

Although Boehme insisted on God's independent existence,[78] his articulation of the necessary sequence of the divine self-revelation exposed an underlying shift toward innerworldy perfection: "Almost unintentionally, Boehme had created the symbolic form for the later depiction of reality as a radically intramundane process."[79]

This shift, effected by Boehme's teachings, was a movement away from the philosophic experience of what Voegelin calls the truth of existence. From the experience of man's existence in a state of unrest, Plato and Aristotle articulated the questioning and searching for the ground of all reality. As the ground is not to be found as a thing in the external world, Plato, in the *Republic*, introduced the symbol of the Beyond, *epekeina*, as the criterion of the creative, divine ground.[80] The consciousness of this "questioning unrest in a state of ignorance becomes luminous to itself as a movement in the *psyche* towards the ground that is present in the psyche as its mover."[81] The spiritual person in search of the ground moves between ignorance and knowledge. In the Platonic perspective, the realm of the spiritual is halfway between (*metaxy*) god and man.[82] The ground which man is in search of is not a spatially distant thing, but "a divine presence that becomes manifest in the experience of unrest and the desire to know."[83]

The search itself is the site of the meeting between man and the divine Beyond that is thus at the same time revealed as a reality that is accessible to the philosopher's quest. The Platonic symbolization of divine being as the creating, sustaining, and forming force within the world is expressed as *methexis*, which in medieval philosophy became the *participatio* of the world, including man, in transcendent being.[84] Voegelin summarizes the experience of transcendence as "a movement of the soul, culminating in an act of transcendence in which the divine Within reveals itself as the divine Beyond."[85] Voegelin reformulates Plato's insight in the following words: "the realms of being, as well as the objects within them, are never merely immanent; over their index of immanence there is always superimposed the index of embracing transcendence."[86] Buber, in his early writings, does not understand the divine–human encounter; rather, he elevates the human pole into an absolute. Buber takes many steps before he acknowledges the divine presence within is also the Divine beyond.

Boehme's conception of reality as a single unfolding of God's self-revelation gave rise to a new symbolic form. This symbolism was a crucial step in the movement toward the rejection of transcendence and the emergence of the perversion of immanence, though Boehme himself did not actually take this step. The perversion of immanence, according to Voegelin, is a movement toward "a wilful groundlessness, i.e. a rejection of the transcendent ground already known and a refusal to engage in search of it through faith."[87] The shift that results in the perversion of immanence and the rejection of transcendence, Voegelin argues, is a revolt against the socially dominant perversion of transcendence through the fundamentalism of ecclesiastic Christianity. The meditative search of both philosophy and faith was overlaid by the late-medieval, radical doctrinization of both metaphysics and theology that eventually led to the Enlightenment.

Buber's personal revolt was against the arid, life-denying intellectuality of the ghetto and the overemphasis of official rabbinical Judaism on a rigid ceremonial law. However, Buber recognized that a period in which a culture disintegrates and loses its cohesion can be a time of fruitful chaos in which the seed of a growing religiousness can develop. This emergent religiousness can be a revolutionary principle that destroys old forms and releases suppressed energy.[88] The perversion of immanence and revolt against transcendence were phases on Buber's journey toward recognition of the ground of all reality as a divine presence. It was much later that the search led him to the principle of participation, and he could then declare that the one thing needful for an authentic life is being "true to the being in which and before which I am placed."[89] In many ways, it was a journey back to the real position of Boehme, of whom Martensen wrote: "It is undeniable that there are few men whose life and thought so pregnantly express the saying of the Apostle, that 'in God we live, and move, and have our being.'"[90] This journey toward recognition of the fundamental connection between the divine presence as the ground of the *metaxy* and also as the ground of the "Between" (*das Zwischenmenschliche*) of interpersonal relations is the path that we will now begin to trace.

"ÜBER JAKOB BOEHME" 1901

This essay on Boehme was published in the *Wiener Rundschau* in June 1901. It is not published in an English translation, although some excerpts from it have been included in the works of commentators.[91] I will argue that the influence of Nietzsche prepared Buber at this time to accept Valentine Weigel's notion of the "Becoming God" and Feuerbach's conception of the "new God we create" and blinded him to those elements of Boehme's conception that would later assume great importance in the formation of his own philosophy. However, I submit that Boehme's question concerning the manifestation of God's presence in reality takes hold of Buber, and this in turn connects with his personal search to understand presence as a result of his mother's absence. I will endeavour to make explicit the implicit question of presence that I believe underlies Buber's early writings.

In his opening sentence, Buber claims that "Boehme's basic problem, about which all his thoughts gather, is the relationship of the individual to the world."[92] This interpretation represents Buber's own involvement with this question, an involvement that was already manifest in his association with the New Community, rather than Boehme's concern to elaborate the process through which God's presence is manifest in all things.

In what may be taken as a statement of his personal position, Buber writes: "The world remains the mystery, which has an influence on us and on which one has an influence and which yet is always distant and strange. The individual consumes himself in dumb hopeless loneliness." The isolation of the person and the desire to overcome this isolation are evident. What constitutes the "mystery" and the "strangeness" of the world for Buber? There is the closed, hopeless solitude that betokens separation, alienation, and a lack of belonging. One is reminded that Buber described this period in his life as a "World of Confusion." Buber was to find the rootedness he needed, partially in his relationship with his wife, Paula, and also in the restoration of the connection with his own Jewish community and through his participation in Zionism.[93]

Later, referring to historical periods when the human spirit becomes solitary and the universe appears alien and uncanny, Buber writes that man finds "he can no longer stand up to the universal forms of present being; he can no longer truly meet them."[94] Finally, having sought a divine form of being with which he can communicate, man "reaches a condition when he can no longer stretch his hands out from his solitude to meet a divine form. That is at the basis of Nietzsche's saying, 'God is dead.'"[95] We may note here a comment made by Nietzsche in a letter: "For all those who somehow had a 'god' for company, what I know as solitude did not yet exist."[96] Experiencing the profound effect of his mother's absence and his estrangement from his roots in Judaism in 1901, Buber perhaps identifies with this experience of solitude and remains under this influence of Nietzsche.

Buber then claims that for Boehme God and nature are one, as soul and body or as energy and organism form unified beings. Boehme portrays the world as a tree that from root to flower and fruit is permeated by one life-giving sap, and which is formed and ordered from within by its own germinal activity.[97] Although the tendency to pantheism is inherent in this symbolism, Boehme repeatedly stresses God's independent existence.[98] He writes that the two principles of love and anger proceed from the one source and are dependent on each other. Boehme adds:

> Not that we mean that God thus receiveth a beginning: but it is the eternal beginning of the manifestation of God, viz. how the divine understanding doth manifest itself with power in distinct variety, and worketh itself forth into a kingdom; which is an eternal generation. We only speak here how the invisible, unperceivable God doth introduce himself into perception for his own manifestation.[99]

Boehme is careful to avoid the charge of pantheism; he does not wish to be considered to be speaking *"heidnisch,"* but rather insists that his meaning is to be interpreted as *"philosophisch."*[100] He does not attempt to identify God and nature, but tries to draw attention to the necessity of their separation as the necessary condition for divine self-manifestation. Boehme considers his understanding to be theosophy, *theosophisch*. In his later dissertation on Cusa and Boehme, Buber argues that when Boehme protested against the assertion that he identifies nature with God, this may be partly due to the limitations imposed on free expression at that time.[101] This statement serves to illustrate Buber's own position.

Boehme explains that the relation between God and the soul is like that between the sun and a pane of glass: the sun shines through glass and yet the glass is not turned into sun. He also uses the image of fire glowing through iron, where the two are intimately conjoined, yet both remain separate, and the iron exercises no power over the fire.[102]

THE GROUNDLESS WILL: THE *UNGRUND*

Buber turns his attention to a significant statement from Boehme concerning the eternal will: "Nature cannot become distinguished from the power of God, it is all one body. We recognise that God in his own nature is not a being but only the power or the reason for being as a groundless [*ungrundlicher*] eternal will."[103] Boehme argues that the search for the origin of all reality arrives at its goal when it encounters a ground that is not itself based on any further ground. This he calls the groundless *Ungrund*, which contains all other realities within itself. Boehme emphasizes its utterly unknowable character as that which it-self has no ground. His conception of the *Ungrund* is similar to earlier notions such as Anaximander's "boundless" (*apeiron*) or Eckhart's ex-perience of God as the "abyss" (*Abgrund*).[104]

The crucial Boehmean conception—which will exercise a massive influence on subsequent thought—is that will precedes being. The *Un-grund*, the groundless Godhead, is understood as a "dark primordial will to self-revelation,"[105] which in order to know itself must unfold itself in the process of reality. The change that the principle—according to which will precedes being—brings about in speculative thought on the nature of man and reality is highlighted by Walsh:

> This notion constituted a sharp reversal of the classical and medi-aeval contention that, from the perspective of transcendent real-ity, being is prior to will, that the fullness of divine Being is not involved in a process of becoming. It arose from the underlying shift of focus from the perfection of being beyond time to one that can be more tangibly realised within it. Of necessity, this im-plied the conception of reality as a process in which will or desire is a moving force that universally precedes the fullest actualiza-tion of being, and it involved the construction of reality on the analogy of finite and especially human development.[106]

Buber's early writings are shaped by this notion: will and becoming are prior to being.

THE MANIFESTATION OF GOD

The question then asked by Buber is "How, out of the unity of power, the world, the individual and different things, or—which means the same thing—how out of God the human being comes into being?" Ac-cording to Buber, Boehme explains this Becoming (*Werden*) through the element of play that is innate to the unity of power. God goes into nature "that his power may come into separateness and sensitiveness and that there shall be a movement and play in him because the energies play with one another and thus reveal, find and feel themselves in this play and wrestling." Thus, Buber continues, out of the playing original power (*Urkraft*), the forms that slumber in it evolve. Thus "all being exists because of play and the creative struggles; the world has no other meaning and purpose than this."[107]

Buber next concerns himself with the question of how the One is revealed in the Many because this is the question that is of primary interest to him. This allows him to outline the process and to claim that play and creative struggles are the meaning and purpose of the world without stating the ultimate reason. This interpretation is in accordance with the ideals of the New Community. However, Boehme's more fundamental question is "Why does God go into nature?" The answer to this question is the key to Boehme's symbolization:

> No thing can be revealed to itself without opposition [*Wiederwartigkeit*]. For if there is nothing that opposes it then it always goes out of itself and never returns to itself again. If it does not return into itself, as into that from which it originated, then it knows nothing of its origin [*Urstand*].[108]

This principle and its implications have a twofold effect on Buber. As a reason for God creating the world, it obstructs him in his search for presence; as a principle in the development of self-consciousness, it is eventually incorporated into his mature philosophy. According to Boehme: "The darkness is the greatest enmity of the light, and yet it is the cause that the light is manifest. For if there were no black, then white could not be manifest to itself; and if there were no sorrow, then joy were also not manifest to itself."[109] This knowledge is the result of Boehme's central experience of the flash (*Blitz*) in which the divine light breaks through the dark selfishness of the soul, and in a glance (*Blick*) in which the soul realizes that all reality is constituted by the same struggle to give birth to the light of divine revelation.[110]

Again, Boehme claims that all essences are but the manifestation of God, and it is only of this that he can write "and not of the unmanifested God, who, without his manifestation, also were not known to himself."[111] If God, the divine One, did not reveal himself in the multiplicity of the world, he would remain unknown to himself. As Boehme asks: "How can there be knowledge of self in one single will?"[112]

The transmission of Boehme's perspective and its incorporation and expansion in Hegel's system led to a more radically innerworldly appropriation of the Boehmean symbolic structure.[113] Hegel achieves this through the elimination of any separately existing divinity outside of the unfolding process of history. Buber also, for his part, confirms his estrangement from the notion of a transcendent God in his appropriation of the positions of Valentine Weigel and Ludwig Feuerbach.

VALENTIN WEIGEL

Turning next to Weigel, Buber claims that as "Boehme's teacher, the strange Valentin Weigel argued [that] it is only through the creation of the world that God becomes God, therefore the world is not Being [*Sein*] but Becoming [*Werden*]."[114]

As Valentin Weigel is a little-known figure in the history of philosophy, I will give a brief outline of his position. Weigel [1533–88] was a Lutheran mystical writer who recycled the doctrines of mediaeval mysticism through secretly circulated tracts expounding the idealism of Meister Eckhart.[115] At this time in the Renaissance, the "theoretical element of recognising in Nature the creative divine power came forward pure and unmixed."[116] Weigel attempted to combine the mystical tradition represented by Meister Eckhart with the philosophy of nature taught by Paracelsus.[117] The doctrine of the analogy between macrocosm and microcosm was revived in various forms. The general metaphysical principle was that the divine nature was held to be fully and entirely contained in each individual manifestation.[118] From this emerged the key inference of the current theory of knowledge. Weigel argues that one can only know that with which one is ontologically identified: "man knows the all in so far as he is the all."[119] The principle is derived from Eckhart's belief that God is in all places, in each with His entire essence. Though Eckhart added that insofar as God is in all things as their intelligent principle, He is also above them.[120]

This principle of Eckhart's mysticism now took on a definite form, using the Neoplatonic triple division of man and thus yielding a scheme for a metaphysical anthropology.[121] As body, man belongs to the material world and unites in himself the essences of all material things in a superior and most compact form. Because of this, he is able to understand the corporeal world. As an intellectual being, he belongs to the "sidereal" world and is therefore able to know the intellectual world.

Finally, as a divine spark, a partial manifestation of the highest principle of life, he is also able to become conscious of the divine nature
whose image he is.[122] It is important to note that for Eckhart, the Godhead, the Absolute, is distinguished from God. The Godhead "has no
predicates and is above all understanding, incomprehensible, and inex-
pressible."[123] The Godhead is "in so far a nothing, a not-God, not-spirit,
not-person, not-image, and yet, as the negation of negation, he is at the
same time the unlimited '*In se*,' the possibility to which no species of
essence is wanting, in which every thing is (not one, but) unity. The
Godhead as such cannot be revealed. It becomes manifest first in its
persons."[124]

We may note how close this understanding of the Godhead is to
Boehme's notion of the *Ungrund*. There is already a withdrawal from
this conception in Weigel's writings or at least in Buber's interpretation
of Weigel's work. In the remainder of the essay, Buber moves further
away from Boehme's notion of the world as the unfolding process of
God's self-revelation. Significantly, in doing so, Buber loses sight of
the ground or origin of the multiplicity of things. For Buber, God *is not*,
but only comes into existence through the becoming of the world.

It can be argued that Buber was inclined toward this interpretation
by his appreciation of Nietzsche. At the end of a short appreciative
essay written in 1900, "Ein Wort über Nietzsche und die Lebenswerte"
(A Word on Nietzsche and Life Values), Buber writes: "To the creator
god he brings a great opponent: the becoming God in whose development we can participate, the dimly glimpsed product of future evolutions."[125] In his essay on Boehme, Buber argues that we create the
world: "Reality is new every day and each morning it offers itself anew
to our creating hands. We already create the world by unconsciously
lending to our perceptions concentration and solidity that make it into
a reality, when in every moment an unconscious existential judgement
speaks in us about the things, i.e. about sense impressions: this is
[*Dieses ist*]."[126] Furthermore, Buber explains that in a deeper and more
inward way, we form the world consciously in that we deliberately intervene in the becoming. He argues that we ourselves intervene in the
fate of the world and are part of the great becoming event. Then the
changes that our creativity brings about become themselves sources of
countless new liberating sense-impressions of many beings. Therefore,
we are not slaves, but the beloved of our world. This is Buber's understanding of Boehme's words: "thus everything is still in the process of
creation."

It is now man who is the creator of all things in a process in which there is continual creation. Thus man is the ground or source of all that he creates, and himself takes part in creating the "great becoming event," which according to the previous section, is the becoming God. This creative force is realized when man asserts his own uniqueness as a creator; only in this way does one overcome individuation. Buber's friend and hero, Gustav Landauer, in a contemporaneous essay, claims that "I am the cause [*Ursache*] of my own person, because I am the world. I am the world when I am totally myself."[127] One of the founders of the New Community, Julius Hart, wrote at the time: "Why do you seek the thing-in-itself and then declare it inscrutable, unfathomable? You are the thing-in-itself! You are God—the hub of the universe—the center of the sun—the core of matter—substance!" and "You should know that you are not created spirits, but rather you are creating spirits."[128] This echoes Nietzsche's call to human beings to become creators rather than mere creatures of the flux.[129] This call to creativity presupposes that man has a "creative Eros," an inner force only realized by each person in daring to assert his or her individuality.[130] Buber has shown the origin of this creative force and that it is intrinsic to human nature. There is no doubt that the manner in which Buber interprets Boehme is distinctly Nietzschean.

If we now reconsider the opening section of the essay where Buber claims that for Boehme "God and nature are one" and "we recognise that God in his own nature is not a being but only the power or the reason for being as a groundless, eternal will," we can argue that this "God" is identifiable with that creative force, the eternal will to create located only in human beings. It is groundless because it has no ground beyond the human beings in whom it is present. It has no ground in a transcendent deity. There is no acknowledgment of the presence of a transcendent God.

THE UNITY OF OPPOSING PRINCIPLES

Proceeding with the essay, Buber writes that for Boehme, all things are moved through two basic energies: the "struggle-longing" and the "love-longing." These, however, writes Buber, are not the old Empedoclean powers that have nothing in common and which tear the world from one extreme to the other, depending on which one becomes master.[131] For Boehme, on the other hand, struggle and love are united in a yearning motion toward each other that adopts different forms.[132] The motion of struggle leads to individuation and the motion of love to God. According to Boehme, these two forces reveal God. They are both present in the variety of forms of creatures and therefore the One is revealed in the many. Man is "created both out of time and eternity, out of the Being of all beings, and made an image of the divine manifestation."[133] Each person is a microcosm of the divine nature; the same forces of conflict and love are present in him or her as in God. Boehme continued the notion of the coincidence of opposites present in Nicholas of Cusa's writings. Boehme, as I have indicated, is affirming a transcendent God. Buber, in keeping with the tradition of speculative mysticism, will avail himself of Boehme's theosophical speculation in his own account of the becoming God.

Before continuing with the essay let us note two points. One is Boehme's notion of the struggle that leads to individuation, and the love that leads to God may be understood as the key to Buber's later understanding of "Distance and Relation." Buber argues that the principle of human life is not simple, but twofold. It is a twofold movement in which the one movement is the presupposition of the other. The first movement is the "setting at a distance," and the second is the "entering into relation." The first movement is the presupposition of the second because one can enter into relation only with a being that has been set at a distance; more precisely, a being that has become an independent opposite. Buber adds that it is only for man that an independent opposite exists.[134] This principle is remarkably similar to the dialectical principle explained by Boehme. Without discussing all the similarities at length, it is enough to draw attention to the following. Both struggle and love are parts of the unity, as distance and relation are parts of the one principle; struggle and distance lead to individuation; love and relation lead to God, whether as Boehme's conception or as the eternal Thou; neither the concept of love nor of relation leads to union, but rather to a mutual dependence in which the individuals remain independent but related opposites. The other is that Boehme repeatedly stresses that man is made in the image of God. It is precisely this point that Buber mentions in his reading of the testament of the Baal-Shem-Tov, who was as previously mentioned, one of the founders of Hasidism:

"Man's being created in the image of God I grasped as deed, as becoming, as task. And this primally Jewish reality was a primal human reality, the content of human religiousness."[135] In Buber's awakening, in his mid-twenties, he recognized the primal Jewish reality as a primal human reality, and this led to his study of Hasidism. This recognition may have been helped by his previous study of Boehme. In the Hasidic tradition, he would certainly have discovered many ideas also present in the German mystical tradition.[136] (However, it was at least another ten years before he rediscovered and accepted the root of both traditions—that is, the presence of a God who is both immanent and transcendent.)

Having mentioned that the motion of struggle leads to individuation and the motion of love to God, Buber comments that he would like to dwell for a while on this "peculiar path-destination [*Weg-bestimmung*]." Buber's comments are selective because he fails to include Boehme's grounding of the two forces in an existing transcendent God. He quotes Boehme as follows:

> It is in nature always for one to be put against the other, that one is the enemy of the other, and not with the final purpose that they are hostile towards each other, but that one moves the other in conflict and reveals the other in itself. Because if there was only one will then all beings would do but one thing, but in opposition [*Widerwillen*] each thing raises itself in itself to its victory and elevation [*Erhöhung*]; and in this conflict stands all life and growth.[137]

Buber presents this quote from Boehme, but omits the remainder of the quotation, which continues: "and thereby the divine Wisdom is made manifest and comes into form to contemplation and to the kingdom of joy; for in the conquest is joy. But one only will is not manifest to itself, for there is neither evil nor good in it, neither joy nor sorrow; and if there were, yet the one, viz. the only will, must first in itself bring itself into contrary, that it might manifest itself."[138] This key Boehmean conception on the necessity of a contrary position is similar to Buber's later emphasis on confrontation in the "Religion as Presence" lectures. According to Boehme, wisdom proceeds from the eternal will; it is the manifestation of God.[139] Buber, in leaving out this statement, is again refusing to perceive the ground of the manifestation and concentrating on the results as if they were self-creating.

Next, Buber denies the presence of a transcendent God and His revelation in the world through his agreement with Feuerbach's position:

> Every being yearns for the other, the higher towards the lower and the lower towards the higher, for they are separated from each other and in this hunger they embrace one another in the desire. This however, according to Boehme, is the right way to the new God whom we create, to the new unity of forces. [*Dies aber ist nach Boehme der rechte Weg zum neuen Gott, den wir schaffen, zur neuen Einheit der Kräfte.*] This opinion finds in a phrase of Ludwig Feuerbach its affirmation and completion: "Man for himself is man (in the ordinary sense); Man with man—the unity of I and Thou——is God." Feuerbach wants to see the unity, of which he speaks, resting on the "reality of the distinction of I and Thou." We however stand today nearer to Boehme than to the teaching of Feuerbach, to the feeling of St. Francis of Assisi who called the trees, the birds and stars his brothers and sisters and still nearer to the Vedânta.[140]

The quotation from Feuerbach is from the *Principles of the Philosophy of the Future*. The full principle, number 60, reads: "Solitude is finiteness and limitation; community is freedom and infinity. Man for himself is man (in the ordinary sense); the unity of I and Thou—is God."[141] Following, but also going beyond Hegel, Feuerbach took the step in which God was fully humanized in all humanity, and the existence of a transcendent God was denied. Feuerbach explains:

> Religion is the childlike condition of humanity; but the child sees his nature—man—out of himself; in childhood a man is an object to himself, under the form of another man. Hence the historical progress of religion, consists in this: that what by an earlier religion was regarded as objective, is now regarded as subjective; that is, what was formerly contemplated and worshipped as God is now perceived to be something *human*.[142]

While Buber will later criticize Feuerbach's "anthropological reduction, the reduction of being to human existence,"[143] in this early period, he actually welcomes it. Indeed, welcoming Feuerbach's affirmation of the new God whom we create as the highest subject of philosophy, Buber only dismisses Feuerbach's idea that this unity should rest on the distinction between the I and the Thou. This is expressed in principle 59:

> The single man for himself possesses the essence of man neither in himself as a moral being nor in himself as a thinking being. The essence of man is contained only in the community and unity of man with man; it is a unity, however, which rests only on the distinction between I and Thou.[144]

Later, Buber will write that these words "introduced that discovery of the Thou which has been called 'the Copernican revolution' of modern thought. . . . I myself was in my youth given a decisive impetus by Feuerbach."[145] In 1901, Buber shows his overwhelming desire for unity and his rejection of any form of dualism in his statement dismissing the distinction between man and man: "We however stand today nearer to Boehme than to the teaching of Feuerbach, to the feeling of St. Francis of Assisi who called the trees, the birds and stars his brothers and sisters and still nearer to the Vedânta."[146] The Vedânta refers to the central tradition of Hindu philosophy based on the Vedas. This states that reality is nondual and that the seeming multiplicity of the world is actually *maya*, or the illusion of creation.[147] However, the assumption of a multiplicity of diverse beings is present in Boehme's conception. Buber states that struggle unfolds the individual thing to personality [*Der Kampf entfaltet das Einzelding zur Personlichkeit*]. He adds that love leads the individual thing toward a reborn unity of powers [*Die Liebe aber führt das Einzelding der wiedergeborenen Krafteinheit zu*]. The latter is the aforementioned "new God whom we create." This conception, however, implies a mutual dependency in order to achieve harmony: "Out of the intertwining of both [struggle and love] life comes into being, in which things stay not in rigid isolation but also not fused with each other, but mutually dependent on each other."[148] Buber is not yet content with this position because it is not in accordance with his view or the views of the New Community. These views are strongly influenced by Schopenhauer and Nietzsche. Buber studied Schopenhauer's book, *The World as Will and Representation*, while he was at the University of Leipzig prior to writing his essay on Boehme.[149] He then studied in Berlin under Dilthey, who, as already mentioned, emphasized the continuity between the mystical tradition and German Idealist philosophy. Buber was very familiar with Schopenhauer's work, as we will discover when considering *Daniel*.

The idea that individuation is "a veil of Maya," a terrible illusion fraught with pain, is advanced by Schopenhauer. For him, the eyes of the "uncultured individual" are clouded by the veil of Maya: "To him is revealed not the thing-in-itself, but only the phenomenon in time and space, in the *principium individuationis*, and in the remaining forms of the principle of sufficient reason. In this form of his limited knowledge he sees not the inner nature of things, which is one, but its phenomena as separated, detached, innumerable, very different, and indeed opposed."[150] This view of opposition and separation as part of the veil of Maya may have clouded Buber's eyes to the importance of Boehme's emphasis on opposition and Feuerbach's insistence on the distinction between the I and Thou. Schopenhauer claims that the thing-in-itself can be experienced and known, and therefore there is a way of going beyond Kant's position. This way is a path through interiority, and it is precisely this that interests Buber. Like Schopenhauer, he wants to go beyond Kant's restriction of knowledge to the realm of appearances. He wishes to have immediate experience, *Erlebnis*, of the thing-in-itself, that is, the *noumenon*. According to Schopenhauer, the subject of knowing appears as an individual through his bodily identity. However, this body is given to him in two different ways. First, it is given in intelligent perception as representation, as an object among objects, or we could add as an object to a subject. Second, it is also given as what is known immediately to everyone and is denoted by the word *will*; here we could add that it is given as subject to subject.[151] The will reveals itself directly to each person as the in-itself of his or her phenomenal being.[152] Schopenhauer's concept of will is broader than that commonly used:

> For as the *known* in self-consciousness we find exclusively the *will*. For not only willing and deciding in the narrowest sense, but also all striving, wishing, shunning, hoping, fearing, loving, hating, in short, all that directly constitutes our own weal and woe, desire and disinclination, is obviously only affection of the will, is a stirring, a modification, of willing and not-willing, is just that which, when it operates outwards, exhibits itself as an act of will proper.[153]

Schopenhauer claims that this immediate consciousness of self is instantiated in all human beings and in the cosmos as a totality: "But only the *will* is *thing-in-itself*. . . . It is the innermost essence, the kernel, of every particular thing and also of the whole. It appears in every blindly acting force of nature, and also in the deliberate conduct of man, and the great difference between the two concerns only the degree of the manifestation, not the inner nature of what is manifested."[154] Man is therefore considered by Schopenhauer to be the microcosm who contains both will and, as a knowing subject, representation:

> Thus everyone in this twofold regard is the whole world itself, the microcosm; he finds its two sides whole and complete within himself. And what he thus recognises as his own inner being also exhausts the inner being of the whole world, of the macrocosm. Thus the whole world, like man himself, is through and through will and through and through representation, and beyond this there is nothing.[155]

Schopenhauer thus considers the will or the thing-in-itself to be groundless; it is free from all plurality, although its phenomena and manifestations in time and space are innumerable. It is itself one, yet not in the manner in which an object is one. Whereas a concept originates only through abstraction from plurality, the will is one as that which lies outside time, space, and the *principium individuationis*, that is to say, outside the possibility of plurality.[156] Schopenhauer's viewpoint bears a close similarity to that which Buber extracted from the writings of Boehme, as we will discover in the next section of the essay.

Buber claims that Boehme is not satisfied with love and struggle as bridges between the individual I and the world. Buber admits that in this dissatisfaction, Boehme is closest to him. Boehme, Buber claims—and we know that Buber himself shared this perspective—longed for a deeper unity: "It is not enough that the I unites itself to the world. The I is the world."[157] However, this is not to be understood in the manner adopted by Berkeley or Fichte, but "in the meaning of that great Renaissance teaching of the microcosmos, which through Leibniz and Goethe still has an effect."[158] Buber claims that this teaching was hinted at in antiquity, that it was present in schematic and lifeless form in scholasticism and was deepened by Cusa, Agrippa, Paracelsus, and Weigel. It was Boehme, according to Buber, who proceeded with it in the most beautiful and most intuitive form. Buber quotes Boehme: "God is not compartmentalised but is everywhere whole and where he reveals himself there he is wholly revealed." Buber then adds: "And since God is the unity of all forces, so each individual thing bears the qualities of all things in itself, and what we call individuality is only a higher grade of development of some one or other quality." Each individual thing possesses all the qualities, but only one quality is principal and this dominates all the others. Buber invokes Boehme's example of a stone or a piece of earth to elucidate this point:

> When I take up a stone or clod of earth and look upon it, then I see that which is above and that which is below, yea, [I see] the whole world therein; only, that in each thing one property happeneth to be the chief and most manifest; according to which it is named. All the other properties are jointly therein; only in various diverse degrees and centres.[159]

For Boehme, the presence of all qualities in each thing constituted "the manifestation of God, according to love and anger, eternity and time."[160] He was not satisfied with a description of the divine cosmic powers without any reference to their origins in eternity, explains Walsh.[161] Boehme criticized the astronomical and alchemical sciences that explain much about the "branches" of the cosmic tree, while "the root of the tree remains hidden to them."[162] Buber identifies the immanent creative forces in each thing as God and omits any reference to the "root of the tree": the Being who is manifested.

Buber then quotes Boehme—who repeatedly refers to the inclusion of all these properties in the human being: "That in man the whole creation lies; but heaven and earth with all beings even God himself lies in the human."[163] This is the general metaphysical principle of those Renaissance writers mentioned by Buber—Cusa, Agrippa, Paracelsus, and Weigel—that the divine nature was entirely contained in each of its finite manifestations. Buber then identifies with the experience of this unity:

> This wonderful world feeling has become peculiarly our own. We have woven it into our inmost experience. When I take a piece of fruit to my mouth, I feel: this is my body; and when I put wine to my lips, I feel: this is my blood. And we are sometimes overcome with a desire to put our arms around a young tree and to feel the same life-rhythm or to read in the eyes of a silent animal our innermost mystery. We experience the maturing and wilting of the most distant stars as something which is happening to us. And

there are moments in which our organism is an altogether different piece of nature.[164]

Schaeder argues that the "youthful candour of the pantheistic confession in this essay on Boehme, reminding us of the words with which
Christ ordained the sacraments required for salvation, could be regarded by hostile critics as a form of literary blasphemy."[165] She adds
that in reality, however, it expresses a "naïve pan-sacramentalism"
found in the works of many poets and later described by Buber as a
preliminary stage for the "sacramental existence" of the Hasidim.[166] It
has also been described as a curious fusion of Renaissance mysticism
and turn-of-the-century vitalism.[167] It points toward Buber's experience
of ecstatic states that, he later writes, prevented him from being present
to another.

Finally, toward the end of the essay, Buber adds that if for Boehme
all is in man, then for him the development of man can only be an unfolding: "It all grows out of our interior being." We know the world
because we have it in ourselves. Buber finds that Weigel has expressed
something similar: "One might think the outer objects [that is, the objects of our perception] are able to bring to the human being some kind
of knowledge, though it is only the awakening of it [the knowledge];
what man is and shall be through nature and grace, that he must have
and possess in himself."[168] The potential is totally within man and requires actualization through its own unfolding. What is it that begins
this unfolding? According to Boehme, "God instils no new or strange
spirit in us, but only opens with his spirit our spirit." If God unlocks
the potential that is inherent in man, then man would be ultimately dependent on God. How does Buber, however, reconcile this statement
with his understanding of God? Buber then adds that above all he believes that nothing can be introduced into the human being from an external source, but rather that everything can be drawn out because we
have the world in us. As Boehme considers everything is in everything,
Buber claims that for Boehme there is no distinction in the value of
things. For this reason, Buber concludes that Boehme considers "Giving" [Schenken] to be a natural quality and a necessary condition of
self-unfolding. This condition would then be constitutive of the creative
forces present in each person.

On the other hand, there remains the question of whether man is actually dependent on a more ultimate ground. Both possibilities may be
argued from the ambivalent last paragraph of the essay:

Because for [Boehme] everything is in everything, thus for him the giving [as a present] is a natural quality and a necessary condition of self-unfolding. "The sun," he says, "gives herself with her energy without gradation, she loves each piece of fruit and plant and withholds herself from no thing; she wants nothing other than from each and every plant, or whatever it is, to raise up a good fruit; because she accepts all things, whether they are bad or good, and gives to them her will to love; that she can not do otherwise, because she is no other being than what she is in herself."[169]

CONCLUSION

In considering Buber's essay on Jacob Boehme, we have noted how Buber's interpretation shifts away from Boehme's position on the transcendence of the Godhead to an acceptance of the becoming God, largely due to the influence of Nietzsche and Weigel. That Boehme created the symbolic form that was to influence subsequent generations of thinkers is without question. The important conclusion for this investigation is that we have established Buber's own position on transcendence and immanence. We can claim the following:

- Buber, in adopting the notion of "the becoming God whom we create," denies the being of any transcendent deity.
- Buber does not even admit the existence of an immanent God.
- Buber accepts the existence of a God who is created by the unity of the creative acts of human beings.
- Buber, in adopting the principle that God himself lies in the human being, identifies the human being and God; they are one, not two beings present to each other.
- Buber thus affirms the divinity of the human being.

However, Buber's experience of his mother's absence remains a limitation; the deaths of loved ones concern all human beings and put this elevation of humanity into question. It is at this time that he wrote to Paula, saying, "ever and always I have been seeking my mother."[170] A question remains as to whether there is a meeting that will never be a mis-meeting, a presence that is always present. As Balthasar argues, the ancient world had "sought to keep before its eyes the dark shadowy, even terrible aspects of reality, but also to find a *locus standi* from which, without closing one's eyes to anything, it would be possible to say a bold and decisive Yes to the whole of experience."[171] Buber's search for a *locus standi* from which he might understand absence and presence continues.

Buber remains interested in Boehme's writings and in the question of individuation. His doctoral dissertation is on a section of the history of this problem.[172] His intention was to write on the whole history from Aristotle to Leibniz; however, the dissertation is only on Cusa and Boehme. Intending to write the remainder, he argues that the section on Cusa and Boehme "could not receive a critical summary because such a summary could only emerge through a complete presentation of the historical connections."[173] It is impossible to determine Buber's personal position without such a summary. I will therefore only briefly summarize some of the main points and then draw attention to Buber's comments on Weigel.

Buber's Dissertation: Zur Geschichte des Individuationsproblems (Nikolaus von Cues und Jakob Böhme)

In 1904, Buber presented this doctoral dissertation to the University of Vienna. Buber chose to write on Cusa and Boehme in order to prove that they were two of the founders of the new metaphysics of the individual—true representatives of an era—whose drive toward personality has been convincingly portrayed by Dilthey. He also saw them as among the first thinkers who created the foundations for the ethics of personality, which Buber claims has found its most harmonious intellectual expression in Schleiermacher, and its most ecstatic literary expression in Emerson.

Cusa and Boehme share, writes Buber, an answer to the questions of the origin and meaning of the plurality and diversity of things:

> Both represent that point of view, which Lasswitz [*Geschichte der Atomistik* 1.264] calls one of the two fundamental ideas of the renewal of neo-Platonism in the Renaissance philosophy, "the concept of a development of plurality and diversity of the world of the senses out of the unity and simplicity of the idea," only that for Cusa this development means the emergence of a relative reality out of an absolute reality, with Boehme on the contrary it means the actualisation of the absolute possibility.[174]

Cusa was, according to Buber, the thinker who straddled the transition from scholasticism to the modern age. It is because Cusa took up anew the question of individuation and the uniqueness of each individual that he is to be considered the first modern thinker. The persistence (*Beharren*) of the individual in its distinctiveness and the absolute irreplaceable worth (*Unersetzlichkeits-Wert*) of the individual are the core of Cusa's contemplations.[175] This irreplaceable worth indicates an intrinsic connection between the individual and infinity. Each individual is charged with the perfection of its own nature although its "self-persistence" (*Selbstbeharren*) may lead to conflict. It is only from the powerful unfolding by each thing of its own being that the harmony of the world-process grows, that the One God appears in the numberless (*zahllosen*) diversity.[176]

This harmony has its justification in Cusa's pantheistic monism in which the world is the *deus sensibilis*: "All is God: the undivided origin, the unfolded world and the unified destination [*Einungsziel*] of all being. . . . In him are all things, even the opposites are included: he is the *complicatio contradictoriorum*."[177] This pantheism is a system "that sees God in everything but also outside everything." In it, all individual beings are divine; however, they are an "outflow from a unified origin, whose unity and wholeness suffer no harm [*Abbruch*] through this radiation or unfolding." The connections between Cusa's system and Plotinus are evident.[178]

Buber writes that Boehme took over the teaching on the microcosm from Paracelsus. Weigel's influence, however, was also crucial in the development of this problematic. Although Buber comments that Weigel's writings "dissolve into prayer, a sermon or an outpouring of an ecstatic experience," he adds that perhaps no one in his time leads so directly from Plato to Leibniz. Boehme, in what Buber interprets as his oscillation between theism and pantheism, treats the problem of the One and the Many as a problem of creation. It is in Weigel's teaching that a transition takes place that, according to Buber, surpasses that which is found in Boehme's speculation. This transition is the teaching that God, through the creation of the world, becomes God; that God, through the development of creation, comes to that self-knowledge that completes consciousness.[179]

This teaching is found in Weigel's little book *Erkenne Dich Selbst* (Know Thyself). Buber claims that this book had the greatest influence on Boehme, but he did not develop the thought. "Hegel still found it unused—however even he has grasped it and has in his way built it into complex ideas. Thereby some elements of the profound originality of Weigel were lost, above all the previously indicated idea of a development of God in the world."[180] Buber's statement that Weigel excelled Boehme and even Hegel, points to his judgment in favor of an immanent becoming God. Buber chooses in favor of the conceptions of Weigel and Feuerbach. In a short comment on Buber's dissertation, Franz Rosenzweig quoted this section concerning Weigel. He wrote that Buber had to break through the whole conceptual-fence (*Begriffszaun*) of Immanence-Transcendence to the freedom of real relations—the addressed and that which has addressed.[181]

Buber refers in his discussion of Boehme's *Ungrund* to Schopenhauer's "Sentences on the Ground" in book two, part eight of *The World as Will and Representation*. Schopenhauer in this section refers to the original forces that are present in everything in nature and for which no explanation is possible. Schopenhauer writes of the character of man that may be thought to explain each manifestation of his will: "But no reason can ever be stated for his having this character, for his willing in general, for the fact that, of several motives, just this one and no other, or indeed any motive moves his will. . . . That which for man is his unfathomable character . . . is for every inorganic body precisely its essential quality. . . . Its particular manifestations, by which alone it becomes visible, are subject to the principle of sufficient reason; it itself is groundless. Its essence was correctly understood by the scholastics, who described it as *forma substantialis*."[182] Buber, in his early writings, follows Schopenhauer's lead in considering the forces manifest in himself and in attempting to attain unity with the "unfathomable something." However, in his desire for unity, the full reality of the unfathomable in each other person is not immediately evident to him. The intrinsic value of each person is inextricably entwined with the fullness of relation. The *forma substantialis* represents the unknown innermost reality of beings, that is, their intrinsic value. It is only when Buber arrives at an understanding of the unfathomable effect or the fullness of presence of the other being that he appreciates relation. Substance in its presence is essential to relation.

3. The One Thing Needful

"Ecstasy and Confession," "The Teaching of the Tao," and
the Early Addresses "On Judaism"

Introduction

Between 1904, when he completed his dissertation on Cusa and
Boehme, and 1909, Buber withdrew from his activity in the Zionist
party and stopped writing articles and giving speeches. Having read the
testament of Rabbi Israel Baal-Shem in *Zevaat Ribesh*, Buber took five
years away from his normal activities and immersed himself in gathering and studying Hasidic literature.[1] During this period he published
two books on Hasidism: *Die Geschichten des Rabbi Nachman* (Tales of
Rabbi Nachman) and *Die Legende des Baal-Shem* (The Legend of the
Baal-Shem).

Buber retained his early interest in the mystical tradition. He collected the mystical confessions of people from many different cultures
and mentioned a plan for a work on European mystics in a letter to
Landauer on 10 February 1903. Buber envisaged that this work would
comprise a collection of mystical writings by German, Slavic, and Judaic mystics. In fact, when published in 1909, *Ecstatic Confessions* also
included Indian, Dutch, Italian, French, and Chinese ecstatic confessions. For the publication of this book, Buber wrote an introductory
essay called "Ecstasy and Confession." In it, Buber gives his interpretation of the mystical experience. He later repudiated his treatment of
unity in this introduction in favor of his discussion of unity in *Daniel:*

Dialogues on Realisation. The introductory essay therefore affords us an insight into Buber's early understanding of the mystic's experience and his conception of God.

Buber also repudiated his essay, "The Teaching of the Tao," which introduced his 1909 translation of selected *Talks and Parables of Chuang-Tzu*.[2] This essay deals with the oriental teaching that recognizes "the one thing needful": that the world's inner destiny, that is, unity, depends on the action of the human person for its realization. In this teaching, Buber found the elemental drive toward unity, which he was already familiar with in a religious form, in the mystical tradition.

Between 1909 and 1914, Buber gave a series of influential addresses on various elements of Judaism. These addresses are significant for our discussion because they contain what Buber later termed "inexact" or indeed "inaccurate" expressions. In the "Preface" to the 1923 edition, written when Buber had formulated his mature philosophy and published *I and Thou*, he "clarified" many of these expressions. Indeed, in editions subsequent to 1923, some sections of the addresses were changed or omitted. They remain, however, a guide to Buber's early position on the presence of God. These addresses and others were collected in the book, *On Judaism*.[3] The early addresses are Buber's communications to young Jewish intellectuals and Zionists before and during the First World War. The first three addresses were given to the Prague Bar Kochba Union, an influential Zionist association; subsequent addresses were delivered to a similar group in Berlin.

These writings are crucial to an understanding of Buber's position on the nature and presence of God. Together with *Daniel: Dialogues on Realisation*, which I will examine in the next chapter, they represent the period between the early writings on Nietzsche, Boehme, and Cusa and the events during the war that led to Buber's conversion to presence and dialogue. They also each contain Buber's leitmotiv: "the one thing that is needful." Buber drew this saying from the gospel of Luke (10:42) and interpreted it as expressing "Judaism's soul,"which "knows that all meaning-contents are null and void unless they grow into a unified one, and that in all of life this alone matters: to have such unity."[4] The key elements of Buber's mature philosophy of dialogue are in the context from which this saying is drawn. Buber, at this stage of his development, overlooks them in his desire for unity. It appears as if the only manner in which the loneliness, isolation, and separation that result from individuation, and especially from Buber's experience of the absence of his mother, can be overcome is through unity, but this is not so. It is through love, not a consuming love in which one is absorbed by the other being, but rather a love in which there is mutual delight in and respect for the unique otherness of each being. Love implies relation. Absence is overcome by presence, not by unity. The unity Buber desires and enjoys is such that it removes the mystic from the everyday commotion of the world and unites all in the self. Both characteristics dismiss the importance of the presence of oneself and the relation to another being. There are many stepping-stones on Buber's way to discovering "the one thing that is needful." Each of these appears as a resting place at the time to Buber. Each is repudiated until he finally discovers presence: "Being true to the being in which and before which I am placed is the one thing that is needful."[5]

In examining Buber's interpretation of Boehme's writings, I have established that at this stage of his development, Buber does not acknowledge the existence of either a transcendent or an immanent God. Nevertheless, Buber accepts an eternal will that is grounded in human beings and that enables them to realize "God." This God is identified with the human being in creative living experiences. The human being is therefore deified. Buber's roots were in the German philosophical tradition, especially in the writings of Boehme, Cusa, Schopenhauer, and Nietzsche. His interest in Hasidism led to his wish to know his own Judaic tradition. In the period in which the texts, which are the subject of this chapter, are written, Buber examines and writes on mysticism in different cultures. From these writings, with the knowledge of Buber's early position, we can extract the fundamental form of Buber's conception of God. This form, we will discover, also underlies his understanding of God in Judaism.

Part I: *Ecstatic Confessions: The Heart of Mysticism*

Plato, in the Myth of the Cave, describes the confusion and disorientation experienced by the person who returns to the cave to communicate what he has seen to his fellow prisoners. Buber's interest is in the ecstatic person who attempts to return from the experience of boundless unity and tries to express the ineffable in language. Buber writes that in these confessions "the power of the experience, the will to utter the ineffable, and the *vox humana* have created a memorable unity."[6] He thought that confessions that bore witness to these elements were worthy of inclusion. He is not concerned with explanation, but with the unclassifiable aspect of ecstasy. Buber appreciates that the ecstatic individual may be explained in terms of psychology, physiology, or pathology; however, he is more concerned with what is beyond explanation, the individual's experience: "We are listening to the human being speak of the soul and of the soul's ineffable mystery."[7]

In this collection of ecstatic confessions, Buber has recognized the equivalent experiences of human beings across time and cultures. He is collecting utterances of *the* human voice. These utterances are the attempts at articulating experiences that are ineffable. The experiences are of a descent into the depth of the psyche that may be expressed as an ascent to the vision of being, as in Parmenides' case. The movement is in search of the ground of reality. The depth that is ineffable, that is beyond articulation, was experienced by the Hellenic thinkers, Heraclitus, Aeschylus, and Plato.[8] Voegelin comments that the experience of the depth of the soul does not add a substantive content to our experiences of God, man, the world, and society, of existential tension, and of participation. The experience, however, does afford an insight into the process of reality from which the equivalent experiences and the articulating symbols emerge. As a philosopher, Buber is interested in these insights into the process of reality. As a person who has experienced ecstatic states, he is interested in communicating his understanding of the experience.

What is the essential character of this ecstatic experience for theistic mystics? In his book, *Studies in the Psychology of the Mystics*, Joseph Maréchal remarks that serious enquirers have reached an agreement to distinguish between the essential and the inessential in mysticism.[9] For Maréchal, the core of the mystical experience is the direct feeling of God's presence, or the intuition of God as present. He concludes: "We are thus compelled . . . to take as our centre of perspective the culminating point of these states—that is, the feeling of the immediate presence of a Transcendent Being."[10] Another understanding of this experience is expressed by Lonergan: "When finally the mystic withdraws into the *ultima solitudo*, he drops the constructs of culture and the whole complicated mass of mediating operations to return to a new, mediated immediacy of his subjectivity reaching for God."[11] Voegelin analyzes the classic experience of the differentiation of the human psyche and the

symbols created to articulate its structure. The unrest caused by ignorance of the ground and meaning of existence leads to the search for
the ground: "The consciousness of questioning unrest in a state of ignorance becomes luminous to itself as a movement in the psyche toward
the ground that is present in the psyche as its mover."[12] Mysticism is a
human experience and is an element in all major religious traditions.
Evelyn Underhill summarizes the general nature of the experience:
"Mysticism, in its pure form, is the science of ultimates, the science of
union with the Absolute, and nothing else, and the mystic is the person
who attains to this union."[13] Parmenides' experience is considered to
be mystical by Voegelin. *Nous* was the name given by Parmenides to
the human being's faculty of ascending to the vision of being, and *logos*
was the name given to the faculty of analyzing the content of the vision.
Voegelin writes of Parmenides' ascent: "the experience was so intense
that it tended toward the identification of *nous* and being, of *noein* and
einai [B3]; in the rapture of the vision the knower and the known would
fuse into the one true reality (*aletheia*), only to be separated again when
the *logos* became active in exploring the experience and in finding suitable language symbols for its expression."[14]

There is no doubt that Buber had ecstatic experiences. He states this
clearly in the autobiographical fragment "Conversion." What happens
in the ecstatic experience is of the greatest importance to him. These
experiences were the high points of his life at the time: "Over there
now lay the accustomed existence with its affairs, but here illumination
and ecstasy and rapture held, without time or sequence."[15] The hours
of religious ecstasy he considered "true life," and everyday life he regarded as an "obscuring of the true life."[16] Instead of an integration of
life, there was a fleeing from everyday existence into "the detached
feeling of unity of being, elevated above life."[17] I am not investigating
the experiences themselves, but rather Buber's interpretation of them.
This will give us an insight into his concept of God at the time.

"ECSTASY AND CONFESSION"

At the beginning of his introduction, Buber writes: "The commotion of
our human life, which lets in everything, all the light and all the music,
all the mad pranks of thought and all the fullness of memory and the
fullness of expectation, is closed only to *one* thing: unity."[18] This commotion or "hustle and bustle" (*Getriebes*) mixes together an experience

of pure astonishment with thousands of memories; it mixes "the quiet-est suffering" with "the hissing of a thousand questions." It builds a "vortex of objects and a vortex of feelings" that we experience throughout our entire lives, but we still do not achieve unity. Buber claims that the commotion prevents us from reaching a unity of the world or of the I: "I, the world, we—no, I the world am what is moved out of reach, what cannot be grasped, what cannot be experienced."[19] Note that Buber is pointing toward the experience of "I the world'" that he identified as his own personal experience in his essay on Boehme: "in man the whole creation lies; but heaven and earth with all beings, even God himself lies in the human."[20]

"THE INWARD"

However, the commotion is only "the outside of an unknown Inward which is the most living thing of all." Buber adds that this "Inward" can "withhold the experience of itself from knowledge," which he de-scribes as a "daughter of the commotion," but it cannot withhold itself from the "vibrant and self-liberating soul." The "Inward" cannot be known, but it is present and can be felt in the soul. Boehme uses the expression "the inward" to indicate man's true nature. He states that man "is created both out of time and eternity, out of the Being of all beings, and made an image of the divine manifestation."[21] Therefore, man should not seek his fulfilment elsewhere but locate it in himself: "the place of the eternal paradise is hidden in this world, in the inward ground; but manifest in the inward man, in which God's power and vir-tue worketh."[22]

Buber argues that the "Inward" cannot be known, but it is present and can be felt in the soul. He claims that it is the soul that has "tensed itself utterly to burst through the commotion and escape from it that receives the grace of unity."[23] In this concentration of itself to make the transition from the commotion, the soul is "self-liberating." It is, therefore, the whole being of the person that is ready for the experience of unity, and the experience is then brought about through grace."[24] Is Buber implying here that this grace of unity, which the person receives, is beyond the control of the person? Where or what is its source? Buber explains that this "grace catches fire" through another being: the expe-rience is attained through the soul meeting someone or something else; the examples given are a loved human being or a wild landscape of heaped-up stones. In the meeting with another being, the spark is kindled, and the soul experiences unity. When this has happened, the soul no longer experiences anything particular, such as the hand of the beloved or the appearance of the rocks; it experiences "unity, the world: itself." The relation of the person to the beloved or to the stone as separate beings therefore no longer exists. The particular beings are not experienced as other than the person, but are "psychologised" as elements in an immanent experience of unity: all the powers of the soul "come into play, all its powers unified and felt as one, and there in the midst of the powers lives and radiates the beloved human being, the contemplated stone: the soul experiences the unity of the I, and in this unity the unity of I and the world; no longer a 'content,' but what is infinitely more than any content."[25] This experience is not concerned with the other person or being as a distinct and unique entity, but only uses him or her as a catalyst of the experience of the unity of "I and the world." There is a return to the "unity of powers," out of which the forms have come. This unity is wholly present in each person, and Buber had already identified it as "God in nature" in the essay on Boehme. The striving to return to this "unity of powers" is a striving for the "original state" (*Urzustand*). It is a cosmic striving; it is innate in nature and is one aspect of the original divine twofold will, proposed by Boehme, the other being the striving toward individuation.[26] The striving for unity attempts to overcome individuation and all multiplicity.

THE SOUL ITSELF

However, this situation of dependence on other beings, which, as we have discovered, Buber did not find fulfilling in Boehme's conception, is not the goal here either. This is because it is not a complete escape from the commotion. According to Buber, it is not yet complete freedom for the soul, as it is dependent on another being, and this being remains subject to the commotion. Any incident, such as a thought that transforms the face of the beloved or a cloud that transforms the face of the rock, can spoil the unity "so that it stands once again abandoned and enslaved in the vortex of feelings and objects."[27] Buber is not satisfied with a unity that requires another being as catalyst; he is seeking a unity that is totally beyond the commotion. The unity required is one in which the soul is independent and is not affected by anybody or anything outside itself. He claims that there is such an experience; this is the experience of the depth of the psyche:

> But there is an experience which grows in the soul out of the soul itself, without contact and without restraint, in naked oneness. It comes into being and completes itself beyond the commotion, free of the other, inaccessible to the other. It needs no nourishment, and no poison can touch it. The soul which stands in it stands in itself, has itself, experiences itself—boundlessly. It experiences itself as a unity, no longer because it has surrendered itself wholly to a thing of the world, gathered itself wholly in a thing of the world, but because it has submerged itself entirely in itself, has plunged down to the very ground of itself, is kernel and husk, sun and eye, carouser and drink, at once. This most inward of all experiences is what the Greeks call *ek-stasis*, a stepping out.[28]

This experience is a stepping out of the bonds of the *principium individuationis*. Buber explicitly writes that the other has no part in this ecstatic experience. It is beyond the "commotion," free of any contact or interference by any other being. It needs no nourishment, so it is not rooted or grounded in any other being. It is entirely within the self. Yet the soul experiences itself "boundlessly," or without limits (*schrankenlos*), explains Buber. This boundlessness may be interpreted in a number of ways: as identical with the boundless (*apeiron*) of Anaximander; as the absence of differentiation; as the identification with the infinite, as, for example, in Spinoza's concept of the unique substance; and as the Hellenic understanding of the depth of the psyche as unbounded.

If there are no boundaries, there is no differentiation of subject and object. There is no awareness of oneself as oneself, and no presence to oneself differentiated from the presence of another to oneself. One could debate whether Buber is correct in saying that the soul experiences *itself*. All that can be said is that the person has an undifferentiated experience in which there is consciousness, but without either consciousness of self as a limited, finite person, or of any other being. This is confirmed by Buber's later comment: "For he who in the act or event of absorption is sunk beneath the realm of all multiplicity that holds sway in the soul cannot experience the cessation of multiplicity except as unity itself. That is, he experiences the cessation of his own multiplicity as the cessation of mutuality, as revealed or fulfilled absence of otherness."[29] If there is no experience of otherness, neither is there any consciousness of self as this particular, limited person. Mauthner, who was a friend of Buber's, as already mentioned, attempts to express this absence of any sense of self in describing an ecstatic experience:

> In the highest mystical ecstasy the Ego [*das Ich*] experiences that
> it has become God. . . . Why not? Shall I quarrel about words?
> For a decade I have been teaching: The feeling of the Ego [*das
> Ichgefühl*] is a delusion. The unity of the individual is a delusion.
> If I am not me, yet exist, then I am entitled to believe that all other
> beings only appear to be individuals; they are not different from
> me; I am one with them; they and I are one. Are these mere philo-
> sophical word sequences? Games of language? No. What I can
> experience [*erleben*] is no longer mere language. What I can ex-
> perience is real. And I can experience, for short hours, that I no
> longer know anything about the *principium individuationis*, that
> there ceases to be a difference between the world and myself.
> "That I became God." Why not?[30]

Gilson argues that this type of experience is "a downward exstasis, wherein finite acts of existing are merely felt in themselves, wholly unrelated to their essences and therefore deprived of all intelligibility."[31] Gilson explains that there is "no concept there, nor even judgement, but the bare experiencing of an is which is not yet a being."[32] This experience, however, of an "is which is not yet a being" represents for Buber an experience of God because God is the "unity of an irrational dynamic potentiality, not the unity of a total absolute substance" and "a groundless eternal will which is silent and in itself without essence."[33] As we have already discovered, Buber believes that God is wholly present in each being. When the person experiences God, the phenomenal self and the unlimited self are united and the experience is "boundless." It is an experience of "nothingness" or "all" because there is no consciousness of differentiation.[34] Gilson remarks that "such an experience is but too real, yet it merely proves that essence and purpose are part and parcel of actual being. Should they be removed, be it for a split second, what is left no longer makes sense: it is that whose only essence and meaning is to have neither essence nor meaning."[35]

A similar experience is expressed in the tract, "Sister Katrei," which is ascribed to Meister Eckhart. This example is used by Schopenhauer and included by Buber in the "Supplement" to *Ecstatic Confessions*. This experience drives the mystic to express to her confessor: "My lord, rejoice with me, I have become God."[36] Schopenhauer comments: "Theism, calculated with reference to the capacity of the crowd, places the primary source of existence outside us as an object. All mysticism . . . draw[s] this source gradually back into ourselves as the subject, and the adept at last recognizes with wonder and delight that he himself is it."[37] Schopenhauer argues that the "pantheistic consciousness, essential to all mysticism," appears in Christianity in a secondary way, as a "consequence of the giving up of all willing, as union with God."[38] The danger of the pantheistic understanding in mysticism is very real because of the experienced union with God. Voegelin even refers to the exuberant joy of touching immortality present in Aristotle's *Metaphysics*. The danger present in the "momentary sameness with the divine" was later recognized and exploited by Hegel.[39]

Buber indicates that the soul experiences itself, not as a limited, finite person, but rather as, in Kantian terms, the "thing-in-itself." He is pointing toward the kernel of the self, the unlimited, which unites with the husk, that is, the self as a finite, limited being. Buber claims that the soul "has plunged down to the very ground of itself," that is, to the kernel. This ground of itself is in itself, as Buber claims that the experience grows out of itself. However, if the soul has plunged down to the very ground of itself, it was in a different "place" prior to this "plunge." There are now three elements of the soul: the "Inward," that is, the ground of motion, the part that is moved, and the motion itself. In this description, there is an understanding similar to Voegelin's analysis of the classic experience as "a movement in the psyche toward the ground that is present in the psyche as its mover."[40] Buber's ground, or the "Inward," is itself groundless and is the moving force; there is a movement in the soul toward this ground. Is this ground, however, understood as the manifestation of the transcendent God, the unmoved mover, and therefore as one pole in the tension experienced by the seeker of the ground? Or is it understood as the purely immanent *Ungrund*, as Boehme's groundless Godhead that is primal, preexistential, and beyond the categories of human thinking? Or is it understood as Plato's *anima mundi*, the cosmic spirit?[41] In order to come to a conclusion regarding Buber's concept of God, we must proceed to the next step in his essay.

THE PHENOMENON OF PROJECTION

In this step, Buber attempts to undermine the common understanding of the experience as a union with a God who is both immanent and transcendent. This goal is achieved through an application of the phenomenon of projection. Buber writes that if, "as people say," religion has developed, "then one may regard as an essential stage of this process the change which the conception of God has undergone."[42] He then explains his understanding of these changes: "At first human beings seem to have explained with the name God primarily that which they did not understand about the world; then, however, oftener and oftener, that which they did not understand about themselves. Thus ecstasy—that which humans could least understand about themselves—became God's highest gift."[43] Buber echoes Feuerbach in his understanding of this phenomenon of projection. The idea of a transcendent God outside oneself and beyond this cosmos is therefore a human construct, according to Buber. It is merely a projection of the mystery discovered in human life. According to Buber, this phenomenon is demonstrated in its purest form in ecstasy, which is the most inward experience and therefore is placed the furthest away. Buber remarks that for the believer of the Christian age this experience can be placed only at the poles of his cosmos—it must be ascribed to God or the devil. He gives the example of Jeanne Cambry, who did not know whether to ascribe her experience to a divine or diabolic power.

However, Buber adds, it was not only "in those times" that people divided life between the divine and the diabolic because they "did not know the power and breadth of the human and failed to grasp the inwardness of ecstasy"[44] In other words, if the full power of the human were known, this ecstatic experience would not need to be ascribed to any power other than oneself. It was through ignorance that it was ascribed to what was thought of as the divine or the diabolic. Buber claims that there is almost no ecstatic who has not interpreted his I-experience as God-experience (and however they tried to make God inward, scarcely one took him wholly into the I as the unity of the I).[45] Buber is implying that he understands the unity of the I to be God. The person therefore becomes God in this experience, the human being is deified. The divine pole of the tension experienced in the psyche is transferred to the divinized psyche.

The need to interpret ecstasy as God-experience, when God is a transcendent Being who is also immanent, seems to Buber to be grounded in the nature of the ecstatic experience itself. He considers that in this experience, there is nothing that points inward or outward: "whoever experiences the oneness of I and the world knows nothing of I and the world."[46] Schopenhauer expresses a similar understanding when he says that the mystic finds himself as the eternal and only being. He explains that if we remember the essential "*immanence of our knowledge and of all knowledge* . . . it becomes easy to explain that all the mystics of all religions ultimately arrive at a kind of *ecstasy*. In this, each and every kind of *knowledge* together with its fundamental form, *object and subject*, entirely ceases."[47] There is no knowledge based on the distinction of subject and object because there is no self-consciousness or consciousness of any other being. Buber explains this point by drawing on the Upanishads: "just as a man embraced by a woman he loves has no consciousness of what is outside or inside, so the mind embraced by the primal self, has no consciousness of what is outside or inside."[48] This is a parable of unification. Here Buber explicitly understands the experience to be unification with the primal self (*das Urselbst*), or as expressed in the Upanishads: Brahman, the Self of being, is identical with Atman, the self of the human person.[49] The equivalent of Brahman in Boehme's writings is the *Ungrund* and in Anaximander the *apeiron* (boundless). The person experiences oneness with the primal self, which Buber also calls the "universal mind," "the world-I," or the "absolute."

This experience of identification with the primal self is the soul's ineffable mystery that cannot be communicated. "But" adds Buber, "the human being cannot help placing even what is most subjective and free, once it has been lived, in the concatenation of the commotion, and forging for that which, timeless and fetterless as eternity, passed through the soul, a little past (the cause) and a little future (the effect)."[50] It becomes more difficult to locate the experience in the ordinary commotion when it is more authentic and unbound, thus it is "more natural and irrefutable" to ascribe it "to one who is above the world and outside all bonds." Buber suggests that this error is understandable when one compares the ordinary experiences of a human being with the experience of ecstasy:

> The human being who trudges along day by day in the functions
> of bodiliness and unfreedom receives in ecstasy a revelation of
> freedom. One who knows only differentiated experiences—the

experience of meaning, of thought, of will, connected with one another, yet still separate in this separation and conscious—comes to know an undifferentiated experience: the experience of the I. One who always feels and knows only particulars about himself suddenly finds himself under the storm cloud of a force, a superabundance, an infinity, in which even the most primal security, the barrier between the self and the other, has foundered. One cannot burden the general run of occurrences with this experience; one does not dare to lay it upon his own poor I, of which he does not suspect that it carries the world-I; so one hangs it on God.[51]

This "hanging it on God" is the purest form of projection. Buber is suggesting that projecting the content of the experience onto a nonexistent God is simply another instance of the tendency to explain with the name God that which is not understood about oneself. It is a useful idea, but is not a reality. The reality to Buber is the I that bears in itself the world-I. The cosmic spirit is thus in the soul of man. The phenomenon mentioned above—"that someone who has experienced his I announces to himself and others that he has experienced God"—Buber suggests, must appear arbitrary to many people. To those who do not believe in God, it seems "the arbitrariness of a superfluous theism (or impure pantheism); to the pious it seems the arbitrariness of presumption and blasphemy."[52]

Buber is advocating a pure pantheism because he understands God not as a transcendent and infinite being, but rather as the cosmic spirit. The cosmic spirit is Boehme's *Ungrund* made immanent. In the experience of unity, there is only one infinite being. This is an identification of oneself as God. In the context of theistic mysticism, the nature of the experience of union with God was expressed by John of the Cross when he wrote that although "all the things of both God and the soul become one in participant transformation, and the soul appears to be God more than a soul. Yet truly, its being (even though transformed) is naturally as distinct from God's as it were before, just as the window, although illumined by the ray, has being distinct from the ray's."[53] This distinction of two beings is essential in the understanding of the experience. It points toward self-transcendence, in which there is a movement of the self to encounter the other, God or other people, rather than ego-transcendence in which the movement is into the deeper psychic resources of the self.[54] Ego-transcendence considers what is experienced to be an exclusive and all-absorbing unity of one's own self.[55] This understanding renders absolute the human element of the relation to the ground of the soul.[56] Gregson's explanation of the psychologically reductionist tendency present in some of Jung's disciples clarifies the issue:

> The "self" as the locus of the indefinite resources of the human psyche is the most powerful personal image of the Infinite . . . the "self," however is not the Infinite. . . . The Jungian tradition offers stern warnings about the inflation which not infrequently occurs when the resources of the self come into consciousness . . . at this point, however, Jungians, such as Edinger, succumb to inflation themselves. They become so fascinated by the God image of the "self" and by the process of coming to psychic wholeness—the "ego" coming to terms with the "self"—that they effectively interpret that very process to be salvation. The intentionality of the "self" beyond the "self," particularly in terms of an Absolute beyond the "self" is truncated.[57]

There is no doubt that intentionality is truncated in Buber's interpretation of the mystical experience. There is no intending of anything; there is no distinction between oneself and any other being; there is no relation to anything as there is no experience of anything outside of the inflated self. As we will discover, Buber's understanding of unity leads to absolute solitude.

THE CREATION OF A MYSTERY

After the descent from the ecstatic experience, what one thinks, feels, and dreams about God is added to the experience. These additions create "around the experience of unity a multiform mystery."[58] Many "forms and sounds" gather around "the fire" in the soul; this fire is the sole trace of the experience. The mystic, in whom "the Word burns," must speak and use images, dreams, and visions to attempt to say the "unsayable," and she does not lie in doing so. These ways of explaining the experience are grasped by the ecstatic as she tries to understand herself. This desire to understand which was extinguished in the experience is reawakened after it. Although the person uses images and words, she realizes that she "is not saying the experience, not the ground, not the unity," and she would like to stop the saying, but cannot. Buber is stating that the ecstatic experience is independent of the thoughts, feelings, and dreams one may have of God; these are outside the experience because they belong to the commotion and are used only as a means to understand the experience. It is not, therefore, through an insight into the experience itself that one comes to have these thoughts, feelings, or dreams about God. One adds these human constructs around the center of the experience of unity and creates a "multiform mystery."

For Buber, union with God is the elementary notion in this constructed "mystery." Rarely, he adds, is the I proclaimed that is one with the universe. It is found only in the most ancient Indian sayings and in rare utterances of some individuals. One of the ancient Indian sayings, an instruction from the *Mahabharatam*, is also included in the supplement to Buber's book. It explains the "turning inward which brings about a hidden existence."[59]

> As fire fed with kindling wood, blazes up with a great brightness, so the great Atman [self] blazes up when the sense organs are suppressed.
>
> When one contemplates all beings in one's heart with a calm self, then he serves as his own light, and from the hidden he arrives at the highest of all hidden things. . . .
>
> This terrible, unfathomable vast ocean called delusion—one must put it aside, annihilate it, and bring the immortal world within one to its awakening. . . .
>
> Desire, anger, fear, greed, guile, and untruth, all these he throws off through subjection of the sense organs, although they are difficult to throw off. . . .
>
> Then, free of all frailties, one contemplates that highest thing, enclosing its Manas [here: the will] in one's own Manas and seeing the Self in one's own self. Omniscient in all beings, he finds the Self in himself by transforming himself into one or into many, now here, now there.
>
> Then he sees through the forms completely . . . then he is creator and orderer, the Lord, the omnipresent, then he will radiate as the heart of all creatures, the great Atman . . . .[60]

In this saying, the blaze represents the ascent of the self into union with the Self. Here all the frailties of the senses are overcome, and one can contemplate the highest thing. In this contemplation, one finds that the highest thing brings its powers into one's own, and one sees the Self in

one's own self. The highest thing, God, goes into the I, and is not fragmented, but the entire Self is in one's self. This is equivalent to Buber's
interpretation of the process in Boehme's writings where God, the creative force, goes into nature and is "not compartmentalised [*abtheilig*]
but is everywhere whole, and where he reveals himself, there he is
wholly revealed."[61] As Buber claimed in the essay on Boehme, one
then recognizes or knows the world because one has it all in oneself.
The ecstatic is the creator and lord, omniscient and omnipresent. He or
she is God. The original Godhead in Boehme's conception, which was
an irrational essence-less unity unable to know itself, has become the
ecstatic as the unity of all beings. Buber stresses the absolute solitude
of this unity when he writes:

> But not merely in comparison to his early plurality has the one
> who has experienced ecstasy become a unity. One's unity is not
> relative, not limited by the other; it is limitless, for it is the unity
> of I and the world. One's unity is solitude, absolute solitude: the
> solitude of that which is without limits. One contains the other,
> the others in oneself, in one's unity: as world; but one no longer
> has others *outside* oneself, no longer has any communion with
> them or anything in common with them.[62]

The ecstatic experience, according to Buber, "is unity, solitude,
uniqueness." It cannot be translated into the language of common experience. "It is the abyss that cannot be fathomed: the unsayable."[63] The
confession of the ecstatic may seem arbitrary. However, it is the expression of one who tries to match what is innermost and most personal
with the given language of human beings: it is a "battle of the irrational
with the rational." It arises out of the enormous contradiction between
the inner experience (*Erlebnis*) and the commotion, out of which the
mystic ascends only to fall back into it.[64]

SILENCE AND SPEECH

Ecstasy is the one experience that is ineffable, according to Buber,
since the human being has become a unity in which all powers have
come together into one force. It is no longer merely a "bundle," but
has become a fire in which "all sparks have blazed together into one
flame."[65] There is no duality, such as subject and object, present in this
unity; it is removed from the multiplicity of ordinary living and thus

separated from language. Language is tied to the multiplicity; it is the expression of knowledge of nearness or distance, sensation or idea. Knowledge is the work of the commotion: "in its greatest miracles a gigantic co-ordinate system of the mind. But the experience of ecstasy is not a knowing."[66]

Rather than speak of the experience, one may try to stay silent. Silence, Buber argues, is a "*symbolon* which protects us from the gods and angels of the commotion, our guard against its aberrations, our purification against its impurity."[67] Referring to the Apathanatismos—the mystic's guide to the highest initiation——Buber suggests that when one keeps silent about the experience, it is a star that illuminates the paths of the traveler.[68] However, if the experience is spoken of, it is "thrown down under the tread of the market." Buber then adds that "when we are quiet to the Lord, he makes his dwelling with us; we say Lord, Lord and we have lost him." How are we to understand this phrase of Buber's in which he seems to suggest that there is a relation to another being in the ecstatic experience? Who is this Lord who makes his dwelling in us? Is Buber using a biblical phrase to indicate that one destroys the experience if one introduces the duality of subject and object by speaking of it? Is he saying that in the unity of the experience, one becomes Lord as in the Indian saying quoted above? He is at the very least suggesting that something happens in the experience, which no words are adequate to explain. Nevertheless, he continues: "We have to speak. And our speech builds a heaven over us, over us and the others a vault of heaven: poetry, love, future. But one thing is not beneath this heaven: the one thing that is needful."[69] As mentioned in the introduction to this chapter, Buber is aiming at "the one thing needful." What can be said of it if it is above this vault constructed by speech?

The apparent contradiction introduced into the essay by Buber's use of the phrase, "when we are quiet to the Lord, he makes his dwelling with us," indicates Buber's hesitation concerning the interpretation of the ecstatic experience. This hesitation is implicit in the recognition of the experience as the illuminating star that remains with one on one's journey and is also evident in his use of the phrase, "the Word," which burns in the mystic after an ecstatic experience and makes him attempt to speak of the experience:

> For the Word burns in him. Ecstasy is dead, stabbed in the back
> by Time, which will not be mocked; but dying, it has flung the

Word into him, and the Word burns in him. And he speaks, speaks, he cannot be silent, the flame in the Word drives him, he knows that he cannot say it, yet he tries over and over again until his soul is exhausted to death and the Word leaves him.[70]

Who speaks this Word? What is it?[71] Is there a connection between the Word that is flung into the mystic and burns in him and the Lord who makes his dwelling in him? Both happen to the person during the experience according to Buber. Earlier in the essay, Buber draws attention to the Jewish sage, Hai Gaon, who rejects a popular opinion of what happens in the experience when he speaks of the adept who has surmounted the ten rungs of mystical ascent: "Then heaven opens up before him—not in order that he may ascend into it, but something happens in his heart, whereby he enters into the contemplation of things divine."[72] What is this "something" that happens? This question cannot be answered because one is not present to oneself in the experience. There is, however, "another, most silent speech, which wants not to describe existence, but only to communicate it."[73] Buber adds that this speech is not guilty of a betrayal because "it says only that something is." Is this a recognition by Buber of some thing or force other than the unity of the I in the ecstatic experience? Bernard de Clairvaux provides an example of this type of speech. Buber reports that once Bernard halted during a sermon and spoke softly, "without boasting and without being humble, it is no artistic device, rather memory has come over him, and speech has broken in his mouth: *Fateor et mihi adventasse verbum:* I confess that the Word has approached me too." Buber adds that Bernard continued speaking and expressed "how he felt that it was there, how he recalls its having been there, how he sensed that it would come, yet did not feel its coming and going. How it could not enter through any sense, being non-sensible, and how it could not have originated in him, being perfect."[74] Buber then quotes Bernard: "When I gazed out, I found it beyond all that was outside me; when I looked in, it was further in than my most inward being. And I recognized that what I had read was true: that we live and move and are in it; but he is blest in whom it lives, and who is moved by it."[75] In a personal admission, Buber then writes: "I believe his confession. I feel that once, at a time when he could not speak as today, he had hours when he too suffered the divine."

If one suffers the divine during an ecstatic experience, one is not identical with the divine. It is clear from this saying of Bernard that it is something that happens to one. The mystic is passive, and, as Bernard says, the divine, which is equated with the Word, comes and goes and is therefore beyond one's control. However, Bernard felt the presence of this other and sensed its coming. This agrees with the essential element in mysticism mentioned by Maréchal. Buber admires this speech of Bernard because he "does not fling down the Word as fodder for the words, but bears witness for the Word with his silence as a martyr bears witness with his blood." Buber returns to the importance of the "Word" in the next essay that I will consider: "The Teaching of the Tao." Is there a contradiction between Buber's approval of Bernard's confession on the one hand and his interpretation of the ecstatic experience on the other hand? I think there is, and that this hesitation in Buber is expressed again in the final section of the essay.

In the final paragraphs of the introduction, Buber suggests that for some people who have experienced unity, their testimony may go beyond Bernard's "silent speech." The mystic's "will to say is not mere impotence and stammering; it is also might and mastery." The mystic wants to "tow the timeless into the harbor of time" and to "make the unity without multiplicity into the unity of all multiplicity."[76] Buber, though, takes a step further in asking whether the great myths are merely symbols of the mystic's experience. Whereas he considers that positive religion subdues the fullness of existence, myth is the "expression of the fullness of existence, its image, its sign; it drinks incessantly from the gushing fountains of life."[77] Buber defines myth as a tale of a real event in the material world, conceived as a divine, an absolute event.[78] Therefore, Buber is asking whether the mystic's experience of unity finds expression as a divine, absolute event in the telling of a myth. Buber, in mentioning the great myths, draws on his familiarity with Boehme:

> The thought of the great myth awakens, a thought which runs through all the times of humanity: the myth of unity which becomes plurality because it wants to gaze and be gazed at, to know and be known, to love and be loved, and which, while itself remaining a unity, embraces itself as multiplicity; of the I which begets a Thou; of the primal self which transforms itself into the world, of the divinity which transforms itself into God. Is the myth proclaimed by Vedas and Upanishads, Midrash and Kabbala, Plato and Jesus, not the symbol of what the ecstatic has experienced?[79]

The masters of all times, as Buber calls those who created and recreated the myth, drew on their own experiences of unity. For these masters who have also passed out of unity into multiplicity, ecstasy was not an overwhelming experience, but "an ingathering and deep upwelling and a familiarity with the ground, the Word did not lie upon them like a driving conflagration; it lay upon them like the hand of a father."[80] It guided them to insert the experience into their lives and to create from it a new poem of the primal myth. Buber ends this essay with questions concerning the myth:

> But is myth a phantasm? Is it not a revelation of the ultimate reality of being? Is not the experience of the ecstatic a symbol of the primal experience of the universal mind [world-spirit]? Are not both a living, inner experience?
>
> We listen to our inmost selves—and we do not know which sea we hear murmuring.[81]

Although these questions imply Buber's pantheist beliefs, he nevertheless broaches a theme that is present in his earlier writings and becomes crucial in his later writings: the connection of the individual with the universal. This is both a philosophic and religious theme. One experiences the reality of one's own wholeness of being, and one is connected through the fact of one's being with the whole of being. The "myths" proclaimed by Vedas and Upanishads, Midrash and Kabbala, Plato and Jesus concern the question of the One and the Many and the One in the Many. The human person is the place of the coincidence of opposites. Both the experience of particular being and that of universal Being are located in the person. At this time, Buber is concerned with these experiences as internal to the self, and it is the goal of the person to raise the self to unity with the Self. (This element of realization by the person is clarified further in the next essay that I will examine and particularly in *Daniel,* which is a set of five dialogues on realization.) Rather than participation by the particular being in the universal being, Buber identifies the particular self with all reality. The I is the absolute. Later he will recognize the relatedness between oneself and all reality. This relatedness is the basic insight in his philosophical understanding of the fundamental connection between the I-Thou relation to God and the I-Thou relation to one's fellow human beings. It is the key to the dialogical reality.

Buber's pantheism is also evident in *The Legend of the Baal-Shem* that was written in 1907. In a footnote, Hans Kohn identifies the changes in later editions that repudiated the pantheistic elements present in the first edition.[82] For example, the sentence "God is the essence of all things" was replaced by "God is in each thing as its essence." In the old edition, it is granted to the human being everywhere and at any time to "unite himself with God"; in the new edition, this mystical formulation is replaced by to "receive the divine." The change is made explicit when "pantheistic" is replaced by "panentheistic." However, at the end of his introduction to this book, *The Legend of the Baal-Shem*, Buber distinguished myth and legend and recognized that dialogical relationship is present in the latter:

> The legend is the myth of the calling. In it the original personality of myth is divided. In pure myth there is no division of essential being. It knows multiplicity but not duality. Even the hero only stands on another rung than that of the god, not over against him: they are not the I and Thou. The hero has a mission but not a call. He ascends but he does not become transformed. The god of pure myth does not call, he begets; he sends forth the one whom he begets, the hero. The god of legend calls forth the son of man— the prophet, the holy man.
>
> The legend is the myth of I and Thou, of the caller and the called, the finite which enters into the infinite and the infinite which has need of the finite.[83]

This is the essential element in the tales of the Baal-Shem—that there is a calling. The kernel of the call is "Where are you?" The answer is presence: "Here I am."[84] Although Buber recognizes here the essential difference between the partners and the independence of man, he has not yet realized the full implications of the call or answer.

CONCLUSION

In our examination of his essay, we have found that Buber did not believe in a mystical union with a transcendent, infinite God. He maintains the essential position in the essay on Boehme—that there is only an innerworldly divinity. This divinity is the "unity of powers" and the creative force present in the "kernel" of each person. This force is the "unmoved mover" with which the finite self is united in ecstasy. Neither did Buber accept that the ecstatic experience should be "hung" on God and explained as a gift of God due to our lack of understanding.

Ecstasy, according to Buber, is an experience of the unity of the I in which consciousness of differentiation and individuation is lost. The unity of the I then appears as the unity of all. The oneness of the I is understood as the I or the mind being embraced by the primal self or universal mind. Thus Buber accepts a movement of ego-transcendence, but not one of self-transcendence, in which there would be a meeting or encounter with another being.

However, I have drawn attention to a hesitation on Buber's part. The experiences of some of the mystics suggest to him that there is something more involved in an ecstatic experience. "Something is." This something has an impact on the person during the ecstatic experience and he or she has no control over it: the person "suffers the divine." This "suffering" is similar to the primitive man's experience of "that which effects," that is, *Mana*, which Buber mentions in *I and Thou*. The mystical experience results in the receipt of a "Word" that remains with the person. This "Word" is given in a "speech" that differs from the speech of the community. It is prior to, or beyond, speech. Is this "Word" an address to the person, that he or she then wants to transmit to others?[85] It is the call that is expressed in the legend.

Buber claimed that the possibility of a God with whom one can have a relation was a question for him, especially since he began his study of Hasidism.[86] In the ecstatic experience as understood by Buber, one loses consciousness of the *principium individuationis*, and one is therefore conscious neither of any other being nor of oneself as oneself. One simply is. One does not intend anything else beyond oneself. However, one cannot have a relation to another being if one is not also conscious of oneself. There is a contradiction between Buber's interpretation of the ecstatic experience and his interest in the possibility of a God with whom one can have a relation. This contradiction is the result of his fusion of the atheistic mysticism of his time with his knowledge of theistic writings such as those of Eckhart, Cusa, Boehme, and the Hasidic tradition. In studying the latter, Buber no doubt became aware of the similarities to the earlier writings that he had studied. If he was questioning the possibility of a God with whom one can have a relation in his study of Hasidism, he could not with integrity close himself to this question in other writings. Is this the reason for the hesitation evident in the recognition of Bernard's awareness that "something is," which echoes Parmenides' great outburst? The hesitation is a fruitful one, as it leads Buber to the discovery of the importance of presence.

Part II: "The Teaching of the Tao"

Buber's interest in the Oriental responses to the question of the one and the many continued throughout his life. He appreciated the importance of the third century B.C., in which great forces shaped China and India, Egypt and Asia Minor. These forces are disclosed in the extant remnants of their creations: "the Shi-Ching and the Vedas, the Pyramid manuscript and the Gilgamesh epos."[87] Buber considered that a clearer understanding of the time is possible if the men who arose in the Orient during the period of the Golden Age of Greece are included: "the Jewish prophets as well as the thinkers of the Upanishads, Zoroaster, and Lao-tse." The significance of the unity that is attained in all great Asiatic religions and ideologies, according to Buber, is the understanding that "the unified world must not only be conceived, it must be realised."

This task of realization becomes increasingly emphasized in his writings, especially in *Daniel*. Buber's insight is that the ultimate truth, which is lacking in the West, is "that the world's inner destiny is, to an unfathomable degree, dependent upon the deed of the doer. It is this truth that the 'way' of Oriental teaching connotes: the truth of the word, 'One thing above all is needed.'"[88] The Oriental teachings claim that the authentic life is "the fundamental metaphysical principle, not derived from nor reducible to anything else; they proclaim the way."[89] This principle commands different responses: in the Vedânta, it means to tear the web of appearance and recognize one's true self as identical with the self of the world; one realizes the true, unified world in the all-encompassing solitude of his soul. In Taoism, the way, Tao, is perceived as the single, primal principle in which both the counteracting principles of light and dark are grounded. This is the Tao that the wise person realizes on earth through his or her life, not by interfering with, but by actualizing in this world the cosmic intent of oneness through the significance of both his action and his nonaction. Alternatively, the Persian of the Avesta may direct the response toward an unreserved championing of the light, which by opposing the obstructive, evil principle, serves the breaking through of unity into the divided world.[90] In these three ways, unity is realized.

In the teaching of the Tao, Buber finds a path that has the same dynamic in the realization of unity as the primal myth that he mentioned at the end of "Ecstasy and Confession." It is the myth of the way of unity in the world. It is the same way of unity that becomes plurality in order to be known and loved that concerned Boehme and Western mysticism, but in a very different context. According to Buber, the teaching demands no particular religious beliefs, but is itself the root of the great religions. It is the ground and meaning of Jesus, Buddha, and Lao-tzu. Tao is the only way: "it is *he hodos tou theou* (Mark 12:14), God's way in the world." What the Orient understands is "that the full manifestation and disclosure of the world's inner substance is thwarted; that the primally intended unity is split and distorted; that the world needs human spirit in order to become redeemed and unified; and that this alone constitutes the meaning and power of man's existence in the world." The essence of the Oriental teaching is the demand for realization. Only when the idea of unity is lived is it a reality. The living of unity is Tao: it is the process of realizing God in the world. The realization of God needs the human spirit. [91]

THE COSMIC INTENT OF ONENESS

Buber claims that the realizing person actualizes the "cosmic intent of oneness" in the world. At the end of the essay, "Ecstasy and Confession," Buber referred to "the universal mind." The intention of unity we can understand as an act of intending by the universal mind, or cosmic spirit. We can begin to understand this notion of cosmic spirit through Buber's references to Heraclitus in "The Teaching of the Tao." Tao, which means the way or the path, also has the meaning of speech that corresponds to the Greek conception of *logos*. What it conveys is, according to Buber, related to that of the Heraclitean *logos*: "both transpose a dynamic principle of human life into the transcendent, though basically they mean nothing other than human life itself, which is the bearer of all transcendence."[92] Buber's assumption that nothing other than human life is meant reflects the influence of Feuerbach's position on God as a projection of man. Buber here maintains the position he held in "Ecstasy and Confession," where he states that the I carries the world-I. Transcendence is restricted to the identification of the I with the world-I. It is an innerworldly reality. The second reference to Heraclitus compares him with Chuang-tzu. Lao-tzu wrote the *Book of the Tao and of Virtue*; Chuang-tzu composed the parable of Lao-tzu's teaching.[93] According to Buber, neither of these writings can be excluded if we are to grasp the integral teaching of the Tao: "'the path,' the ground and meaning of the unified life, as the ground and meaning of all." Chuang-tzu accomplishes this because his parable "bears the unity of the teaching into all the world," so that everything appeared full of it and nothing is so insignificant that the teaching refused to fill it. The teaching adds nothing new, but enables what is already present to be actualized: "All strive to comprehend what they do not know, none strives to comprehend what he knows."[94] At the end of his essay, Buber wrote:

> There are words of Heraclitus that could not be associated with any other philosophy with the same justification as with the Tao-teaching: words such as that of the unknowable logos that yet works in all, of the unity that is at once nameless and named, of its manifestation as the eternal order in the world, of the eternal transformation from totality to unity and from unity to totality, of the harmony of opposites, of the relation between waking and dream in the existence of the individual, of that between life and death in the existence of the world. Further, Chuang-tzu may perhaps be compared with the total shape of Greek philosophy that transferred the teaching from the sphere of genuine life into the sphere of explanation of the world, into an ideological structure, thereby, to be sure, creating something wholly individual and powerful in itself.[95]

Heraclitus wrote of the *logos* as the law or order that pervades all things.[96] The truth of the *logos*, the underlying unity of things, is valid for and accessible to all human beings. The *logos* is common (*xynon*), though people live as if they have a private understanding. Some people act as if they were asleep, even when awake. Those who are awake have the *logos* in common and thus form a unity, or community. All people should recognize the *logos* as the "unifying formula," or "structural plan," of each thing and of the whole.[97] It is a universal principle that every rational being should obey. Heraclitus also discerns the unity of opposites: Out of all things comes a unity, and out of a unity all things.[98] God is connected to the pairs of opposites as the common element that remains during change. Heraclitus seems to have "regarded 'god' as in some probably undefined way immanent in things, or as the sum total of things."[99] God, therefore, is not essentially different from the *logos*. Wisdom means understanding the *logos*, but God is the One who is completely wise: "One thing, the only true wise, does not and does consent to be called by the name of Zeus."[100]

In the same period as Heraclitus was presenting his insights to the Western world, the teaching of the Tao became of great importance in the East. Buber claims that in the West, Tao has usually been understood as an attempt to explain the world. The explanation always happens to coincide with the philosophy of the particular time. Tao has therefore been successively understood as nature, as reason, and as energy. However, Tao implies only that the "whole meaning of being rests in the unity of the genuine life, that it is experienced nowhere else, that it is just this unity which is grasped as the absolute."[101] Buber cautions against any attempt to seek what underlies the unified life; nothing will be found but the unknowable, and of this, "nothing further can be said than that it is unknowable." Here is the mystery of the primal source. Heraclitus claimed that the real constitution of the whole is accustomed to hide itself. Buber argues that the "unknowableness" of "Tao in itself," or the "true Tao," is not like the "unknowableness" of some philosophical or religious principle that one then goes on to discuss. Buber stresses that even the word "Tao" does not actually name the unknowable; he quotes from Lao-tzu: "the name that can be named is not the eternal name." There is therefore a "nameless," both in Taoism and in Heraclitus' teaching. Tao is to be regarded as the "one thing needful," whose reality is experienced in unified life; if one attempts to consider it as something separate, one finds that there is nothing to regard: "Tao can have no existence." Tao cannot be represented, as it cannot be thought, it has no image, no word, and no measure: "The right measure of the Tao is its self." It cannot be investigated or demonstrated. Not only can no truth be stated concerning it, but also it cannot be a subject of a statement at all. "We cannot discover it in any being. If we seek it in heaven and earth, in space and in time, then it is not there; rather, heaven and earth, space and time, are grounded in it alone. And nonetheless 'it can be found through seeking' (L): in unified life. There it is not recognized and known, but possessed, lived, and acted."[102]

This Tao that is unknowable "in itself" appears in the becoming of the world as "the original undivided state, as the primal existence from which all elements sprang, as 'the mother of all beings . . .' (L) as the 'spirit of the valley' that bears everything."[103] Is this the universal mind or cosmic spirit that Buber mentions in "Ecstasy and Confession"? Buber states that always in Tao-teaching, "consciousness effects being, spirit effects reality." It is the One, the cosmic spirit, that effects reality. In the becoming of the world, it is the One, the unity out of which comes the multiplicity of all things. It is a different "face" or aspect of the same Tao. In the being of the world, Tao appears as "the constant undividedness: as the united transformation of the world, as its order." In the connection of the successive moments in the life of the world, Tao verifies itself—"in the coming and going of all things, in the unity of their eternal changes." Like the Heraclitean *logos*, Tao is the unity in all change: "Tao is unloosing, it is transition to new shape, it is a moment of sleep and contemplation between two world lives. All is becoming and change in the 'great house' of eternity. As in the existence of things, separation and gathering, change and unity, succeed each other, so in the existence of the world life and death follow each other, together verifying Tao as unity in change. This eternal Tao, which is the denial of all illusory being, is also called non-being."[104]

In particular things, Buber claims that Tao appears as "undividedness." Tao is the path of things, their manner, their peculiar order, and their unity. Each thing reveals the Tao through the way of its existence, through its life. "There is nothing in which the whole Tao is not present as this thing's self."[105] This statement essentially agrees with Buber's statement in his essay on Boehme that "God is not compartmentalised but is everywhere whole and where he reveals himself there he is wholly revealed." It is an identification of the absolute with each thing. Tao, which Buber claims is comparable with the *logos* of Heraclitus, lies wholly in each thing. It is the thing's self. This is a pantheistic position. As Boehme claims that in each thing, the latent qualities of all things are present, the Tao also exists in things only potentially. It first becomes active in its contact with other things: "If there were metal and stone without Tao, there would be no sound. They have the power of sound, but it does not come out of them if they are not struck. Thus it is with all things." Tao is the power present in things. This power is latent in them; it only becomes living and manifest through their contact with other things.

Two comments may be made here. First, as Jonathan Herman points out, this is an instance in which Buber gives an indication "that he is discerning in *Chuang Tzu* a concept of unity predicated on relationality, as though he were on the threshold of breaking free from a self-annihilating pantheism."[106] This confirms our recognition of a hesitation on Buber's part in "Ecstasy and Confession." I would add that the activity and passivity involved in the contact of things with each other in order for Tao to become living is a step toward the activity and passivity present in the I-Thou relation,[107] in which the Eternal Thou becomes present.

Second, Robert Wood recognizes the notion of nonaction as one of the central notions of *I and Thou.* Both action and nonaction, according to Buber, are characteristic of the presence of Tao in things. Wood explains nonaction [*wu-wei*] as follows:

> As in any graceful performance, there is a coincidence of opposites: conscious and unconscious, mind and body, where "it acts in me" as much as "I act." To attempt to force one's actions from the outside, as it were, by a detached picturing of positions, remembrance of prescriptions, marshalling of multiple forces and deliberate willing of movement is to issue in an extremely ungraceful performance. "Grace" is a gift, the gift of instincts and of situations. And it is only by allying oneself with one's gift, by creating in ourselves the conditions for "letting things be," that graceful performance ensues.[108]

Tao appears in human beings as "purposeful undividedness: as the unifying force that overcomes all straying away from the ground of life, as the completing force that heals all that is sundered and broken, as the atoning force that delivers from all division." The goal of purposeful undividedness, of Tao, is its own fulfillment. It wills to realize itself, as Boehme's *Ungrund*, the eternal groundless will, willed to realize itself. It can realize itself in human beings while it cannot do so in the realm of things. It is only the person who reaches Tao in silence and fulfills it with his being who actually possesses it, and "he does not have it as his own but as the meaning of the world." This person out of his or her unity beholds the unity in the world: "the unity of the masculine and the feminine elements that do not exist for themselves but only for each other, the unity of the opposites that do not exist for themselves but only through each other, the unity of the things that do not exist for themselves but only with one another. This unity is the Tao in the world."[109] It is the person who is unified that recognizes the unity in the world.

THE UNITY OF THE PERSON

It was stated above that the unified person beholds the unity of the world. However, Buber adds: "But that is not to be understood as if the world were a closed thing outside of him whose unity he penetrates. Rather the unity of the world is only a reflection of his unity; for the world is nothing alien, but one with the unified man. 'Heaven and earth and I came together into existence, and I and all things are one.' But since the unity of the world only exists for the perfected man, it is, in truth, his unity that sets unity in the world."[110] Buber maintains a mystical position here: the person beholds the unity of the world, but this unity is only a reflection of his own unity because he and the world are one. He is thus free of distinctions and is joined to the infinite and out of his unity is able to bring unity to the world. In his unity with the All, knowledge is attained. It is only the undivided person who knows; for only in him or her in whom there is no division is there no separation from the world. Only the person who is not separated from the world can know it. Buber then states, "only in the unity with the all is knowledge possible. Unity is knowledge."[111] This person is the wholeness of being, and knowledge is attained through this wholeness. Relation is overcome in the unconditionality of the all-embracing nature of the wholeness. This implies that no relation remains, and the wholeness is unconditional. Buber is stating that the relation between the One and the Many is also overcome. Does this confirm that it is the Unknowable as it is in itself that the person has become in attaining unity? This is the only wholeness: it is the Godhead that in Boehme's terms is prior to the separation of God and the world. Further analysis will enable us to answer this question.

Buber states that in human beings Tao can become pure unity, but it cannot in things. In the perfected being in whom Tao is pure unity, "Tao no longer appears but is."[112] Tao is an immediate reality in the unified person. This reflects the status of the person as both absolute and human. It parallels again Boehme's understanding of the nature of the person as divine and human. The unified person has become unconditioned in fulfilling the teaching. This sets the world of the conditioned against him or her. Since the unity of the world only exists for the perfected person, it is he or she who brings to life the Tao that is latent in them. "The perfected man is self-enclosed, secure, united out of Tao, unifying the world, a creator, 'God's companion': the companion of all creating eternity."[113] This person "reconciles and brings into accord the two primal elements of nature, the positive and the negative, yang and yin, which the primal unity of being tore asunder."[114] By becoming unified, the perfected person, and only he or she, possesses eternity: "The spirit wanders through things until it blooms to eternity in the perfected man." This coming to fruition of the spirit is also symbolized as a returning to the root in the following quotation cited by Buber from Lao-tzu:

> Ascend the height of renunciation, embrace the abyss of rest. The numberless beings all arise. Therein I recognize their return. When the being unfolds itself, in the unfolding each returns to his root. To have returned to the root means to rest. To rest means to have fulfilled one's destiny. To have fulfilled one's destiny means to be eternal.[115]

Each thing returns to its root. Is this root the unknowable or the One out of which all things have come? Buber answers: "The unknowable and the unified human life, the first and the last touch one another. In the perfected man Tao returns to itself from its world wandering through the manifestation. It becomes fulfilment."[116] It is the unknowable and the unified human being that touch. In the returning to its root, the Tao in the person has completed the circle. The first and the last, the beginning and the end, join together. This is the path of Tao in the world. The touch, however, of the unknowable and the unified human being signifies their identification: Tao is fulfilled in the person. The person has become free of the distinctions between himself or herself and all other beings and joins himself or herself to the infinite; he or she restores both the things and himself or herself to the primal existence.[117]

Remembering Buber's comparison of Taoism with Heraclitus, we also discover the "return" in Heraclitus in a phrase that reflects "the first and the last": "Common [*xynon*]—beginning and end [*arche kai peras*]—in the periphery of the soul."[B 103]. Voegelin comments that this phrase articulates more adequately the thought of Anaximander that "the things" perish into that from that they were born.[118] This is the abyss mentioned above. It is the womb, mentioned by Buber in another essay, which gives birth to and devours all multiplicity and all contrast.[119] Voegelin continues: "The Milesian search for the beginning in the horizontal line of the flux of things is now bent back, through the symbol of the circle, so that the beginning and the end will meet in the permanent presence of the *xynon* that is experienced in the vertical direction of the soul toward the 'All-Wise.' For Heraclitus and for Tao the dynamic principle is a process of ascent: 'Human wisdom is not a completed possession but a process. The participation in the divine wisdom that is apart from all things, cannot be achieved through a leap beyond all things; it is the result of the occupation with these very things, ascending from the manifold to the One that is to be found in them all."[120]

ALL-EMBRACING LOVE

Although, as I have mentioned, Buber gives an indication that the importance of relation is beginning to emerge in his understanding of the teaching of Tao, the One is found in all things as a result of the unity of the perfected person. As I have mentioned, it is not in separation, but in the unity of being that there is knowledge. This knowledge is had in the embracing of all things in unity. This knowledge is being, and the person is every thing as he or she is the wholeness of being. In this wholeness things are known because he or she regards them from the inside out, not from their appearances, but "from the essence of this thing, from the unity of this thing that it possesses in its own unity." Everything is subjective; there is therefore immediate knowledge of all. As the person is the wholeness of being, all things are lifted with him or her out of appearance into being. This knowledge embraces all things in its being; that is, in its love. "It is the all-embracing love that overcomes all opposites."[121] There is no distinction here between one person and another; there is no relation.

This embracing love is the action of the perfected person. What is commonly called action, Buber claims, is not action. It is not done out of the whole being, but from single intentions and is dispersed in many aims. If the action is approved, it is commonly called virtue, but it is not virtue. It exhausts itself in "love of mankind" and "righteousness." However, these expressions of "virtue" have nothing in common with the love of the perfected man. What is generally called love is perverted because "it comes forward as an ought, as the subject of a command." Love, though, cannot be commanded. Furthermore, these expressions of action, that is, "love of mankind" and "righteousness" have nothing in common with the love of the perfected man because they "rest upon a man's standing opposite the other men and then treating them 'lovingly' and 'justly.'" But the love of the perfected man, for which each man can strive, rests upon unity with all things."[122] Buber is again dismissing the distinction and difference between one person and another—even in the context of love. Here love, rather than being a relation, is identification. Love is not recognized as a movement toward the other, but as an overcoming of all distinction in one's unity with all things. There is no presence of oneself to oneself or to another. The wholeness of this unity precludes any relation.

In his essay, "With a Monist" [1914], Buber draws on the connection between knowledge and love in the Hebrew word "to know," which also means "to embrace lovingly." However, in 1909, when he wrote "The Teaching of the Tao," Buber has one foot in the camp of unity while the other is attempting to reach relation. The embracing of all things is in the unity, the "being all" of the unified person: "This knowledge embraces all things in its being." It thus denies the differentiation of oneself from the other person or thing standing over against one. The unified person is not present to himself as a limited person, but is infinite, is unconditioned, is absolute. No other person or thing is present to this person as a unique other that is not included in the perfected person's "I." The perfected person is being, and there is nothing outside being.

The only way in which the unity of the unknowable can be experienced and grasped is through the unity of the perfected person. The person knows that this unity is all-knowing and all-embracing love. Why then does "Tao in itself" appear in the becoming of the world as the primal existence from which all elements spring? Why does it make this appearance and not remain unknowable? In the smaller perspective, why does the person who experiences this unity "set unity in the world"? Why does he through his action actualize the latent Tao in things?

As the true knowledge is called by Lao-tzu "not-knowing," so the true action is called "non-action." This "nonaction" is an "effecting of the whole being. To interfere with the life of things means to harm both them and oneself. But to rest means to effect, to purify one's own soul means to purify the world, to collect oneself means to be helpful, to surrender oneself to Tao means to renew creation."[123] The will of the person concentrated into a whole becomes pure power, pure effecting; there is no longer any division between this person and what is willed: being. Buber claims that the "nobility of a being lies in its ability to concentrate itself into one." This action is in harmony with the nature and destiny of all things, that is, with Tao.[124] It does not interfere with the growth of things. The person guards and unfolds what wills to become. Each thing is embraced: this love is totally free and unlimited, it does not depend on the conduct of men and knows no choice; "it is the *unconditioned* love. 'Good men—I treat them well, men who are not good—I treat them well: virtue is good. True men—I deal with them truly, men who are not true—I also deal with them truly: virtue is true' (L)"[125] What wills to become is what is in agreement with the primal nature (*Urbeschaffenheit*) of things and persons. This position has dangerous consequences that become evident in Buber's attitude to the First World War.

The will of the Tao reveals itself to the person through "the need and drive" of the community of beings. This person does not impose command or compulsion on the community, but "submerges himself in it, listens to its secret message, and brings it to light and to work, he rules it in truth. He performs the non-action; he does not interfere, but guards and unfolds what wills to become."[126] This is a revelation of the will of the cosmic spirit, or universal mind, that Buber mentioned at the end of his introduction to the *Ecstatic Confessions*. It is also, as I will later discuss, the kernel of Buber's concept of realization, which leads to the I-Thou relation. The choices that he or she makes therefore affect the world.

The perfected person, the unified one, is the one who directly experiences Tao. However, naked unity, just like ecstasy, is "dumb."[127] It takes place in solitude and leads to the person bringing the word to others or to a life of concealment. A word stirs in the person who is submerged "in wordless wonder, in the hour of stillness, before the break of day where there is yet no Thou other than the I, and the lonely talk in the dark traverses the abyss across and back."[128] The picture that Buber paints is that of the primal I who is alone and has no response from the other side of the abyss. The abyss is the *apeiron* out of which the multiplicity flows and to which it returns. On one side of the abyss is the unknowable and on the other side is the world. However, if there is only I, there is only the unknowable identified with the person. This unity is undifferentiated, and there is only consciousness of the I as the One.

INEFFABILITY: "NAKED UNITY IS DUMB"

The teaching is inaccessible through subject and object, content and form, or is and ought, because its way is not the way of knowledge, but of the pure fulfillment in a human life. In other words, one can only "know" it by doing it. Naked unity, just like ecstasy, is "dumb." However, echoing Bernard de Clairvaux's experience, Buber claims that in the experience of unity, a word stirs in the ground of the person, "where there is yet no Thou other than the I."[129] Already with the stirring of the word, the unity is touched by parable: the words do not proceed from pure unity because the multiplicity has already entered when the person attempts to speak the word.[130] The teacher in using the parable attempts to express the unity through things, events, and relations, as all speech concerns these things.[131] The person who has achieved unity seeks out those who remain in a simple unity and speaks to them in parables. Here the parable becomes a prism and leads to the dissolution of the teaching, whereas to those who have become unified, it is a "glass through which one beholds the light framed in a border of colours."[132] The teacher's life itself becomes a myth after his death; here myth is "the insertion of the world of things into the absolute." After this fulfillment, the teaching mingles with elements of science and law and forms religion. However, this contributes to the dissolution of the teaching, but again and again there is an awakening in the souls of the religious that leads them to the teaching. This does not mean, though, that there is one content of the teaching that takes different forms. Buber argues that the dialectical opposition of content and form does not clarify history, but confuses it. In the same way, this opposition does not clarify the apperception of art. Buber uses the example of art recurrently. The mere extraction of content and form in the appreciation of a painting limits the experience to the realm of I-It.[133]

There is a symbol, a sign of truth, however, that stands against the encroachment of this dialectic of content and form on the teaching: "the Logos of the Johannine Gospel, the symbol of primal existence taken significantly from the world of speech." This primal existence is the mysterious one from which emanates the many. Buber claims that "'The Word' is 'in the beginning' because it is the unity that is dialectically dissected."[134] This symbol of primal existence, "The Word," which is unity, is a companion to every genuine human word. Each such word is a unity that has been dissected into content and form. Nevertheless, this dissection means that the word cannot "reach beyond the province of conceptual classification."[135] It cannot, therefore, go back before the multiplicity with which it is concerned and reach the one.

Buber claims that the same holds for the teaching. When each teaching is dissected, we get the "content," not the unity. The content is "the

talk about the kingdom of heaven and the adoption by God; or the talk
about the release from suffering and the holy path; or the talk about Tao
and non-action."[136] This is inevitable, Buber claims, because the unity
is more than Jesus, Buddha, and Lao-tzu tried to express; it is their
ground and meaning. Just as unity is the ground and meaning of the life
of the great teachers, it awaits discovery as the ground and meaning of
all life. In revealing the teaching in its essence, the parable "bestows
on each the possibility of also discovering and animating the teaching
in himself." The person can discover the unity already present as a potentiality in himself or herself and bring it to life.[137]

CONCLUSION

The teaching of the Tao is in Buber's presentation another form of the
primordial myth of the path of the Ultimate. It is a formulation that
parallels Boehme's to a very significant extent. It remains a creation
myth. There is a source: the Godhead, the eternal, unchangeable Unity,
the *Ungrund* in Boehme, which is the "Tao in itself," the Unknowable
in the teaching.[138] Whereas Boehme stresses that he can only write
about the manifestation of the Godhead in the world—and in writing of
this manifestation, he uses the name God—Buber distinguishes between the unknowable "Tao in itself" and Tao as it appears in the becoming of the world: the primal existence that is open to relation and
the becoming of many. In Boehme's conception, there is the Holy
Spirit, the power or will operative in all things that is equivalent to the
presence of Tao as the core of all beings in the world. For Boehme,
there is also the third presence of the Trinity: the delight, the Son, who
is the incarnated substance of the will.[139] Buber claims that, according
to the teaching of Tao, each person is the substance and place of the
actualization of the will that desires itself. Here unity attains being, is
actualized. This is another form of the becoming God. Through the
human being, according to Buber, the will for unity manifests itself as
an all-embracing love and knowledge and thus returns to or becomes
itself. However, it is not the Tao as it appears in the being of the world
to which it returns, but to the Unknowable in which there is no possibility of relation. It is this unknowable unity, Buber claims, that is reached
in the experience of the unified person. This unity is wholeness without
any duality or multiplicity, without any relation to anything.[140] In the
experience of the unified person, there is no differentiation between

oneself as a limited human being and any other being. In identifying the unified human being with the source, with the Godhead, Buber must deny the value of human relationality. There is no relationality in identity, in unity with the Tao as it is itself. There is therefore no knowledge in the common sense as it depends on a knower and a known. This person attains an absolute knowledge through the embracing of all that is called "unconditioned love." This is the love that has no relation to anything because it is everything; it is the love of itself. In being all it knows all. "To be and to know are one and the same thing," as both Parmenides and Plotinus held.[141]

Part III: *On Judaism*

In the collection of Buber's essays published as *On Judaism*, the addresses delivered before 1914 concern a number of ideas that are relevant to our investigation. Unity remains the most important goal for Buber, and he identifies this as the most fundamental desire of the Jewish people. This desire is innate; it arises out of the latent natural tendencies of the people. The idea of God, according to Buber, emerges out of the striving for unity. The actualization of this idea of God remains dependent on the actions of human beings.

As I mentioned in the introduction to this chapter, Buber clarified many of the "inexact" or "inaccurate" expressions in these addresses in the preface to the 1923 edition. Nevertheless, the addresses themselves indicate Buber's position on some conceptions relevant to our discussion. I will consider these under three headings: Religiosity, Striving for Unity, and God and Godhead.

Religiosity

During the period 1906 to 1912, Buber was editor of a series of monographs on social psychology; the series had the title, *Die Gesellschaft*. Buber's professor and friend Georg Simmel contributed a volume, *Die Religion*, to this series. In this work, Simmel made a distinction between "religion as the objective world of belief, and religiosity as a category of feeling, an innermost quality of being that colors one's entire experience, a force that creates religion out of itself."[142] Buber adapted

this distinction and used religiosity as an expression for the feeling of
the person who discovered and animated the unconditioned in himself
or herself. Buber defines religiosity and religion as follows:

> Religiosity is man's sense of wonder and adoration, an ever anew
> becoming, an ever anew articulation and formulation of his feel-
> ing that, transcending his conditioned being yet bursting from its
> very core, there is something that is unconditioned. Religiosity is
> his longing to establish a living communion with the uncondi-
> tioned, his will to realise the unconditioned through his action,
> transposing it into the world of man. Religion is the sum total
> of the customs and teachings articulated and formulated by the
> religiosity of a certain epoch in a people's life; its prescriptions
> and dogmas are rigidly determined and handed down as unalter-
> ably binding to all future generations, without regard for their
> newly developed religiosity, which seeks new forms.[143]

The concept of religiosity is therefore also applicable to Buber's understanding of the mystical experience in which the mystic seeks unity and
to the experience of the person who discovers the Tao in himself or
herself. Whatever the unconditioned is, the person wishes to realize it
in the world. It is something that remains unrealized without the action
of man. The crucial thing about this action is not so much what is done,
as whether it is being done in human conditionality or divine unconditionality: "Whether a deed will peter out in the courtyard, in the realm
of things, or whether it will penetrate to the Holy of Holies is determined not by its content but by the power of decision which brought it
about, and by the sanctity of intent that dwells in it." Indecisiveness
and inertia are the root of evil. To be acted upon is to be conditioned;
this means to be in bondage, to be in sin, rather than to live in freedom,
which is to make decisions. This indecisiveness means one does not
realize God. Acting unconditionally, the person becomes unconditioned, and the fate of the "God-idea," that is, the abstract truth, is entirely dependent on his or her decision:

> God is an unknown Being beyond this world only for the indo-
> lent, the decisionless, the lethargic, the man enmeshed in his own
> designs; for the one who chooses, who is aflame with his goal,
> who is unconditioned, God is the closest, the most familiar being,

whom man, through his own action, realises ever anew, experiencing thereby the mystery of mysteries. Whether God is "transcendent" or "immanent" does not depend on him; it depends on man.[144]

Buber stresses the absolute importance of the action of man when he argues that "God is not something to be believed in but to be fulfilled."[145] Furthermore, the extent of the reality of God is dependent on man's decision: "the more man realises God in the world, the greater His reality." Therefore, as the only reality of God is that created by man in the world, this reality is restricted to the world. The decision is a religious act; in fact, it is *the* religious act because it is the realization of God by man. Buber's first address, "Judaism and the Jews," gives us an example of the immanent realization of the "God-idea" in the world.

Buber asks: "Is there an inherently Jewish religiosity? Is there not dogma or norm, nor cult or rule, but, alive in men of today and manifest in a community of Jews, a unique relationship to the absolute which can be called essentially Jewish?"[146] Pursuing this line of inquiry, Buber asks of his own time: "Where is there among Jews a divine fervor that would drive them from the purposive busyness of our society into an authentic life, a life that bears witness to God, that, because it is lived in His name, transmutes Him from an abstract truth into a reality?"[147] Buber's concept of God is that of "an abstract truth," but this idea may become reality. The human being has to decide whether this idea is realized. God is merely an idea until it is realized by man. We will shortly discuss how man arrives at this abstract truth. In this bearing witness to the idea, the person brings the idea to reality. One is not bearing witness to something that already is, but to something that is becoming through one's actions, through one's life. The influence of the idea of the "becoming God whom we create," present in the essay on Boehme, is also felt here.

What is the content of this idea of God? In answering this question, Buber first introduces a theory of the development of the "I" that he maintains in his writings through *I and Thou*. He claims that "the child first experiences the world around him and only gradually discovers his I, only gradually learns to differentiate between the mass of objects and his body as a separate existence."[148] The individual adult repeats this process of perceptual orientation on the level of intellectual orientation.

The adult first experiences the changing world of impressions and influences, the surrounding world, and lastly discovers his or her own self, the enduring substance, amidst all the changes. What is this enduring substance? The person comes to an awareness of his own self and to a sense of belonging to his native surroundings and community. But he or she may be led on from there. "What leads him on is an innate desire, blunted in some people but growing and maturing in others, for perpetuity, for lasting substance, for immortal being. He discovers that there is a constancy not only in the forms of experience, but also a constancy of existence which steadily sustains all being."[149] Buber claims that just as the child discovers the I of his physical being last, so the adult finally discovers the I of his spiritual being as an enduring substance. As the person discovers her I, her desire for perpetuity guides her range of vision beyond the time-span of her own life. A person "stirred by the awesomeness of eternity" experiences within himself the existence of something enduring. This something is the "unconditioned bursting forth from his core" in accordance with the above definition of religiosity. He experiences it still more keenly in its "manifestness and its mystery" in the succession of generations.[150]

According to Buber, in this "immortality of the generations a community of blood" is sensed by the person, which he feels to be "the antecedents of his I, its perseverance in the infinite past." Added to this sense is the discovery "that blood is a deep-rooted nurturing force within individual man; that the deepest layers of our being are determined by blood; that our innermost thinking and our will are colored by it."[151] The person senses that he belongs to the community of those whose substance he shares. His people are now his soul, and together with past and future generations, they constitute a unity. "It is this unity that, to him, is the ground of his I, this I which is fitted as a link into the great chain."[152] This unity is the unconditioned, it is realized through each person absorbing it as his own truth and making a decision that affirms it. The unity of the community of blood, which is the ground of the person's I, is, according to Buber, the reality that manifests the transmutation of God from an abstract truth. Just as in the essay on Boehme, Buber wrote that the unity of creative forces was "the new God whom we create," here God is manifested as a reality through the decision of each person to affirm the unity of the successive generations.

Immediately following Buber's discussion of the unity of the generations, in the same paragraph, a section was omitted from all editions of this address subsequent to the publication of *I and Thou*.[153] The omitted section states that as the Jews of the past freed themselves of the fall of their souls through devotion to the one God, so in these days, Buber and his contemporaries free themselves from it. "But not through devotion to a God, which is no longer possible for us, but through devotion to the ground of our being, to the unity of the substance in us."[154] The ground of all beings in "The Teaching of the Tao" was the Tao, the unity of all. Buber is now claiming that the ground of all beings is the unity of the community of blood, which again is a substitute for God.

Buber believes that devotion to this unity will free Jews of duality. He states that something has been planted within the person that does not leave at any hour of life, "that determines every tone and every hue in our life, all that we do and all that befalls us: blood, the deepest, most potent stratum of our being."[155] This determinant is explained by Buber: "the innermost stratum of man's disposition, which yields his type, the basic structure of his personality, is that which I have called blood: that something which is implanted within us by the chain of fathers and mothers, by their nature and by their fate, by their deeds and by their sufferings; it is time's great heritage that we bring with us into the world."[156] This connection with past and future generations therefore replaces the devotion to the one God of past generations. The transmutation has given rise to a substitute reality. And this reality eclipses the reality of a transcendent God.[157]

Whoever decides for the substantial community of blood affirms himself and his whole Jewish existence; "then our feelings will no longer be the feelings of individuals; every individual among us will feel that he is the people, for he will feel the people within himself."[158] Here again, Buber is emphasizing that the unity of the whole community of people is the unity experienced by the person within himself or herself. The person is the whole. This relegates the relations with members of this community to a position of lower value and importance. The past of the community is now viewed as the early history of this person's life; the present of the community is his present. "My soul is not by the side of my people; my people *is* my soul," writes Buber, and by the same process, "every one of us will then become aware of the future of Judaism and feel: I want to go on living; I want my future—a new, total life, a life for my own self, for my people within me, for myself within my people."[159] "What matters for the Jew," writes Buber, "is not his credo, nor his declared adherence to an idea or movement, but that he absorb his own truth, that he live it, that he purify himself from the dross of foreign rule, and that he find his way from division to unity."[160] Absorbing one's own truth is discovering and animating the unity of the community in oneself; this is "the unconditioned bursting from his core" mentioned by Buber in his definition of religiosity.[161] The overcoming of duality through commitment to this unconditioned is the redemption that the person can achieve for himself.

An analysis of this address indicates a striking similarity, in the Jewish context, to Friedrich Schiller's understanding of universal history. Remembering that Buber's grandmother read Schiller's periodicals, and that he chose an extract from Schiller for his bar mitzvah ceremony, the influence of Schiller here is not surprising. Schiller wrote that there "is a long chain of events reaching from the present moment back to the beginnings of the human race, interlocked like cause and effect."[162] However, there are gaps in the knowledge of world history. It is the task of the "philosophical intellect" to connect the fragments by artificial links, so that "the aggregate will be raised to the rank of a system, to a rationally coherent whole."[163] I suggest that this is what Buber has achieved in the above outline of Jewish self-understanding by stating that the community of the dead, the living, and the yet unborn constitutes a unity, devotion to which will overcome duality. This unity is the unconditioned, and realizing it leads to the unity of the I—the I that is the All. The I therefore becomes unconditioned.

Voegelin's comment on Schiller's understanding enables us to appreciate the similarity: Schiller believes that the reduction of man to an "individual of the species" and the submersion of the mortal individual in the immortal stream of human history will gain for man an immortality for which as a person he has no hope. The barriers of birth and death that are felt to be the walls of a prison cannot be abolished, but they can at least be made invisible by the "optical illusion" of participating in universal history. "The occupation with universal history turns out to be the opium for an intellectual who has lost Faith."[164] At this time in his development, Buber is just such an intellectual.

STRIVING FOR UNITY

In the second address, "Judaism and Mankind," Buber extends the question of duality to all humanity. He writes that mankind has needed and still needs Judaism as "the most distinct embodiment, the exemplary representation, of one of the mind's most supreme elemental drives."[165] According to Buber, there is more at stake here than the fate of a people; at stake are "archhuman and universally human matters." Buber argues that "Man experiences the fullness of his reality and his potentiality as a living substance that gravitates toward two poles; he experiences his inner progress as a journey from crossroads to crossroads."[166] These two poles are the sublime and the debased: "often the yea wrestles with the nay within the same individuals who, through singular upheavals, crises, and decisions, may attain either of the two poles." Buber continues by arguing that this tension in man between the "two opposites of his inner striving" is one of the essential, determining facts of human life; perhaps, he adds, it is even the most essential. Buber claims that this essential fact of human life "conveys the awesomeness of the primal dualism." This primal dualism is a reference to the conflict and love discussed in Buber's essay on Boehme. Although the two opposites may be given different names and have various meanings and the choice at the crossroads may be considered a personal decision, an external necessity, or a matter of chance, the basic form is unchanged. Buber asserts that in the Jew, this basic form is more central and dominant than in anyone else. It is the striving for unity that makes Judaism a phenomenon of mankind and changes the Jewish question into a human question.

Throughout Jewish history and writings, Buber claims, one will find a "sense and knowledge of disunion and duality—and a striving for unity."[167] It is the inner duality and the striving for unity that are permanent. The strongest expression of the duality is that between the elements of good and evil presented in the myth of the fall in the Book of Genesis. Here the task of the human person is presented as a choice, as a decision on which his fate depends. This striving is for unity within the individual person, within and between nations; between mankind and every living thing; and between God and the world. Then Buber asserts:

> And this God Himself had emerged from the striving for unity, from the dark impassioned striving for unity. He had been disclosed not in nature but in the subject. The believing Jew . . . had

drawn Him not out of reality but out of his own yearning, because he had not espied Him in heaven or earth but had established Him as a unity above his own duality, as salvation above his own suffering.[168]

God is not present as one of the poles of the tension experienced in the psyche because God is not a reality when the tension is experienced. God emerges only from the striving for unity that overcomes the duality. This God that emerges is not a reality, but an idea, or an ideal, in the Kantian sense,[169] arising out of the desire for unity. This ideal of the *ens realissimum* is arrived at through the internal striving of the person. There is no understanding of the presence of the divine in oneself or beyond oneself as a reality in itself. There is no question of the revelation of the divine to oneself. The emergence of the idea of God and the realization of this idea of God by human beings stands opposed to the concept of revelation.

In another address, Buber claims that Judaism is a spiritual process. This process is manifested in history as "the striving for an ever more perfect realisation of three interconnected ideas: the idea of unity, the idea of the deed, and the idea of the future."[170] However, these ideas are not abstract concepts. They are "innate predispositions of a people's ethos that manifest themselves with such great force and so enduringly that they produce a complex of spiritual deeds and values which can be called that people's absolute life."[171] This absolute life is the reality; it is the life lived in the world of the wandering and searching human spirit, and becomes part of the consciousness of mankind. The relative life of manifold appearances exists solely in order for the absolute to arise from it. The spiritual process of Judaism therefore takes the form of "an ideological struggle (*Geisteskampfes*), an eternally renewed inner struggle for the pure realisation of these folk-tendencies (*Volkstendenzen*)."[172] Buber argues that the struggle comes from the fact that the virtues, which determine the life of the individual person, are simply his or her her reformed, redirected passions elevated to ideality. In the same way, the determining ideas in the life of a people are simply its inherent tendencies elevated to the spiritual and the creative planes.

In other words, the idea of God has nothing to do with the relation between man and an existing transcendent and immanent God, but it arises out of the desire of the person to overcome his or her own duality:

unity is "born out of one's own duality and the redemption from it."[173] God for Buber at this time is a name for an idea of unity, which is an element in the ideological struggle of human beings.

The first of these ideas, the striving for unity, deserves more investigation. The idea of unity, explains Buber, originates in two sources. First is the fact that the Jew perceives more keenly than others the "context in which phenomena appear than the phenomena themselves, he sees the forest more truly than the trees."[174] Being more inclined to conceptual thought than to imagery, he is "impelled to conceptualize the fullness of things even before he has fully experienced it." However, he does not stop with a concept; he is driven to continue to "a highest unit that sustains as well as crowns all concepts and binds them into one, just as the phenomena has been bound into a single concept."[175] Kant's claim that the "business of reason to ascend from the conditioned synthesis, beyond which the understanding never proceeds, to the unconditioned which the understanding can never reach" is clearly evident here.[176] Buber adds that the second deeper source for the Jew's unitary tendency is "the longing to rescue himself from his inner duality and raise himself to absolute unity. Both sources converge in the God-idea of the prophets. The idea of a transcendent unity springs into being: the world-creating, world-ruling, world-loving God."[177]

This explanation of the coming into being of the idea of God leaves no doubt that for Buber at this time there is no question of an encounter with the presence of God. God is not a Being, a Thou whose presence is encountered in relation. Buber claims that this "springing into being" of God as the idea of transcendent unity was a peak in the spiritual process. The idea of unity underwent changes. Another peak was Spinoza's synthesis between the faculties of conceptualization and that of yearning. Here transcendent unity became immanent—"the unity of the world-permeating, world-animating, world-being God: *deus sive natura*." Each peak was followed by a decline in which the tendency to unity fades. For a while, it arose again in Hasidism, then weakened, and the sterile period in which Buber writes began. Even here, however, the yearning for unity is not dead, and therefore there is a call for renewal.

Once the basic elements of Judaism, which Buber identifies as the primal dualism and the striving for unity, are present, then the creativity of Judaism can continue in its task which is to offer, ever anew, a unification of mankind's varied striving and ever new possibilities for synthesis. It has already offered a religious synthesis at the time of the prophets and early Christianity; an intellectual synthesis at the time of Spinoza; a social synthesis at the time of socialism, when the Messianic ideal was reduced in scope, made finite, and called socialism.[178]

As Kant's highest idea of reason, the being of all beings, is called God, each of the syntheses, which Buber mentions, can be called "God." Those who offered a religious synthesis referred to the unity as "God"; Spinoza named the "most unified world structure," or the one substance, "God." Finally, in a letter to Landauer, Buber wrote: "I have just come across a wonderful saying in Pliny (apparently quoted from Poseidonios); it might virtually serve as a motto for the Socialist league: *Deus est mortali iuvare mortalem* [God is the helping of man by man]. Probably the finest definition of God!"[179] Judaism is getting ready for another synthesis, but its form is still unknown, according to Buber. Nevertheless, one thing is certain: it will demand unity. We conclude that it will be called "God."

At the end of this address, Buber refers to a saying of Jesus that remains Buber's leitmotiv: "A Jew once said: 'One thing above all is needed.'"[180] Buber's interpretation follows: "With this saying he expressed Judaism's soul which knows that all meaning-contents are null and void unless they grow into a unified one, and that in all of life this alone matters: to have such unity." This, Buber claims, was one of the great, eternal moments of Jewish history. At these moments, Judaism was the Orient's apostle to mankind because it drew from its experience of inner duality and its redemption from it, the power and fervour to teach the world of man the one thing above all that it needs. "Judaism set up the great symbol of inner duality, the separation of good and evil: sin." However, Judaism also taught the overcoming of this separation—in God, in the life of the holy man, and in the Messianic world. Judaism's fundamental significance for mankind, concludes Buber, is that being conscious of primal dualism and knowing division more than any other community, it proclaims a world in which dualism will be abolished, "a world of God which needs to be realised in both the life of individual man and the life of the community: the world of unity."[181] This implies that it is the task of human beings through their creative striving to bring to reality the world of God, which is equated with the world of unity.

Buber corrected this notion of the realization or becoming of God "either within man or within mankind," which he calls a "hopelessly

wrong conception," in the "Preface" to the 1923 edition of the addresses.[182] He then wrote: "I call such a theory, manifest today in a
variety of guises, hopelessly wrong, not because I am not certain of a
divine *becoming* in immanence, but because only a primal certainty of
divine *being* enables us to sense the awesome meaning of divine becoming, that is, the self-imparting of God to [H]is creation and His participation in the destiny of its freedom, whereas without this primal
certainty there can only be a blatant misuse of God's name."[183]

GOD AND GODHEAD

The question of God's name arises for Buber in his explanation of the
biblical origin of Jewish monotheism. Buber claims that there are three
clearly distinguishable strata: "The first of these three religio-historical
strata . . . is characterized by its use of the name Elohim, the second by
the use of the name YHVH, and the third by its use of both names, to
indicate a truly nameless divine being's twofold manifestation as universal God and national God."[184] The name "Elohim," Buber states,
appears as a singular in the Bible, but it was originally unmistakably a
plural, meaning approximately "the powers." Buber claims that there
are several traces of this plural divinity, which is "not differentiated
into separate, individually existing beings, each with its own nature and
own life, but representing, as it were, a plurality of cosmic forces, distinguished in their nature, united in action—an aggregate of creating,
sustaining, and destroying powers, a God-cloud moving above the
earth, deliberating within itself, and following its own counsel." This
"God-cloud" of cosmic forces that create, sustain, and destroy reminds
us again of Buber's conclusion regarding the "Boehmean God," which
he defines as "a potential infinity of powers which constitute no multiplicity but only an irrational unity, within which is a striving towards
actualisation."[185] Buber continues by adding that out of the plurality
of Elohim emerges a "single dominating force, a single name-bearing,
overruling being that seizes more and more power and finally detaches
itself as an autonomous sovereign, adorned with the mythical insignia
of an old tribal god: YHVH."[186] This being carries with it the powers
of Elohim. Then Elohim sinks to the level of a mere attribute. YHVH
Elohim is called the One: "YHVH is the divine hero of His people, and
the ancient hymns . . . praise His triumphant deeds, every one of which
is a genuine myth." Buber argues, however, that Judaism's tendency to

seek an ever higher, perfect unity continues. The cosmic-national YHVH is expanded into the God of the universe, the God of mankind, the God of the soul. YHVH is no longer a corporeal reality, though, and the old mythical images in which he is glorified are now only metaphors for his ineffability. Thus, writes Buber, "the rationalists seem to be vindicated after all, with the Jewish myth apparently ended. But this is not true, for, even millennia later, the people have still not truly accepted the idea of an incorporeal God."[187] However, the position of the rationalists is untrue, Buber adds, for a more important reason, that is, their definition of the concept of myth is too narrow and too petty. The rationalist definition of myth is that "only a tale of the actions and passions of a god who is presented as a physical substance may be properly called a myth." Nevertheless, the Platonic definition of myth—"a narrative of some divine event described as corporeal reality"—really means, according to Buber, "that we must designate as myth every tale of a corporeally real event that is perceived and presented as a divine, an absolute event."[188] Buber's interpretation requires further examination of the origin of myth. Buber's analysis is important because it is an insight into his concept of realization that he develops in *Daniel* and which leads to the meetings of *I and Thou*.

Buber argues that the civilized person's interpretation of the world is based on his understanding of the working of causality, whereas the primitive person's understanding of causality is poorly developed. Here we recognize Buber's desire to go further than the appearances of Kant to the "thing-in-itself," or *noumenon*. The primitive understanding is particularly weak in relation to dreams and death, "which for him denote a realm he is powerless to penetrate by investigation, duplication or verification."[189] Sorcerers and heroes also intervene in this person's life with a power that he is unable to interpret. The primitive person does not set these phenomena in a causal relationship, as he does with everyday incidents. Buber argues, instead, that "he absorbs, with all the tension and fervor of his soul, these events in their singularity, relating them not to causes and effects but to their own meaning-content, to their significance as expressions of the unutterable, unthinkable meaning of the world that becomes manifest in them alone."[190] Buber is arguing that the primitive person experiences these events with the intensity of an *Erlebnis*:

As a result primitive man . . . has a heightened awareness of the nonrational aspect of the single experience, an aspect that cannot

be grasped within the context of other events but is to be perceived within the experience itself; of the significance of the experience as a signum of a hidden, supracausal connection; of the
manifestness of the absolute. He assigns these events to the world
of the absolute, the Divine: he mythicizes them. His account of
them is a tale of a corporeally real event, conceived and represented as a divine, an absolute event: a myth.[191]

Buber concentrates on the experience of the person. It is in his or her
own experience that the absolute is grasped as manifested. This is the
experience of realization that we will discuss in the next chapter. Buber
adds that the ability to create myths does not cease with the passing of
primitive peoples. He argues that myth is an eternal function of the soul.
This ability to create myths remains in later civilizations even when
there is a far greater understanding of causality. Buber asserts that in
times of high tension and intense experience, the "shackles" of the
awareness of causality fall away, and the person "perceives the world's
processes as being supracausally meaningful, as the manifestation of a
central intent, which cannot, however, be grasped by the mind but only
by the wide-awake power of the senses, the ardent vibrations of one's
entire being—as palpable, multifaceted reality."[192]

The beginning of the I-Thou relation is present in the element of
confrontation in the primitive person's experience. In *I and Thou*,
Buber recognizes the confrontational character of the experience that
he has outlined.[193] However, at the time of writing "Myth in Judaism,"
Buber mentions that the primitive person *absorbs* the unusual events
that he experiences; this absorption is a way of explaining one of the
key elements of Buber's understanding of realization. Nevertheless, to
the primitive person these experiences remain a sign of something other
than himself—of the absolute. At this time, the teaching of Hasidism is
becoming evident in Buber's understanding of the relation of the person
to the world. In this teaching, he discovers that this "sign of the absolute" has to be realized by man. At the end of this address—"Myth in
Judaism"—Buber claims that the ultimate expression "of the influence
man and his deed have upon God's destiny" is found in Hasidism. This
teaches that the Divine is dormant in all things:

> Corporeal reality is divine, but it must be realised in its divinity
> by him who truly lives it. The *shekinah* is banished into conceal-
> ment; it lies, tied, at the bottom of every thing, and is redeemed

in every thing by man, who, by his own vision or his deed, liberates the thing's soul. Thus, every man is called to determine, by his own life, God's destiny; and every living being is deeply rooted in the living myth.[194]

Finally, what do these addresses indicate concerning Buber's understanding of God? The divine is dormant, that is, it is a potential in each thing, but man is necessary to realize it in its divinity. Thus God is not present except through the action of man. Through this action the world is redeemed. This means that the reality of the world is heightened and given the "great reality." This is a phrase used by Buber to signify that intensified reality is functionally dependent upon the intensity of the person's experiencing and realizing.[195] Although Bergman relates Buber's phrase "the Great Reality" to the "Great Experience" of Zen Buddhism,[196] it is also a phrase used by the early Kabbalists for the hidden God, the Infinite, or "En-Sof."[197] Is it this "great reality" that man realizes in the world, according to Buber? This reality is the equivalent of the "Unknowable" in Tao and of the Godhead for Eckhart and Boehme. Buber does not accept the presence of a transcendent and immanent God who is other than man in every way. He recognizes the ability of man to realize, to make actual, the dormant divine wholly present as a potential in all things. Whether this is the Godhead or not we will discover in the next chapter.

Later, Buber summarized the teachings of Hasidism in a single sentence: "God can be beheld in each thing and reached through each pure deed." He added that this should not be considered a pantheistic world-view. However, in his earlier writing this is exactly how he understood it.[198]

4. REALIZATION

Buber's first work of original philosophical thought is *Daniel: Gespräche von der Verwirklichung* (*Daniel: Dialogues on Realization*), published in 1913. This book of five dialogues is a pivotal work. It draws on Buber's past experience and contains the seed that will flower in *I and Thou*. In *Daniel*, Buber attempts to give a philosophical basis to the theme of "realization"—a theme that I have shown was already present in the addresses *On Judaism*. This basis is established through the five dialogues: Direction, Reality, Meaning, Polarity, and Unity. Each of these dialogues takes place in a different setting, and the main character, Daniel, who represents Buber himself, converses with a different friend in each. These dialogues are poetical and mystical as well as philosophical. Landauer, Buber's friend, wrote to Buber concerning them: "the reader cannot immediately grasp everything you say; here and there you have little more than a grey, vague feeling, and in addition an attempt to make fixed terminology develop a life of its own."[1] Referring to the fourth dialogue he added: "there is much said in rapid succession about settling, embracing, transforming, rather the way declining and conjugating are spoken of in school. But I feel somewhat like a student who has unfortunately missed the early classes and who gathers from the definite tone that these are established terms which cannot be amended; but he has no experience with them or examples of them and yet is supposed to keep up and build on the basis of this."[2]

Despite the difficulty in interpreting them, the dialogues form a significant step in Buber's intellectual journey. All of the works that we have examined lead up to this book. It outlines a mystical approach to the world, but does so from the perspective of the experience of the person. It identifies the aim of an authentic life as the realization of unity. It disagrees, however, with the manner in which Eastern thought and German idealism reach this unity.

My examination of these dialogues is extensive, as they are not widely known, although they are an important step on Buber's intellectual journey. Understandably, most of the secondary sources concentrate on Buber's mature dialogical philosophy. However, an appreciation of *Daniel*, which contains many symbolic references and allusions, will aid the clarification of many of the statements made by Buber in *I and Thou*. There, and in "The Religion as Presence" Lectures, he repeatedly critiques his own previous thought.

Although first published in Leipzig in 1913, an English translation of *Daniel* was not available until 1964. Buber agreed to the publication of an English translation on condition that it should include an introduction explaining that *Daniel* "is an early book in which there is already expressed the great duality of human life, but only in its cognitive and not yet its communicative and existential character. This book is obviously a transition to a new type of thinking and must be characterised as such."[3] Following his study of Hasidism, the locus of his search turns from the individual's experience of ecstasy to human action in the world. In this action, the person harnesses an innate power to bring about the transition from the potential to the actual. In examining the decision to act, Buber develops his understanding of the distinction between *Erlebnis* and *Erfahrung*. The person's response to life-experience decides whether the unconditioned will be realized.

The motto chosen by Buber for the title page of the first edition of *Daniel* comes from Scotus Eriugena's *De Divisione Naturae*: "Deus in creatura mirabili et ineffabili modo creatur" (God is created in his creatures in a marvellous and ineffable way).[4] As Kohn notes, the paradox contained in the motto embraces a mystery.[5] It implies that God and the human being are allied in mystical sonship. Copleston explains that Scotus Eriugena's meaning is in terms of God manifesting Himself in

His creatures: they are a "theophany."[6] Buber's understanding of realization implies that God is made real through the action of the human being.

The late-medieval mystic Meister Eckhart had already elaborated this notion in his reflections on the birth of God in the soul.[7] Eckhart has a great influence on Buber's reflections. For Eckhart, the analogy of birth illustrates the "breakthrough" of the individual into a realization of God's immediate presence. Eckhart calls the single unified and transcendent element in the person "the soul," a "light," "the ground of the soul," the "spark of the soul," or more generally, simply "intellect."[8] It is this element that is the image of God, and indeed God's Son, in human beings.[9] The birth of God, the Son, is intellective in character. It signifies a changed state of being that is fundamentally a "changed state of knowing."[10] The image of God is a transcendental potentiality within us that enables us to enjoy a cognitive unity with God.[11] In this state, "the soul in its essence and God are one."[12] However, this is not to say that we are God; Eckhart's appeal is to the potentiality that is never totally fulfilled.

According to Eckhart, the virtuous person is one who is detached. Detachment here includes not only freedom from attachment to physical things, but also a cognitive freedom.[13] The virtuous soul withdraws from the "multiplicity of its powers" into its unified ground. "There it loses selfhood, which is the primary obstacle to the practice of virtue, and merges with the oneness of intellectual essence."[14] In losing selfhood and becoming one with God, as in ecstasy, there is no experience of the presence of a distinct other. Buber moves from the unity of the self in ecstasy to unity with the whole world. The human being creates this unity when she bears in herself the tension of all duality in the world.

The motto from Scotus Eriugena's work was later omitted, presumably because of the pantheistic implications. Kohn states that it was omitted in all reprints.[15] However, I have located a second edition, published in 1919 in Leipzig, in which the motto remains. My aim in examining *Daniel* is to attempt to discover Buber's conception of the presence of God at the time that this text was first published. Thus I shall confine myself to this early edition, using the 1919 reprint. The Friedman translation of *Daniel* differs, sometimes significantly, from the 1919 Leipzig text. For example, certain omissions, especially in the first dialogue, obscure Kant's influence on Buber (an influence always acknowledged by Buber[16]) and the extent to which he was attempting to move beyond Kant in *Daniel*. Another highly significant difference in Friedman's translation—given my aim—is the omission of the sentence: *"Dieses Ich ist das Unbedingte"* (This I is the unconditioned.)[17] This sentence, which appears in the fifth dialogue, confirms our perspective on Buber's position on the nature of God at this time. However, to understand this position, the entire context of the argument in Daniel must be taken into account.

I will proceed by examining in turn each of the five dialogues, and I will formulate my understanding of Buber's developing conception of the presence of God. I will indicate the significant alterations and omissions between the 1919 Leipzig edition and the Friedman translation.[18] In a final section, I will come to a conclusion regarding Buber's conception of God and His presence at the time of writing Daniel. If my understanding of Buber's conception is correct, the intervening years between *Daniel* and *I and Thou* should clarify the development of Buber's thought.

Part I: On Direction: Dialogue in the Mountains

This dialogue takes place between Daniel and a woman as they climb a mountain. Daniel begins by saying, "Let us go further" [7]{49}. He speaks of the ascent of the mountain as a striving to liberate himself from the multiplicity of space and the rhythm of time. He wants to go further as the rocks tower over him like a call. Only if he goes further will the rocks become "brothers." The mastery achieved in the plains does not apply here. This mastery is the knowledge of the world ordered according to space, time, and causality. To establish that mastery in the mountains—that is, at a higher level—would be to fail to appreciate the true meaning of things [7]{49}. The woman mentions to him the joy of recurrence in the world:[19] "Would we not be miserable— creatures flung into a stale existence—if we were not born again every morning out of the abyss of sleep?"[9]{50}. Daniel agrees that this rhythm is "the breath of the earth, the indispensable" for human beings. Usually, we are content with this rhythm of "being submerged and awakening," but Daniel has experienced liberation. This liberation is the life-experience (*Erlebnis*) that has been the most valid reality for him and the only way by which he can measure all other life-experiences. It is liberation from the prison of direction-building (*dem Bann des Richtungsbaus*). The experience of liberation is explained before the meaning of "direction" and "direction-building" is discussed. This is the initial step in Buber's distinction between "realisation" and "orientation"; a step that precedes the distinction between the "I-Thou" and "I-It" attitudes.

Daniel gives an account of his first experience of liberation, using the image of the cross: "What happened? A crossbeam detached itself from the cross of the space to which I was bound, and soon my feet were also free: I stood up free in the vertical, and I was the vertical" [8–9]{50}. Daniel notes that only then did he feel in truth the meaning of his upright body, my upright "body-soul" (*Leibesseele*). Lifting his arms above his head in order to intensify this uprightness, he claims that the example of a powerful cathedral's buttress could not compare with the experience of the intensification of life. This liberation is described by Daniel as an ascent into a "spaceless" realm. The woman questions the possibility of thinking of a "spaceless" domain.[20] Is it possible to imagine or represent an overcoming of our spatial limitations? Daniel asks: "Is not space the clearest form of the great occurrence in which the One is intersected by the Many? And is not this, our way, a passionate image of that free remaining in the One that is denied us?"[9]{51}. Daniel explains that certainly in this experience (*Erlebnis*) he remained in space, but reflected therein was a kingdom in which there was nothing except his self and its completion.

This reflection suggests that the kingdom Buber speaks of is spiritual rather than material. What is the source of the reflection? Focusing exclusively on his direction (*Richtung*), nothing interrupted the flickering of the torch of his tension (*Spannung*) to the zenith: "undiverted, the lightning of the heights hurled down on my head, and earthly fire mixed itself with heavenly fire" [10]{51}.[21] This image, suggesting consecration and transformation, is completed in the next sentence: "And at that time the grace appeared to me which transforms one who is borne into the one who bears." This transformation is one in which the person moves from being passive, like an infant being carried, to being active, walking, and carrying. It repeats Buber's assertion in "Ecstasy and Confession" that in the ecstatic experience, the "I" bears the "world-I."[22] Aristotle's influence becomes evident in this notion of the self-mover. Aristotle uses the example of being carried and being the carrier in a discussion of the self-mover in the *Physics*:

It is impossible for that which moves itself to move itself all over, so as to be both carried and carrier in the same act of locomotion, though one and indivisible in form, or both changed and changer. One would teach and be taught at the same time, or enjoy and bestow the same health. Moreover it has been established that what is moved is the movable, i.e. what is potentially moved but not actually, and the potential proceeds towards actuality. Movement is the incomplete actualisation of the movable. But the mover exists in actuality. . . . Within the self-mover therefore something moves and something else is moved.[23]

The mover, whether external or internal to the person, must exist. When the person moves herself, within her are both the actuality of the mover and the potentiality of what may be moved. Buber writes: "the grace appeared to me *which transforms* one who is borne into the one who bears"—"grace" (*Gnade*) is thus the mover that actualizes the potential to become a bearer. What is meant by this mover and what does Buber mean by saying it appeared? The clue in Buber's image of consecration is that a transformation takes place. The changed state of being is a reference to Eckhart's reflections on the metaphor of the birth of God in the soul, in which each person is made like God. This is a variation on the traditional scholastic and patristic teaching on grace.[24] Eckhart understood grace to be "the uncreated self-communication of God, which is to say as the transcendental union of the human and divine."[25] Eckhart writes of the kingdom of God as hidden by time, multiplicity, the soul's own activity, and createdness. He reflects that the more the soul departs from all this multiplicity, the more the kingdom of God is uncovered in her. Grace is the essential power in the movement away from multiplicity toward oneness:

This can only happen through grace and not by the soul's own powers. The soul can discover the kingdom only with the help of the grace which inheres naturally within the highest image. Here the soul is God, savouring and delighting in all things as God. And here the soul receives nothing from God nor from creatures, since she it is who contains herself and receives all things from herself. Here the soul and the Godhead are one, and here the soul has discovered that she herself is the kingdom of God.[26]

In Aristotle's terminology, the soul is a soul-mover if it contains both the part that moves and a part that is movable. Whether this is Buber's understanding will be considered as I proceed.

Daniel then asks a puzzling question: "For what is it that we feel ourselves surrendered to since the might of our life is still confirmed with immortal seals?" [10] {51}. This is Friedman's translation. It suggests that there is something that we are surrendered to. However, the phrase *"das wir uns ausgeliefert fühlen"* directs our attention to a state in which we feel ourselves to be helpless. In this case, Buber is questioning the feeling of helplessness, since he claims our life force is after all confirmed with immortal seals.[27] As Daniel has been confirmed by the "lightning of the heights," so each person through his or her own direction can achieve the transformation. What does it mean to be confirmed with "immortal seals"? In the experience Daniel has described, he reached a state in which he was the only one present and within that state, the transformation from being the one who is borne to the one who bears took place. Oneness is here considered a stamp of immortality; it is the seal or the impression of the divine in the soul. Further implications of the phrase "immortal seals" will be dealt with later.

Direction

Buber begins his explanation of "direction" by presenting a description of a person making a choice. Daniel asks the woman if she remembers an evening in which she made a particular choice. She begins to speak of leaning on a window in a room that hung over the sea, but Daniel interrupts and takes up the story:

> You leaned on the open window in the evening; the small waves of the sea played against you, and you felt the small waves of your blood in unison with them, felt a mild melancholy and all security. Then you took your eyes away for a moment, you lowered them again half involuntarily, then the world was transformed: instead of the familiar playing of the waves the heavy flood of the night with the horror of its thousand despairings swelled up towards you, and you, who even now were the mistress, felt yourself lost. But when you gazed at the night, as before the sea; with glance and blood you made it into a partner; you tore out of the infinity of its directions the one, that which was yours, and you flung it as a bridge out of the core of your being into the core of the night. Then the horror disappeared; the great being turned its gaze upon you, and the sadness in it was to you,

its kindred spirit, no more terrifying than the sadness in the eyes of your dog. [11]{52}

This is Buber's description of an experience[28] in which one actively chooses one of many possibilities. It is important that we recognize the two perceptions of the situation from the woman's point of view. On the one hand are the small waves, the mild melancholy and total security. In this situation, the woman is called the mistress, she is in control. On the other hand, the deep flood, the thousand "despairings," and the feeling of being lost all give rise to horror. Here the woman is no longer mistress. However, all of this was encompassed by the night, and with this whole the woman made a connection. When she acted by tearing her own direction out of the infinity of possibilities and had the strength to make this her unique way, the horror disappeared. Then the encompassing whole became a partner, a kindred spirit. The woman chose the One from the Many, and through this choice bridged the distance between the core of her being and the core of the night. In making the choice, the woman drew all her innate power together in an act that connected her innermost self with the core of the world.

Daniel claims that it is "the infinite directions, the infinite tensions, the infinite feelings which mislead us, cause us to waiver and deprive us of our rights" [11]{52}. A decision is not made if one is continually wavering between the possibilities. If a decision is not made, no value is brought into being. If one is aware that one is failing to bring some value into being, then the question of responsibility arises even if one attempts to justify one's lack of action.

The infinite possibilities are described as the horizontal that intersects the vertical. Daniel claims that he "lifted their confusion" from his life "like the crossbeam from the cross," and that which bore him is now borne by him as he bears his own body [12]{52}. Being bound to the cross of infinite possibilities prevented his taking decisive action. The transformation meant that he now bears the crossbeam, but he holds it as a vertical. He holds in himself "the clouds of infinity, the waves that go between every pair of the numberless poles of the existent."[29] He not only bears the tension of these possibilities, but also has the power to make his way through the multiplicity. Through decision, one transcends the confusion of the multiplicity; it is not dismissed, but one is able to be master of it. It is not an easy mastery of the familiar and habitual, as in the example given, in which the woman was already mistress within total security. It is a mastery that has faced the "horror of the thousand despairings," and with all one's strength one has chosen to bring about what one considers to be of value.

Buber discusses the question of polarity in the fourth dialogue. Among the polarities considered are life and death, being and counter-being, spirit and matter, form and material, being and becoming, reason and will, and the positive and negative elements in the polarities. Recognizing the polarities, there is only one way to unity for human beings—by appropriating and realizing our direction. However, this way is not a negation of happenings or things, but through full engagement with each of them: "Not over the things, not around the things, not between the things—in each thing, in the experience [*Erlebnis*] of each thing, the gate of the One opens to you if you bring with you the magic that unlocks it: the perfection of your direction"[13]{53}. Buber continues to use the analogy of magic when explaining direction. Through this act of choice, a connection is made between the core of the person and the One. Each person can therefore reach the unity of the One because each has the ability to choose—but is direction alone sufficient to attain unity?

Direction is perfect only when it is realized with focused power: "power alone would give you only the fullness, direction alone only the meaning of the life experiences [*Erlebnisse*]—directed-power [*Richtungskraft*] allows you to penetrate into its substance, that is into the unity itself"[13]{53}. The power is the *kinesis*, the movement from potency to act. If direction gives the meaning of the life-experiences, it is a knowing. Prior to arriving at the meaning of a life-experience, one asks the question: "What is it?" Further, one must make a judgment as to whether one's understanding is correct: "Is it so?" Affirming that it is so, one reaches knowledge of the meaning of the life-experience. However, a further question then arises: "What value is this action realizing and is it truly worthwhile?" It is the right to realize the value that one thinks worthwhile that is denied when one waivers endlessly between the infinite possibilities. The right to create is one of those "immortal seals" present within the person. *Kinesis* is necessary in order to realize the value chosen. Buber claims that through directed-power, one penetrates into the substance of the life-experience. Through this act, one experiences and knows the meaning of the Oneness that transcends multiplicity. The unity found here cannot be found in the "track of the connections" [13]{54}. "Connections" in this context are the diverse strands of "the ingeniously spun net of world-knowledge" link-ing time, place, cause, and effect [15]{54}.

WORLD-KNOWLEDGE AND *ERLEBNIS*-KNOWLEDGE

Buber uses the example of a stone pine[30] to illustrate the distinction between the knowledge attained through the person's directed-power and the knowledge that fails to reach the truth obtained in this way. This illustration clearly anticipates the "I-It" and "I-Thou" attitudes of his mature philosophy. In the scientific mode of "world-knowledge," one compares the tree with others, examines what it has in common with those others, and in what ways they differ. Buber claims that this knowledge will be of benefit "in the useful auxiliary world of names and classifications, of reports about how things arose and how they evolved." However, he insists that in this way one experiences nothing of the truth of the being of the tree. The other way of knowing it is then outlined:

> And now seek to draw near to this stone pine itself. Not with the force of the feeling glance alone—that can present you only with the fullness of an image: much, not all. Not with the direction of a received spirit [*des aufnehmenden Geistes*] alone—that can re-veal to you only the meaning of a living form: much, not all. But with all your directed force, receive the tree, surrender yourself to it. Until you feel its bark as your skin and the springing forth of a branch from the trunk like the striving in your muscles; until your feet cleave and grope like roots and your skull arches itself like a bright, heavy crown; until you recognise your children in the soft blue cones; yes, truly until you are transformed. But also in the transformation your direction is with you, and through it you experience the tree so that you attain the unity in it. For it draws you back into yourself; the transformation clears away like a fog; and around your direction a being forms itself, the tree, so that you experience its unity, the unity. Already it is transplanted out of the earth of space into the earth of the soul, already it tells its secret to your heart, already you become aware of the mystery of the real [*gewährst du das Mysterium des Wirklichen*]. Was it not just a tree among trees? But now it has become the tree of eternal life.[31] [14–15]{54}

Buber distinguishes between the scientific approach to the tree and an approach in which one experiences "the truth of this being."[32] In the former approach, one relates the tree to other trees that are similar and other plants that are similar only in some respects. One examines these relationships and comes to knowledge of how the tree is to be classified. However, this classification is fitting this tree into an already formed net of knowledge. Buber claims that in this approach, one does not experience the truth of the being of the tree. Buber is directing our attention to an experience of the tree, as it is itself. In order to reach this, it is not enough to experience the tree only through one's senses, in this case, the power of sight, nor is it enough only to accept the agreed understanding of the tree. The first would provide the content, the image of this tree, the second would provide a concept of the meaning of a living form.[33] In Kantian terms, Buber is attempting to reach through the phenomenal world to reality itself.[34]

UNITY

Buber is not yet writing of a revelation that takes place in the meeting or encounter with another being as he will in *I and Thou*. He urges one with all of one's directed power to receive the tree, to surrender oneself to it until one is transformed. This is an ecstatic experience. Through one's act of direction, however, one is drawn back into oneself and the transformation disappears. In this drawing back, the tree is re-presented or "absorbed" into the soul.[35] It is in oneself that one gains the experience of the tree's unity. This implies that if the other being is a person, one does not appreciate his or her distinct otherness in the experience of realization, but "transplants"—re-presents—that other within oneself in order to achieve unity. It is in oneself that one becomes aware of the mystery of the real. What is this mystery? Through directed force, one is able to penetrate to the core of the thing and to experience its unity. According to Buber, this unity is *the* unity; it is the One in which everything is united and to which nothing can be added. Therefore, through the response to a single thing with his or her own directed power, the person is able to experience the unity of all in the One. There is in the experience a consciousness of this state of oneness, but it is not thematically known. It is an experience of mystery, the mystery of reality, of what is.

Buber draws attention to the necessity for the act of decision by the person entering into this ecstatic experience. His statement is prompted by the woman's question concerning times when the connection is not "the ingeniously spun net of world-knowledge, but the deep element itself: the mother's lap in which we save ourselves from the cruel laws of isolation, the boundless into which we must dive from the shore of limits in order not to perish in contradiction? Is not all ecstasy a merging into the Other?" [15]{55}. Buber clarifies his position by drawing on the myth of Dionysus and Orpheus. Dionysus was enticed by the Titans and was torn to pieces and devoured. Anyone who surrenders to ecstasy with undirected soul experiences this fate. In contrast, Orpheus entered into ecstasy with a directed soul: "Not enticed: decided, and with the lyre." Orpheus, because he is guided by his own direction, represented by the music of the lyre, becomes creative. He decides to enter into ecstatic death "not in order to regain a beloved but in order to die and rise from the dead with Dionysus" [16]{55}. The transformation in ecstasy is a death and rebirth of the soul. The decision of the person to follow this way toward rebirth is essential. This rebirth is possible because rather than being fragmented in the ecstatic experience, the music of Orpheus's lyre enables him to remain whole.

The soul expresses its own innate direction, its unique melody in the abyss.[36] Whereas music is the "pure word of the directed soul" [16]{55}, melody is the unique music particular to each person, it is the line along which the person in his or her choices decides to move.[37] In the kingdom in which the transformation takes place, the directed soul, with its inner song, rules alone: "Here there is nothing more of the artificial context of linked polarities into which the life-experiences [*Erlebnisse*] are wedged and confined, but also the formless mixture and its isolation are banned from this kingdom. The directed soul alone rules here" [16]{55}. Daniel suggests that this is the kingdom in which there is only the one, the directed soul, who experiences cosmic oneness. As Orpheus with his music could charm the wild beasts, so when one sets one's direction, the other forces arrange themselves around it: they submit to the form of the song. Thus the person can experience the ecstasy of transformation, yet through the magic of its own song, the soul remains intact and is immortal. Immortality is attained through one's direction and is one of the seals of this life force that Buber mentioned earlier.[38] This explains why Buber says the tree, the stone-pine, becomes the "tree of eternal life" [15]{54}. Immortality is not a human condition, except insofar as we are identical to God. Buber is drawing our attention to a conception of the human being in which we can recognize divinity. Eckhart's notion of the birth of God in the soul, where the Godhead is present with all the divine properties, is again the principle that is grounding Buber's reflections.

THE RESPONSE OF THE DIRECTED AND UNDIRECTED SOULS

Before he arrives at a definition of direction, Buber further explains the difference between the directed and undirected soul by reference to the meeting of the soul and the whirlpool of happenings in the world. This whirlpool envelops the soul like "an endless sandstorm that threatens to destroy it" [17]{56}. How it withstands this whirlpool decides the nature of the soul. Again this explanation is a step on the way to his mature philosophy:

> The one thinks only of protection. It surrenders itself entirely to the inherited powers, the traditional arts of self-defence, which educate its senses to perceive in place of the whirlpool an ordered world conceived within the framework of basic principles of experience; which educate its will [*Willen*] to meet a stable system of causality and purposefulness and to fit itself to it rather than succumb to the whirlpool. And indeed this *is* protection. For to the benumbed soul the divine force of the whirlpool is also benumbed. [39] [17–18]{56}

This person is not creatively responding to the uniqueness of the situation or event, but is, rather, inserting the happening into the "useful auxiliary world of names and classifications." The person fears the disturbance that the whirlpool may cause and for his or her own protection, perhaps to remain undisturbed in the pattern of existing life, he or she allows the senses and will to be restricted to the traditional framework of space, time, causality, and purpose. However, in doing so, the life of the "divine force" present in the whirlpool of happenings is deadened. One may perhaps imagine a child who is taught to restrict its notion of "normal" to others like herself. The context in which she lives then determines who she considers to be similar to herself. She may be tempted, when an adult, to continue restricting her concept of a normal human being because she fears that a revision would disturb her whole understanding of happenings in the past and perhaps in the present. She attempts to close off, or numb, that part of her that hints at a different perception. Thus the uniqueness of what is before her is deadened; its truth is buried. However, this turning away may leave unease within her.

The directed soul is sensitive to the unease, to the lack of fulfilment; it finds that the protective response does not satisfy. It treats the whirlpool differently:

> It finds no satisfaction in the protection that the inherited powers accord it. It lets it stand, to be sure, the auxiliary world in which alone it can live with men; it accepts it and learns its laws. But deep within it grows and endures the readiness to go out and meet the naked whirlpool. Armed with what? With nothing other than with the magic of its direction, its own, inborn, unique direction, belonging to it and no other. [18]{56}

Although the "inherited powers" are necessary and the laws are learned, the ordered world and the settled system of causality and purposefulness, which one is educated to accept, do not bring fulfillment. The Kantian system has not answered Buber's questions; it has not satisfied his desire for an unconditional presence. The human person cannot fit herself into this system and be satisfied. There is an intimation of something lacking, something else that may be found by meeting and entering the living divine force of the whirlpool of happenings. Buber then defines direction:

> Direction is that primal tension [*Urspannung*] of a human soul which moves it to choose and act to realise this and no other out of the infinity of possibilities. Thus the soul strips off the net of directions, the net of space and of time, of causes and of ends, of subjects and of objects, it strips off the net of directions and takes nothing with it but the magic of its direction. That is the strength that the soul has found in itself, to which it recalls itself, which it raises out of itself. [18–19]{56–57}

The lack of satisfaction disturbs the other soul. There is a desire within it to go further, as Daniel said at the opening of the dialogue. In wanting to go further, it seeks to meet whatever is to be met in the whirlpool of happenings. In its direction, the soul intends what is real, what is hidden by the protection of the "inherited powers." At the same time, it finds within itself the abilty to choose to respond with openness to the divine force of the whirlpool. As direction is a primal tension (*Urspannung*), it is therefore original, elementary, the ultimate tension that is the cause of the soul's choosing to realize one out of an infinity of possibilities. Direction is that strength or force (*Kraft*) that the soul finds in itself.[40] Buber states that the soul recalls or becomes conscious of this force in itself, and through it the multiplicity of the whirlpool is calmed, and the soul, which has attained unity, knows the multiplicity.

THE NECESSITY OF NATURE

At a time when the importance of the theory of relativity was being discussed, the understanding of the distinction between necessary and contingent laws was undergoing change. Buber points toward the directed soul as the one necessity of nature. He recalls that man succeeded in confining the happenings of the world in the machinery of cause and effect. "When the machinery stood joined fast and the skilfully finished clockwork did its bidden service, then they named the swing of the pendulum, the inexorable [*unaufhaltsamen*] necessity [*Notwendigkeit*], and they were horrified at the necessity" [20]{57}.[41] However, Daniel says that he does not grant the name of necessity to "the demands of human need between birth and grave, nor to the fate of all scattered life in the world, nor to all the counterplay of the elements, nor even to the movement of the stars themselves, not to all these investigated and registered things may I grant the name of necessity, but only to the directed soul" [20–21]{58}. The soul is that which commands, and it points toward its unique goal. It chooses its way, unlike the needle on the compass that *must* point to north out of all the possible points.[42] The soul does not obey the commands of any other power. Whereas humanity has assembled a system through which nature can be understood, Buber claims that the soul can surpass that: "for with its one direction it summons [*ruft*] reality and conjures it around its direction, so that the reality does not organise but reveals itself and gives itself, not to the senses and the understanding alone but from being to being and from mother to child. Thus the directed soul is the necessity of nature" [21]{58}. Buber uses the analogy of a conjuror—who has the power to summon reality. Direction is the power of the soul that enables reality to be revealed. Reality is revealed and gives itself not only in knowledge, but also existentially—from being to being. The directed soul is the necessity of nature because only through it is reality revealed.

Buber points to an existential communication or revelation between human beings. This revelation is a form of knowledge in the same sense as the Hebrew word "to know" can mean the knowing involved in an intimate relation, a loving embracing, as mentioned in the last chapter. The person embraces the nature of each thing; this action is the nonaction or noninterference that we discovered in the teaching of the Tao. The reality of each thing is then fully realized, and the person is one with this reality. Daniel adds that direction is the necessity of the soul. However, direction can only be expressed in deeds, not in words. She manifests herself only through her work, "she, who pulls me up in the morning and drives me into the wilderness, who visits me at midday and sends me to the living, who takes my hand at evening and accompanies [*geleitet*] me to God: the high mistress [*Herrin*] of my all-enveloping solitude."[43] Buber is referring here to direction as the female power, Sophia, or Wisdom. Wisdom in Boehme's writings is the word of the Godhead. Wisdom reflects the glory of man, of the world, and of God.[44] When Daniel says that the mistress takes him into the wilderness, this is the solitude of his own self; when she takes him to the living, it is to the world; she also takes him to God. Buber has already stated that through its own direction, the soul has divine qualities. The divine wisdom is present in each person. One becomes aware of these qualities present in oneself through one's actions. Buber is implying that insofar as the person reveals reality through his or her actions, he or she becomes aware of his or her own divinity.

At the end of this first dialogue, the woman asks Daniel for his hand and indicates that the joining of hands is a horizontal. She then asks Daniel to remove the crossbeam. Daniel replies that this is not the horizontal—the multiplicity—that has to be overcome. It is not compulsion by the other, but the "choice of the other: the direction of the Holy Ghost [*heiliges Gespinst*], the flowering cross of community." Here Buber names direction as one of the qualities of the Holy Ghost. The choice of this direction brings community. This final sentence again suggests a hesitation on Buber's part—he cannot ignore the community that he knows in his own life, in his marriage to Paula, his wife.

Part II: On Reality: Dialogue above the City

Buber has claimed that perfected direction—the primal tension of the human soul that moves it to choose and act to realize one and no other out of an infinity of possibilities—leads a person to the revelation of reality. Buber in this dialogue attempts to clarify "reality" and what he means by the "realisation of reality." A clarification is offered in the discussion of the twofold relation of the human being to experience where the differences between the orienting and realizing functions of the person are explained.

FREEDOM OF THE SOUL

In the first dialogue, Daniel claims that "music is the pure word of the directed soul." At the beginning of the second dialogue, the musical theme is continued when Daniel indicates an awareness of "the longing for the song" present in every person in the city, though unknown to each of them. This longing is the desire for knowledge of the "thing-in-itself," that is, for noumenal knowledge. Daniel is speaking to a friend, Ulrich, during a walk that takes them out of and above the city. Daniel asks Ulrich if he knows "what the moment you allow to fulfil itself brings to you, what a flood of song and light" [26]{62}. Before he tells Ulrich what he learned in such a moment, he relates an experience in which he attempted to open himself fully to a crowd and receive from them their "scattered pain" and fragmentation. He wished to unite their torn pieces in himself. Then, he believed, his soul would become their song. With this will or intention, he went through the crowd. He says this will became actual. He no longer knew himself, but knew only the tumult of forces rushing around. In the center was a heart, like a human heart, receiving blood and then sending it out in all directions. As his self-consciousness returned, he received a song from each individual in the crowd and became faint with compassion. Then he had no longer any will in him other than to be a man again and to take one of these men by the hand and say to him: "Remember, brother, that your soul is a free and mighty firmament that nothing can compel" [27]{63}. Renouncing this position, he again found himself trembling in the crowd. Afterward, he was alone in the garden[45] and was lonelier than before. However, much later, it was revealed to him what he had known at that moment.

The importance of intention in the above account must be noted. Daniel decides that he can unite the pain of the people and overcome their fragmentation in himself so that his soul may become their song. He believes that he can be their liberator, their redeemer. This is his desire. As this intention became actual, Daniel lost self-consciousness and seemed to become a heart, the life force of the tumult of forces around him. When he regained consciousness, he received one song from each of the forces—from the hungry, the greedy, the seeking, and the grasping. However, he became cowardly (*feig*), and his intention changed. What emerges here is the understanding that the other person is free, that Daniel cannot accomplish for them what they have to do for themselves. The soul is free, autonomous, and it cannot be determined. Each has its own song of which it has to become aware. Daniel wants to communicate awareness of this freedom: "your soul is a free and mighty firmament that nothing can compel."

In speaking of the soul as a firmament, Daniel relates it to what is above the world, to what is transcendent. It does not belong to the world of contingency, yet is related to it. As argued in the previous dialogue, the human being is not fully determined by the laws of the phenomenal world. In itself, the soul finds the power to transcend the world of appearances and to summon reality. In Kantian terms, the transcendental freedom of the will belongs to the human being as *noumenon*, not as a phenomenon bound by laws of causal necessity. Freedom brings the responsibility to decide and to act. What Daniel had known in that moment was that "'the human being remains unreal who does not realise" (*Unwirklich bleibt, wer nicht verwirklicht*) [29]{64}. It is through one's own act of realization, in which one responds in a particular way to one's life-experiences (*Erlebnisse*), that one becomes real oneself. One's own reality is a value that can be realized through one's decision. It is one's own responsibility to realize oneself. However, the implication of Buber's theory here is that I can by means of my response to another person benefit from him or her in order to realize myself. The other person is not realized in himself or herself, but is only present as a representation in my consciousness.[46] That other person has the responsibility to realize himself or herself.

TWOFOLD RELATION TO EXPERIENCE

In elucidating this statement, Buber explains that there is a twofold relation of the human being to life-experience (*Erlebnis*) [47]: the orienting or classifying and the realizing or making real [29]{64}.[48] Life-experience is what one experiences in doing and suffering, in creating and enjoying. One may either register this life-experience in the structure of experience for the sake of one's aims or one can grasp it for its own sake in its power and splendor. In the former attitude, the experience is explained in terms of the forms and laws, for example, space, time, and causality. Although the experience "no more occupied a space than the new heaven which John saw at Patmos, . . . you make it into a thing in space." Although it was "no more temporal than the last, already double-directed glance of the dying man," it becomes an event in time, located between a before and after that squashes it flat. Although it was "no more causal than the majesty of the first dream," it becomes a link in a chain where it has just as much meaning as the other links. Furthermore, although it was "no more objective [*gegenständlich*] than God is an object to the human being or the human being is to God, you break it in two so that you injure its core and with superior certainty name the pieces the perceiving and the perceived" [30]{64–65}. A statement of the conclusions of orientation is called the truth. Daniel claims that to a certain extent this is right, "for doubt is at home on journeys of discovery, but truth and error are easily established in reading a map. Only one shall not speak of reality in all this" [31]{65}.

We can appreciate this analogy by reflecting on our use of a map. In this situation, one is considering one's experience according to an already charted terrain. The map and the criteria that led to its formation may not be questioned. It helps one to be oriented, to feel in control, but the map is not reality. If one allows it to dominate and determine one's expectation of what is to be experienced and one's understanding of what is actually experienced, the map may be considered real and the area of which it is a map may be considered unreal.[49] In each of the examples that Buber gives there is a depth of reality that is omitted if one expects simply to insert the experience into an already formed structure of experience. There it would be situated in a place with "an unshakeably fixed relationship to each other point of the world." In each example, the experience is not simply a daily event, but a special unique moment in the life of the person. It is a moment that has not already been mapped. If one expects it to fit into the map, it may be judged as true or false in relation to other events on the map. In this way, one imposes the past on the present and closes off the possibility of appreciating the uniqueness of each present happening. Buber illustrates the damage done to the life-experience by comparing the situating of it between a before and after that squashes it flat with the act of "a boy who violently presses a rosebud flat" [30]{64}.

To break the life-experience into subject and object is to tear apart the intrinsic intimate relation of the person and the event and does not allow for the fact that in this relation one's own temperament is involved. In the experience, there is no split between subject and object. This emerges only at a later stage when one reaches an understanding of what the experience was and, in judging that one's understanding is correct, one affirms what one has experienced. It is in the affirmation that objectification occurs.

SCIENCE AND REALITY

Buber's statement that the scientific method does not reach reality raises the questions of the basis of scientific inquiry and commonsense perception. First, Ulrich asks Daniel if he is implying that science, which is verified in natural happenings and in purposeful acts, is not grounded in reality. Daniel agrees that this is what he means, but asks to be understood correctly. Buber draws our attention to the distinction between the true scientist, who appreciates that his knowledge is grounded in a life-experience, and the use of such knowledge without any awareness of its basis. The creative moment of genius is where knowledge begins. It is for Buber a realizing moment, in which the happening or event and the person each have an input. The inputs cannot be separated or considered as the perceived and the perceiver because there is an intrinsic link between the inputs of both at the core of the creative moment. The scientific hypothesis is based on this moment. Daniel explains that the structure of experience "appears to me ingenious but not artificial; it seems to me an elaboration of life-experience, yet not an arbitrary one" [31]{65}. The elaboration is not arbitrary, as all laws and forms have their origin in a life-experience. The regularities in the structure reflect the deep rhythms of life-experience (*Erlebnis*), although only symbolically. One cannot wish away or wish to go behind the structure without transgressing against the power of the spirit. "For everywhere a knowing was formed, where it began, where it was creative, it was not orienting but realising; immersion in pure life-experience, and what was thus found was widely utilised" [32]{65}. However, where orienting knowledge was dominant, there was an omission, "for it took place at the cost of the mothering, nourishing juices of life-experience and was only able to replace a small need or a little security by the realisation" [32]{66}.

Buber points here to the dominance of technique and the value system commanded by it. Science or technology become autonomous in their aims, and knowledge is used to achieve ends that fail to take into account the whole of reality. The connection with that which nourishes it is broken, so that development may take place in directions that are at odds with the authentic growth of human life. It is the dominance of this orienting consciousness that masks reality.[50] The orienting consciousness is geared toward the questions: "What use is it?" or "What use is it to me?" Every experience is assessed according to this one value and discarded if it cannot be used as a means to the satisfaction of one's needs or as the guarantee of one's security. The organization of means to satisfy needs is part of the good functioning of the world. However, if orienting knowledge rules autonomously, the danger is present that the self-understanding and relationship of human beings will be determined by its values. A disinterested appreciation of each unique being is then no longer possible. It is this danger that Buber is pointing toward. We must also add that his concept of realization is, through the use of another being, in danger of being subject to these same values.

LIFE-EXPERIENCE

Daniel rebels against this exclusive emphasis on orientation for the sake of the realizing, "which creates reality out of the life-experience [*die aus dem Erlebnis die Wirklichleit schafft*]" [32]{66}.[51] Questioning Daniel's concept of the creation of reality, Ulrich asks: "Then you want to understand by reality not the elementary material of the life-experience but a work of the soul?" [33]{66}. Ulrich is pointing to a crucial distinction between what is the most elementary or preliminary given of experience and the process that is the work of the soul and which arrives at a knowledge of reality. In the key paragraph that follows this question, Buber outlines the basics of his epistemology [33]{66}. As already noted, Buber's conceptions of *Erfahrung* and *Erlebnis* are closely related to Dilthey's, but extend beyond his teacher's to claim access to the "things-in-themselves" through life-experiences.

> A work of the soul certainly; but consider that in life-experience
> we are not offered a material that we form and that is detachable
> for our forming, extractable out of it; rather that it sprouts in our

activity and that in the finished plant we can no longer in any way separate out the seed. Life-experience is only given to us to observe and compare in the form which our function, orienting or realising, has developed out of it; in its unformed essence we only experience it, but we do not possess it. To our knowledge, to our memory, to our taking possession of it there lead from experience [*Erlebnis*] only the two bridges of our formation, and when it has crossed the bridge—even though its passage were faster than the speed of light—it is formed; it has become mere experience [*Erfahrung*] or reality. Life-experience is ungraspable like a lightning flash or a waterfall or the formation of crystals; we may not call it reality since we cannot thereby deal with it, draw it forth and regard it. But less will we accord the name of reality to the construction of experience [*Aufbau der Erfahrung*]. [33–34]{66–67}

Buber recognizes that the elementary material, which is the experience, is not knowledge, but rather is the essential presupposition of knowledge. When he asserts that "in its unformed essence we only experience it, but we do not possess it," Buber is making the distinction between the experience, which like the seed has potential, but which has not developed yet, and the developed knowledge of reality, that is, the plant that sprouts through the activity of our inquiry into the unformed experience. As simple experience, we cannot observe or compare it with other formed experiences; we simply undergo it. We cannot circumscribe it in our conceptual and linguistic structures. We cannot hold on to the experience itself, just as a lightning flash or a waterfall or the formation of crystals cannot be held in our hands. The unity of the life-experience, which Buber has argued is not spatial, temporal, causal, or separated into subject and object, is only experienced, it is not known. We therefore cannot call this "unformed essence" reality. Even less than this "unformed essence," however, can the name of reality be applied to the construction of experience in which the subject-object relation dominates. The unformed essence has still the potential to become reality through the process of realization. The life-experience, which has been subjected to orientation, has been damaged and its core has been torn asunder. Its unique potentiality to develop or be realized has thus been destroyed.

From the "unformed essence," two bridges lead to our knowledge, to our memory, and to our possession of the life-experience. First, there is the orienting bridge. As soon as this bridge has been crossed, the unformed essence has been formed into "mere experience" (*Erfahrung*). Here "mere experience" is an object considered in terms of space, time, and causality, which are human constructs. It is an object for use by the person to provide security or satisfy need. Orientation arrives at a type of knowledge, but to Buber, it is a different form of knowledge from that arrived at by the second bridge—realization. Through this second bridge, the unformed essence becomes reality. Therefore, the same life-experience, through different functions of the person, yields both types of knowledge. In the rest of this dialogue, Buber will attempt to explain the difference between the two bridges that represent the twofold relation of the human being to experience.

Before that, however, he briefly deals with Ulrich's second question that concerns the commonsense perception of the world. Ulrich asks Daniel about the common linguistic usage in which *reality* is the existing perceptible world [34]{67}. Here Buber is addressing the question of the dominance of the senses in common sense. Buber does not dismiss this knowledge, but says attention should be paid to it because the communal life of human beings is based on it. The time to accept it again, with or without a qualification, will be when they end the intellectual discussion and move into the business of ordinary life. Buber thus also distinguishes commonsense knowledge from the knowledge reached in realization.

THE INTENSIFIED AND CREATIVE MEANING OF REALITY

Buber then draws our attention to moments in which we are aware of a heightened or intensified reality, which was mentioned in the previous chapter. Daniel indicates the use of a word in a poem where the ordinary meaning of the word is extended. It is this intensified (*gesteigerte*) sense that to him is reality. It is not arbitrary, just as the use of the extended meaning of a word in a poem is not arbitrary. This is because the meaning comes from "intensified existence, intensified humanity, intensified knowledge" [35]{67}. These moments "fix speech" and "renew speech," rather than just fitting into a place in the already formed system of speech.[52] Daniel says that these moments of intensified existence must be consulted when we want to talk of reality and realization in an intensified, creative sense. It is reality in this sense that

Buber insists must not be left aside through a submission to the dominance of orientation.

Ulrich asks, however, how do we take these into account when they are inaccessible to us? Daniel replies that these moments are not more inaccessible "than the hero is to the poet who knows him only because, having met with his face and his gesture in the world, he finds present in his soul what is expressed in this face and gesture" [35]{68}. Between the hero and the poet there is a common human spirit. The story of the hero evokes in the consciousness of the poet the "unformed essence" or preliminary knowing of the heroic experience. The poet must advert to his own becoming conscious of this experience in order to understand it and to know that what he grasps in the heroic story is present in himself. The poet is the one who finds the words to articulate what is grasped so that they evoke recognition of the same reality in others.[53] Thus the words of the poet fix and renew speech.[54] In speech, there is an attempt to express the unknowable Heraclitean logos, which is the meaning of being and which is common to all people.[55]

In order to further explain how these moments of intensified existence are accessible to us, Daniel gives the example of the person who calls forth his whole life in memory. As the two functions of the person bring the experience to knowledge and memory, in what is remembered one should be able to distinguish the result of orientation and realization. Buber mentions the type of remembering that he does not mean:

> I do not mean that resigned laziness which leaves the doors of the past open and turns to every entering shadow the same bittersweet attentiveness; also not that assumed superiority that reckons up what has been like the earlier moves of a game in which the decisive is still to be done; but also not that true and thankful accounting of a human being who judges the decisions and the absences of decision of his life. [36]{68}

The other form of remembering is called the rarest of all; it is the "heightened hour of great evocation," in which the person's life steps up to him or her like a form: "See him possessed by the shudder of the event, of the whole of which he has only now become fully aware; see him compose himself, govern his glance, behold" [36]{68}. The image that the person beholds is woven out of nothing else than that "mysterious material we call time, lived time." Out of these appearances of lived time, the "holy countenance [*das heilige Antlitz*] is unfolded, and the beholder recognises this image which continually changes according to the meaning of life"[36]{68}.

What is the "holy countenance" to which Buber refers? Although the meaning of this phrase is not clarified until later, it is important to note that it is formed out of the person's life as it unfolds. The person's life is the objectification of the decisions he has made. Through reflection on and understanding of his own history, the person comes to self-knowledge. The image that he finds changes according to the meaning of life. The meaning depends on the cultural context of the person; therefore, different people may have different perceptions. Most important is Buber's insistence that it is out of the lived experiences that the image is formed.[56] He is not claiming knowledge or memory of anything that lies beyond the possible temporal experience of human beings. What is known through realization and orientation is grounded in experience. Daniel asks Ulrich to consider which times are recognized as reality by the person remembering. Is it those in which life-experience is inserted into the "inherited context of indirectness (mediacy) as a servant of the alien" [36–37]{68–69} or those times in which the person concentrates his entire self in the moment, as does an athlete? Buber points to the unified action of the whole person in answering this question:

> Or those in which he catches them, as the ballplayer the ball, hurling himself against them, receiving them with hastily collected limbs; in which he embraces them, as the wrestler embraces the body tensed against him, throwing his whole strength into a muscle struggling for victory; in which he completes it as the runner his course, fulfilling, completing it with the swing of his own stride? Which, which does he recognise as reality, the hours in which the Many overshadow and weaken the One or those in which the One shines in the undiminished fullness of its splendour because it is related to nothing other than to itself?[57] Yes, this is what it means to realise: to relate the life-experience to nothing other than itself [*das Erlebnis auf nichts anderes beziehen als auf es selber*]. And here is the place where the power of the human spirit awakens and collects itself and becomes creative. [37]{69}

As the ballplayer is immediately and fully present when catching the ball, the person is also present with his whole being in those moments of life-experience. He grasps them, embraces them, fulfills and completes them. These examples indicate that realization requires the engagement of the whole person in the immediacy of a moment of life-experience. In the engagement, the person does not consider how it relates to other experiences, whether it is similar or different, how it can be classified or used. There is no division in one's consciousness. If the person considers how this experience can be used, he "disturbs the experience, stunts its growth and taints the process of becoming." This concentration or convergence of the human spirit in the life-experience means that the person is unified. This unification of the person, which we have also discussed in relation to ecstatic experiences and the unity of the Tao, again leads to the person's ability to create. Through his or her unity, the person creates reality, that is, the person actualizes the fullness of reality.

The ballplayer, the wrestler, and the runner are called (*beruft*) to their task, and in the same way, the life-experience calls to the person who is ready and willing to realize it [38]{69}. In order to be engaged in this task, the person must be whole and united in himself or herself. In orienting, however, one is living with only part of one's being and can therefore register the experience among others for the sake of one's own aims or goals. These goals have priority, and the experience is slotted in as a step to these goals and not considered as unique in itself. Where orientation rules, claims Daniel, "that crafty economy is at home whose shrewdness stinks to heaven because it only saves and never renews" [37]{69}. In realization, the person who, through orientation, could come to terms with the All, has to focus the whole of his or her being in engaging with one thing or event. Thus both ways are open to the same person. However, it is in the engagement of the whole person in realizing the life-experience that the "power of the human spirit [*Kraft des Menschengeistes*] awakens, collects itself and becomes creative" [37]{69}. This is equivalent to the person plunging to the depth of his or her soul, which Buber described in "Ecstasy and Confession."

When the person is unified, his or her power of realization creates an effective reality: "where the foot of realisation stands, there power is drawn from the depths and collected and moved to action and renewed in work" [38]{69}. The power gives itself to the unified person (*dem Einen*) and becomes creative within him; it creates reality in him and through him [38]{69}. Buber claims "that alone is reality, which is so lived." Furthermore, "all effective reality of the human world is lived thus, has become created like this" [38]{70}. Therefore, it is the decision of the person that determines whether this fullness of reality is achieved. The creative power becomes activated in the unified person, and through his or her act of realization, all reality is realized. This power is the Aristotelian *kinesis*. Buber states that it has been dormant and is awakened through the becoming whole of the person. If this power was a potential that had to be awakened to become active, then either the other part of the soul is a part that is already actual and thus awakened it or it is awakened by another power outside itself. The former cannot be the case, as the person would then have this power already; therefore, the power that moves must be outside the person. Wholeness of being is then the condition of possibility for the power to be awakened by this outside power. This is the meaning of the statement that the life-experience calls to the person who is ready to realize it. There is a summons to the person. In Buber's later philosophy, this will become the call of the other being to whom we have a responsibility.[58]

THE CREATIVE PERSON

Ulrich asks whether what is called creating is only the expression of realizing and whether the creative person is identical with the realizing one [38]{70}. Buber argues for the universality of the possibility of realization in claiming that the spirit is common to all who thus have the power to make real or fulfill their own life-experience. This is again equivalent to the teaching of the Tao, in which the Tao is waiting to be discovered and animated in each person. Daniel claims that no person is totally of a realizing or orienting kind.[59] The creative person, however, is one in whom "that genuine iron ore" that is present in each person, even the most miserable, "becomes steel at red and then at white heat." In this person, the spirit, which is common to all, is fulfilled and becomes effective. In each person there is a tendency toward life and death. As discussed in the teaching of the Tao, these two principles were the positive and negative, yang and yin. In Buber's addresses on Judaism, the duality is understood as good and evil. In each person, the growing and the stifled, the free and the warped, wisdom and folly, coexist. However, when the brilliance of genius flashes, "the sunlike might of what is living turns what is dead into dust."

Buber insists that neither a purely realizing person nor a purely orienting person actually exists:

A purely realising human being would pass into the God [*ein nur Realisierender muste in den Gott vergehen*]; a purely orienting human being would degenerate into nothingness; but realisation and orientation dwell close together, like procreation [*Zeugung*] and pregnancy, like knowledge [*Erkenntnis*] and dissemination, like invention [*Erfindung*] and utilisation. [39]{70}

The mention of God does not confirm that Buber locates the source of power in God, but it does imply that if a person had the fullness of this power he or she would be a being who could be called God. Both potentialities are present in the creative person, in whom realization dominates, but in the most miserable person, orientation would be most evident. If it were possible for a purely orienting being to exist, there would have to be a complete absence of realization.[60] Buber claims that such a person does not exist. It is because of the presence of both potentialities in the person that the total elevation or degeneration is prevented.[61]

In each of the analogies in the quotation given above, something new comes into being through the act of a person. The first step of realization, of procreation, of knowledge, of invention is the presupposition of the second. Realization and orientation are in a relationship in the one person. Both are necessary, Daniel claims, for hours of realization *must be* followed by hours of inserting the attained reality in the structure of experience. Just as the invention must find the niche in which it can be generally utilized, the reality attained through realization must, following its attainment, be integrated in the general context of the experience of both the community and the individual. Buber claims that the reality attained by the individual is not only the highest bliss, but also the heaviest of burdens [40]{71}. The individual creative person in whom the spirit fulfills itself may be compared to the mystic who attains the ecstasy of union with All. Just as the mystic attempts to communicate the ineffable, it is the responsibility of the realizing person to integrate the reality attained in realization in his orher life.

Though no one is entirely of one or the other kind, Daniel agrees that the name "creative person" be given to the person who has the most effective power of realization[62] [40]{71}. The realizing power of the soul is so concentrated in the work of the creative person that he creates reality for all. Looking at the creative person's life, among the ordinary ups and downs, the realizing hours stand out like a line of peaks in a mountain range. These are peak experiences in which the effective power of realization unfolds the meaning of life.[63] The power of realization is so strong that even in his hours of orienting, the impulse or the striving of the actual remains. The unbroken power of realization belongs to the creative person. It is present in the primitive person and the child, as the orienting ability has not matured enough in them to overcome it. They are *still* masters of reality: the young child lives in a world of immediacy, where reality is the immediate experience of sensation—touch, taste, smell, and so forth. In the creative person, orientation has been mastered and become mature as a function dependent on and serving the power of the spirit. The creative person is thus "*newly* master of reality" [41]{71}.

The creative person does not return to the immediacy of the child. He enters a new immediacy, which represents a higher level of differentiation of consciousness. The creative person has at his disposal all those resources that could otherwise be used in orientation. In a similar way, the painter masters the techniques not as an end in themselves, but in order to bring a form of reality into existence in the painting. The child and the primitive person dream reality, but the creative person awakens it. This person is "the vigilant watchtower warder of the earth" [41]{71}.[64] It is the creative person who is able to use the skills that he has mastered in order to bring forth in his creation what he has apprehended in the intimate relation of the life-experience. This creation has the power to awaken reality for all. Inasmuch as the creative person awakens reality, "the inner meaning of realisation is revealed to him as to no other: that the realising human being is the genuinely real. For as the things that stand in his life-experiencing become reality, so also he himself" [41]{71}. Therefore, in the action of realizing or making actual his life-experience, the creative person is also realizing himself. This self-realization is achieved in one's relation to that whirlpool of happenings, the doing and suffering, creating and enjoying of one's life. The inner meaning is that, in the act of realizing, changes take place in the person that mean that he or she becomes an authentic human being. Others who do not realize are therefore not authentic. It is this aim of becoming an authentic human being that Buber points toward. The dominance of this aim would mean the desire to realize in an ever-greater fashion. The subjection of life-experience to the mastery of the many aims of orientation would then be overturned.

THE ESSENTIAL FORM OF EXISTENCE

Daniel then explains the relation between the realizing person and the whirlpool of happenings. He says that it is more appropriate to say that things are real "with" the realizing person rather than "for" him or her: "Is the fire there for the iron or the iron for the fire or both only for the smith? No matter the steel really comes forth and works"[65] [42]{72}. Both the presence of the fire and the ore create the context in which the steel can attain reality. In the unification of the fire and ore, something new is created. Similarly, an essential form of existence is created by the act of the person realizing a life experience:

> Realising life-experience creates the essential form of existence of which we speak; what we call things and what we call I, are both comprehended in what is thus created; both find their reality here; both can only find it here. For all living-experience is a dream of bonding [*Verbundenheit*]; orientation divides and sunders it, realisation accomplishes and proclaims it. Thus all reality is fulfilled bonding; nothing individual is real in itself; all individuality is only presupposition. The creative hours, acting and beholding, forming and thinking, are the combining [*verbindenden*] hours; a bonding person is the hero and the sage, the poet and the prophet; communion names his mystery, and he is real because he shares in the reality, because he in the times of intensity is a real part. A thing is not real for him but with him; out of his life-experiencing reality emerges which embraces him. [42]{72}[66]

The essential form of existence, in which the dream of unity becomes real, is created by realization. Both the things of the world and each person attain reality in what is created through realization. The dream of bonding is the primal dream of returning to unity with everything in the One: of being embraced by reality. Buber argues that individuality or particularity is only the presupposition of the movement into communion: the "I" of the person is united with the whole.[67] Buber insists that this communion is a mystery. Reality encompasses the realizing person as a result of his or her own act of realization.

The fullness of reality is attained through the engagement of the whole person in life-experience. For whom, though, is this reality available? "For all because out of it a seed of realising falls in all? For a Self that experiences us and receives from us nothing other than our reality? For no one? It does not matter: it *is*, and is not less if it is beheld by no eyes" [43]{72}.

In the remainder of this dialogue, Daniel expresses his anger at the effect of the dominance of orientation in depriving people of their "grace-filled right to reality [*dem gnadenreichen Recht auf Wirklichkeit*]" [47]{75}. He admits that there are many people equal in realizing power to the creative people, but perhaps through a lack of the desire and the ability to express or because they choose to live in a narrow circle or to live a reclusive life, few people are aware of their realizing power. He adds that "even the true hermit cannot persist without realising power" [43–44]{73}. In "The Teaching of the Tao," Buber describes the life of Lao-tzu as one of concealment. However, even these people can have an effect in creating reality for all people, "for the paths of effectiveness are a mystery, and it is often revealed to us in all stillness that the deeds of the secret ones are greater than the deeds of those who are in vogue" [43–44]{73}. We do not know the effectiveness of those who themselves attain reality in solitude. As they are part of the unity of the All, or the One, their reality has an influence on the whole.

However, people who realize are few, continues Daniel. They are being replaced by producers (*Leistenden*) [44]{73}. These are "those who work without being, who give what they do not possess, who triumph where they have not fought: the pet children of appearance." They simply keep production going, producing things similar to those that began in times of realization. Bitterly, Daniel remarks that God created the world in six days, but now that the technique of creation has been learned, "the apes of God make the world in one day and find it more interesting" [45]{74}.

Although the power of realization is innate in all people, it has been impaired by the only power with the ability to do so: the predominance of orientation. This has replaced reality by appearance. When orientation has become dominant, people are deprived of their most important right: "the grace-filled right to reality." They submit to a world of appearance and live their whole lives in this world unaware of reality.

These people, Daniel says to Ulrich, looking back at the city, live outside of reality. They have aims and know how to attain them; they have an environment and information about it; they have many kinds of spirituality and talk a great deal. Many people, however, do not grasp the meaning of life: "Their experience is ordered, without having been comprehended" [47]{75}. They can experience and register the experience in the inherited structure without understanding the meaning of the experience. "To each of them eternity calls, 'Be!' They smile at eternity and answer, 'I have information'" [47]{75}. Information is distinguished from the revelation of meaning received in the realization of the life-experience.[68] Daniel says that those who are dominated by orientation live and do not realize what they live: "their destiny, which should have led them to experience living inspiration in a living way and through it to become inspiring themselves, disappears" [48]{75}. In an implicit reference to Heraclitus, he adds that they "walk as unreal men" and they pursue misleading and unworthy goals. Their limitation of reality to information may appear in many guises: culture, religion, progress, tradition, or intellectualization. Buber adds: "Ah, the unreal has a thousand masks" [47]{75}.

This is not the only age in which orientation is present. In the past, according to Daniel, there were a great multitude of realizing people who dispensed "warmth, movement and self-activity" [48]{76}. Furthermore, the "*terra incognita* was always beheld before it was measured, named, and registered." The aims were kept in check and the new experience was not immediately ordered according to them. Daniel here recognizes the wonder of the person who beholds and enters the unknown land. The wanderer suggests a person who sets out without the use of an inherited map to guide him or her. The aims themselves, however, became surrounded by means that acted as aims. The soul can only withstand their domination through realization. As for the person without a map in an unknown country, the way of realization is "full of insecurity and danger" [49]{76}. However, escape from the danger was thought to be secured by orientation. Since being dominated by orientation means being yoked to the multiplicity of their aims, their means, their knowledge—everything is therefore "conditioned by everything, everything is decided out of everything, everything is related to everything, and over all there rules the security of orientation that has information" [50]{77}. This, though, is a "sin against the spirit."

The spirit is realization: "unity of soul, exclusiveness of life-experience, bonding." In place of this, the dominance of orientation brings fragmentation, dispersion, and dissection. Instead of becoming united with reality, those people who allow orientation to dominate know that in this world one "succeeds" by dissecting rather than unifying.

Daniel wishes that he could immerse the unreal and the wretched, for whom he has great compassion, "in the fire of renewal and baptise them to a second birth" [51]{78}.[69] He longs to redeem them to reality. Redemption thus involves the ascent to the liberation from multiplicity into oneness experienced by Daniel. In this liberation, those who are unreal become genuinely real, but each person must accomplish this for himself or herself. What can happen is that all the needs and contradictions, the wrong and madness of the age must be conquered for reality. The realizing person must first of all bring the power of realization to work on the existing chaos. Buber implies that there is no ultimate division between good and evil, and that all can be redeemed. The realizing person has the power of redemption. Daniel explains that one must begin with the world as it is. All that is unreal must become reality; this will be the new beginning of real life. This real life is a "life of immediacy [*der Unmittelbarkeit*] and of human-bonding; for as in genuine solitude, so in genuine community, it is immediacy [*die unmittelbare*] which alone makes it possible to live the realising as real"[70] [52]{78}.

The influence of Buber's study of Hasidism is evident in the desire for the whole world to be redeemed. Buber recognized that what is of greatest importance in Hasidism is the tendency to overcome the fundamental separation between the sacred and the profane.[71] The profane is considered as a "preliminary stage of the holy; it is the not-yet-hallowed."[72] The whole of human life is to be hallowed, but this hallowing, or redemption, begins with the choice of the person. "Hallowing," Buber explains, "is an event which commences in the depths of man, there where choosing, deciding, beginning takes place."[73] It is to this event in the person that essentially concerns meaning that Buber turns in the next dialogue.

Finally, Buber asserts that immediacy or directness alone—whether in solitude or community—makes it possible to live what he considers an authentic life. Immediacy overcomes objectification; it implies the knowledge attained through love. We have already noted the return to immediacy in the unity experienced by the mystic when the principle of individuation and the constructs of space, time, and causality are overcome; the creative person also attains the immediacy—possessed by the child and the primitive person—in a new way when he or she masters the techniques and they become instruments to express the meaning attained through realization. Immediacy is central to the I-Thou relation; it is an openness to the presence of each unique being. However, as we have already found and will continue to discover, Buber has not yet recognized the importance of mutual presence. Realization involves a bonding that enables me to realize myself. Realization takes place in the person rather than between the person and another person.

Part III: On Meaning: Dialogue in the Garden

What is the meaning of human life? In the last dialogue, Buber argued that people dominated by orientation do not grasp the meaning. Dilthey recognized meaning as one of the categories through which we come to appreciate a human life. He argues that every life "has its own significance, determined by a context of meaning in which every remembered moment has an intrinsic value, and yet, in the perspectives of memory, is also related to the meaning of the whole."[74] In the second dialogue, Buber drew our attention to the person looking back and recognizing the significant moments in his or her life. He argues that out of these moments, each person "recognises an image which continually changes according to the meaning of life." The choices and decisions made by the person realize his or her values and purposes. These are objectified in the course of the person's life. The meaning of the different significant moments, which remain in memory, is connected to the meaning of the whole found in looking back. Dilthey's discussion of the continuity between different parts of Augustine's life is particularly apposite to Buber's discussion of meaning and indeed to Buber's life. He writes of Augustine's autobiography:

> Augustine is exclusively orientated towards the dependence of his life on God. His work is, at one and the same time, religious meditation, prayer and narrative. His story culminated in his conversion, and every previous event is only a milestone on the road to

this consummation in which the purpose of providence with this particular man is fulfilled. Sensual enjoyment, philosophic delight, the rhetorician's pleasure in scintillating speech, the circumstances of life have no intrinsic value for him. He feels the content of all these strangely mixed with longing for that transcendental relationship; they are all transitory and only in his conversion does an eternal relationship, untainted by suffering, come into being. Thus, to understand his life, we must relate its parts to the realisation of an absolute value, an unconditional highest good. Looking back, we see the meaning of all the earlier features of his life in terms of this relationship: we find not development but preparation for the turning away from all that is transitory.[75]

Buber's way of realizing an absolute value is the Hasidic way of the redemption of all things rather than turning away from them. Otherwise, Buber's journey is similar to Augustine's, particularly in the point concerning conversion. At this point in Buber's journey, however, the desire for a transcendental relationship with a God who is a really present being is clouded by his exaggeration of the power of the person and his inadequate notion of love. In *Daniel*, Buber is drawing our attention to the power of each person to realize an ultimate value. In this dialogue, Buber argues that meaning is unfolded through the person realizing ultimate meaning in his or her life. Direction—that primal tension that moves one to choose—intrinsically involves meaning and value. Each person has to make a decision as to whether realization or orientation will be the dominant force in his or her life. It is the way of realization that awakens one to ultimate meaning. Buber claims that the person who has direction and meaning touches the ultimate underived truth and can bring this truth to reality. This truth is already present in each person and is intrinsically involved in each choice made with one's whole being. Thus for Buber, direction is a tendency toward what is good, whereas not to choose is evil; it is to remain in the endless whirl of possibilities and not to bring any value or meaning to life.

This dialogue moves from the loss of the naive security of meaning often present in childhood, through the consciousness of the abyss of meaninglessness and duality in oneself, to the possibility of finding a new meaning through realization.

LOSS OF MEANING

Reinold, Daniel's friend, has lost the security of meaning that was present in his childhood. He comes to meet Daniel one morning in the garden. Reinold first explains how his present state of anxiety and restlessness arose and then asks Daniel's advice. Daniel encourages him to speak, saying: "So long as one is in the calm of his becoming, the Thou that he bears in himself may be enough for him. But when the flood comes to him, then his need and summons is to find the Thou to whom he can speak in the world" [56–57]{82}. This recognition of the need for a dialogue partner in times of crisis is a step toward Buber's mature philosophy.

Reinold explains that during childhood he had a sense of the meaning at the heart of his world: "Nothing meaningless happened to me" [58]{83}. All beings and events were in accord. As he left his teenage years, he came to know enmity and love, but the meaning did not fade. However, in his twenty-fourth year,[76] Reinold went out on the sea in a small boat. It was a night with a new moon and starlight. Reinold felt at one with it all: "boundlessness was the bed of my soul, heaven, night and sea its cushion. It was one of those hours in which we no longer know with certainty what we do than what is done about us and with us" [60]{85}. This feeling of unity is similar to the ecstatic experience described by Buber in "Ecstasy and Confession." The feeling of boundlessness means that the boundaries between oneself and every other being have broken down; one is united with all beings.

However, this sense of unity soon vanished; boundlessness turned into nothingness. As Reinold turned the boat around and headed for the shore, he looked up casually and was terrified. The infinity around him seemed threatening. Even within him there was nothing: "where the bed of my soul had been, was the nothingness; seduced, betrayed, rejected, my soul hung in the grey of the night between sea and heaven" [61]{85}. Reinold struggled to affirm his own presence: "I am there, I am there . . . and you cannot annihilate me," and then with renewed strength he rowed for the shore. Although he "knew" that the pieces of earth lit up by the lightning were connected, they appeared like "spectral shrieks." Though he "knew" that life went on in the local village, he "felt no connection, rather shriek, shriek, and in between them the abyss" [62]{86}. His knowledge was not existential. The meaning of the whole has been lost. The abyss of meaninglessness has opened up. The familiar meaning of everything, present since his childhood, has been shattered. Everything was separated from everything else; there was no unity and no meaning:

> My benumbed soul longed for its sacrament, for meaning: for the meaning had burst, a bloody tear ran right through the middle of it. And I saw the ultimate: in me, in my inmost self, was the abyss. I was forever broken; not into spirit and body, which were as integrated as ever; but into the many diverse forms of the bright One and the dark Other, with the eternal abyss in between. [62–63]{86}

Buber names meaning as the sacrament of the soul. Meaning is the manifestation of the spiritual reality—the truth—that is the ground of the soul. When this ground is lost, one experiences a fragmentation of one's innermost self that takes the form of a divided self.[77] This duality, which was one of the major themes in Buber's addresses in *On Judaism*, suggests that of the brightness of good and the darkness of evil.[78] Between them, Reinold claims that there is an eternal abyss. The experience of the abyss shattered Reinold's childlike security. He felt as if he were leaving the last "calm hiding place" and entering the harsh storm that would never end. Since then, Reinold tells Daniel, "the abyss is before me at all times—the nameless that everything that is named proclaims" [63]{87}.[79] One cannot escape the abyss, since it is present in each thing: nothing answers the desire for meaning because meaninglessness and nothingness touch everything. Reinold is lost in the mystery of reality.[80]

The Abyss

When one experiences the depth of the abyss in oneself, all security is lost. One has no certainty any longer. Those who appear to have answers stand around one "in superior equilibrium, like the sober stand around the drunk." The person without meaning and security is like a drunk swaying in this direction and in that direction, listening to various answers. Before coming to Daniel, Reinold has consulted others about the abyss. These people knew of the abyss, "but they also have information" and they are not mean with their information. Reinold asked the "World-knowers" (*die Weltkundigen*), the "God-knowers" (*die*

Gotteskundigen), the "Mind-knowers" (*die Geisteskundigen*), and the "Mystery-knowers" (*Geheimniskundigen*) [64–65]{87–88}. The scientists say that it is the abyss between the things and consciousness and that it is an illusion. This is so because they know that consciousness is a power among powers, and all is one. What good, however, Reinold asks, does it do him that they deny what he has experienced with his being? "Shall I subjugate the storm of my knowledge to a formula, so that they examine and reject it?[81] Shall the truth verify itself to me in a finished agreement, instead of in the totality of my life-experiences?" [64]{87}. This "totality of life-experiences" is a reference to the "holy countenance" that Buber claimed was revealed when one looked back over those significant moments in one's life.

The answer Reinold receives from the "experts" does not deal with the reality of his experience, but rather dismisses it. The "God-knowers," the theologians, say the abyss is between man and God, but they add that it no longer exists, as it has been closed by an act in history at a certain time on a certain day. The abyss no longer exists for each person who believes in this closing of the gap. However, Reinold states that "it is not filled up for me; for me it must be filled up here and now since I behold it here and now" [64]{87}. Reinold's knowledge has been undermined, and in the recognition of the abyss, he perceives that here and now "is infinity and eternity just as sometime and somewhere; and here and now is the abyss." He cannot deceive himself and ignore the abyss present to him here and now: "And I should rather behold it on all days and in all dreams and even in the hour of my death than smear my eye with salve and become blind to my truth" [65]{87}.

The "mind-knowers," the philosophers, say that it is the abyss between the idea and the experience (*Erfahrung*), and that it their task to build a bridge over this abyss. However, only thought can set foot on these bridges of transparent brilliance, otherwise they collapse. However, the abyss that Reinold experiences is not a concept, it is existential: "And it is not, indeed, my thought that beholds the abyss, it is my *being*: this thing made of stone and storm and flood and flame, this whole, weighing down, springing upward—this substance" [65]{88}.

Those who know mysteries say that it is over the abyss between the world of appearance and the true world that they fly. Reinold went with them and felt wonderful, "as though behind all the heavy seriousness there must still hide only a plaything. And so it was. For when we were again below, they said: now we are on the other side. That seemed strange to me, for it was all like this side. And when I looked closely, I noticed that we stood on the same spot as before. Then I went my way" [66]{88}.

Buber's own experience of the abyss began with the absence of his mother; then, as Reinold expressed it, "the meaning had burst, a bloody tear ran right through the middle of it." Separation, isolation, and fragmentation lead to a loss of identity. The loss of the security of meaning present in childhood may be compared to the insecurity present in the adolescent's striving for identity. Reinold cannot go back to the naive meaning of childhood, but must attain a mature meaning. Buber could not undo the loss of his mother; he had to reach a meaning in which even this loss is redeemed. It is at this point in the third dialogue that Reinold asks Daniel for advice. Through Daniel, Buber now comes to the point of explaining what meaning is and how it is discovered in life. Buber draws attention to two different human responses to the unknown—the longing for security and the desire to be fully alive in the present moment.

THE ORIENTING PERSON AND THE REALISING PERSON

Buber uses the device of comparing the responses of two wanderers in an unknown city. One seeks the security of knowing his way about; the other takes the risk of meeting danger. Coming from hours of walking in darkness on the heath, the first experiences the darkness of the city as filled with unfamiliar threatening beings and danger. Here "in the anxious heart of the wanderer one longing is powerful—for security" [67]{89}. For this wanderer, security is the ultimate desire. Because he longs for security, there is one thing that he needs: to know his way about. This is seen as the key to salvation, health, and security. Daniel identifies this longing for security with the longing of those people who are gripped by the "shudder of the boundless" (*Schauder des Schrankenlosen*) or by the glimpse of the contradiction (*Blick des Widerspruchs*) and only wish to protect themselves. Buber's phrase, "being seized by the shudder of the boundless," suggests a sudden experiential consciousness of "oneness" without any limits.[82] This oneness would exclude internal division and external boundaries. If there are no internal divisions, the person glimpses the unity of himself or herself. If there are no external boundaries, then all being is one. This is a glimpse of metaphysical unity. Buber claims that when people reach this point of awareness, "their being is ready for knowledge and the mystery has opened itself to them, but they do not prepare themselves to stand up to it" [67]{89}. This is the moment of choice, but the irrational causes anxiety, so that instead of realizing it—receiving it into life-experience with the whole strength of the moment—some people desire to hold onto their security. Buber is therefore arguing that what is beyond the power of reason to comprehend, that is, the mystery of reality, awaits realization. As mentioned previously, the comprehensibility of the world is only a footstool of its incomprehensibility. This realm is not reached through reason alone.

However, Daniel claims that "all living with the whole being and with unconstrained force means danger; for there is no thing, no relation, no happening in the world that thus known does not reveal its bottomless abyss [*Untiefe*], and all thinking threatens to shatter the stability of the knower" [68]{89}. Through the act of realization, the mystery of the abyss is revealed as present in all reality.[83] Buber claims that when one is living fully, there is no firm ground on which one can find security and peace. All living is precarious as each life-experience reveals a depth that touches the irrational. Specifically mentioned here are "relationships" and the risk and danger inherent in any human relation. As Buber experienced with his mother, one cannot rely on a human relationship to be totally trustworthy, since such relationships are not the ultimate ground. In each situation, there remains the possibility of danger. Thus one is vulnerable to this danger and risks one's stability when one enters it with one's whole being. Likewise, all thinking can lead to this mystery if the person is open to doubt and discovery. The stability of the knower is shattered because the abyss of "the thousand-named immanent duality" is present in all things, even in himself. The contradiction and opposition of the abyss are experienced in oneself. The usual relation of knower to known is disturbed. The irrationality of the mystery causes the disturbance; the firm ground of familiar truths is overturned. However, if life is to be lived "in genuine, realising knowledge," the person must be always prepared to risk everything and start again. This person's truth is not something that he possesses, that he grasps and holds as a fixed system. Thus "his truth is not a having but a becoming" [68]{90}. It is always in the process of becoming, always open to revision, and always uncertain.

Those who wish to avoid danger will "not risk their skin for the sake of a vain problematic." They want the security of a place to remain:

"they do not want to be on the move but at home." They want to hold onto a "solid general truth that will not let itself be overturned" [68]{90}. Buber recognizes the restriction of the desire to know the truth. Some people are satisfied with a truth that enables them to function in the world of orientation. The unrestricted or unconditional in their desires or their search for truth is suppressed. Therefore, they "build their ark or have it built, and they name the ark *Weltanschauung*, and they seal up with pitch not only its cracks but also its windows. But outside are the waters of the living world" [68–69]{90}. Their worldview is a closed system. It is not open to revision or new insights into existing or new situations, beliefs, or meaning. It is not open to the questions that may lead to a deeper truth or reality. It gives protection, as the person has all the answers required within this system, but it remains closed to the living world of change, doubt, and discovery.

The realizing person has a different approach in the unknown city. He is there with wide-open senses, with opened spirit, willing and resolute. He has no wish to know his way about. He wants to "live this here . . . so completely that it becomes for him reality and message" [69]{90}. It is in realizing that he reaches reality and receives meaning through his realization.[84] This meaning is given here "in another language than that in which names exist" [69]{90}. It speaks in the language of the nameless, that is, of the abyss, not in that of rational language of subject and object.[85] Those looking for security want to know the name of the city. The unknown, however, is not sinister. Daniel asks: "does not the uncertain proclaim existing being just as faithfully as the certain? Does not the insidious attest to the holy power as fervently as the reliable?" [69]{90}. Buber is suggesting that the realizing person is open to what is given in what is dangerous as well as what is safe. Openness to the redemption of everything, good and evil, is one of the key Hasidic notions, as I mentioned at the end of the discussion on the last dialogue. This openness is not naive, as there is an awareness of danger and a readiness to meet it when necessary. "But what would life be if it did not everywhere approach the uttermost and threaten to capsize? The script of life is so unspeakably beautiful to read because death looks over our shoulder" [70]{91}. When one takes risks, there is always an element of danger, and one is vulnerable, even to death.

The orienting person has not lived the life-experience down to its ground (*das Erlebnis nicht bis zu seinem Grunde gelebt*). He or she skims the surface, takes only that which can be rationalized and ordered.[86] What is the ground of the life-experience? Rather than just skimming the surface of life, the realizing person "loves danger and the underived truth which he who ventures draws [creates] from the depths" [70]{91}. The "underived truth" (*die unabgeleitete Wahrheit*) is not inferred or deduced from any other source. It is therefore itself a principle, the truth that is a source of meaning. It is that truth that has no conditions. Buber is arguing here that it is possible to reach a knowledge of the truth that is the unconditioned by living each life-experience fully. Buber then reaches an expression for this underived truth attained by the realizing person:

> He does not want to know where he is; how could he, for he is not always at the same place but is ever at the new, ever at the uttermost. Ever at God, I may even say, since in fact, God cannot realise himself to man otherwise than as the innermost presence of a life-experience, and for him therefore it is not the same, but ever the new, the uttermost, the God of this life-experience. [71]{91}[87]

Buber has already argued that in the life-experience, the person only experiences the "unformed essence," the ungraspable givenness. This unformed essence may either be realized or through the imposition of orientation be denied realization. Buber now argues that God can realize himself only as the "innermost presence" of each life-experience, and therefore each experience is a new realization of God. Buber is asserting that there is a God, and that this God can only be present to man in each separate life-experience. However, what is experienced in the "innermost presence" of a life experience is potentially but not actually God. God is not an already existing reality to human beings and cannot become real to human beings other than through the act of realization. This realization must be accomplished in each person if God is to be experienced. We have argued, though, that the power to activate the creative power in each person must come from outside the person. God is merely the potential—present in each person—to be actualized. Therefore, according to Buber, each person can become God. This position will be confirmed later. This conception of God does not allow any notion of the presence of God as an independent being, although there remains the question of the power that activates the latent potential to create in the person.

Buber's clarification begins through a criticism of other positions. When orientation is "all-embracing" or comprehensive, it is absolutely godless. As with the hypothetical individual who was of a totally orienting kind, the absence of realization implies the absence of God as a reality. The person has not actualized the God-potential in himself or herself, and therefore there is no God. Without God also is the theologian who fixes his God in causality, which Buber calls a helping formula of orientation. Also godless is the spiritualist (*spiritualisten*) who knows his way about the "true world" and sketches its topography. Buber claims that all religiosity is reduced "to religion and church"— that is, rigidly determined prescriptions and dogmas—when it begins to orient itself: "when instead of the one thing needful" it gives a summary of this life and the beyond which one is to believe, and in the place of becoming, promises having [*statt des Werdens das Haben . . . verspricht*], in the place of danger, promises security." [71]{91}.

This security is a way of protecting oneself. Buber adds that the realizing person does not want the security offered to the believers of old and new churches; rather, he wants to realize himself. Buber claims that this realizing person is far more deeply connected to reality than the person who is secure. The realizing person is "not at home in the world, yet he is at home at all times; for the ground of each thing wishes to harbor him. He does not possess the world, yet stands in its love; for he realises all being in its reality." When one protects oneself, one places the emphasis on one's separation from others; one may feel secure in a society in which the importance of one's distinction from others is the norm. One is at home in a deeper sense when one is engaged with one's whole being in the act of realization: here one discovers in each thing the oneness of the ground of all being and finds oneself in this oneness.[88] This person does not "have the world" in the sense of using it for his own aims, but he realizes all being—he brings all being from its unfulfilled state to the fullness of reality. He is part of this great reality and is embraced by it.

DIRECTION AND MEANING

Although the realizing person knows no security, yet he or she is never unsure; for he or she has direction and meaning [72]{92}. The person with direction is not bound by a system. He "does not have information as to how the will is determined in cause and effect, nor as to what one

must hold to be good and bad, nor that there is an evolution[89] in which
one is imprisoned; but when he acts, he does his deed and no other, he
chooses his lot and no other, he decides with his being" [72]{92}. The
realizing person is like the wanderer who chooses "with immediate decision as if out of a deep imperative" when he comes to a crossroad.
The person with direction is not bound by causality or evolution; he
transcends the limitation imposed by the dominance of orientation and
feels himself free and acts as a free man. He has the power to choose
and act that arises out of the primal tension. To the realizing person,
"the deed is as magic to the primitive man: as the magic action does
not hang in a chain of occurences but is a world event which begins and
ends out of itself" [73]{93}, so the person who ever begins anew does
the deed "out of himself into being" as an act of creation and a completion. "This is direction: the magic power of unconstrained acting that
wants to realise itself and choose its deed with its own nature [*und seine
Tat mit dem Wesen erwählt*]" [74]{93}. This power that arises from the
primal tension is an unconditional power, nothing constrains or limits
it; it wishes to realize its unconditionality.

What is the meaning of this unconditionality? Meaning is added to
direction: "over it the star shines down meaning and sends its beam
into all occurences." Buber refers to the wanderer, who is the realizing
person, stopping in a clump of trees and looking at the skies. A very
bright star appears that the person greets like a brother: "'All the time
you were turned to me,' he said, 'and now I see you too, distant and
friendly one, ever present one!'"[90] [74]{93}. In the light of this star, the
wanderer understood the truth of all his wanderings.[91] The world around
him was also understood to have its own profound meaning. Meaning,
Daniel continues, cannot be scraped together out of experiences of just
any kind. It is not like the planks out of which the ark of a secure world-
view is constructed. Meaning does not let itself be taught and
transmitted:

> Meaning . . . rather is assigned to the soul as its very own [*er ist
> der Seele ureigen beigegeben*], to become unfolded and proven
> in its life-experience. And as a painter singly wills a painting and
> turns out the work as an expression of the spirit and as witness to
> his daimon [*Dämons*], thus the soul itself, which wills nothing
> other than to live truly from the ground and to establish reality,
> transfigures the lived world in the light of meaning into a holy

mirror in which the symbol of primal being [*Urwesens*] appears. [75]{94}[92]

Meaning is assigned: it is present in the soul, but has its source elsewhere. Thus the recognition by the wanderer of the meaning given by the star is possible because of the meaning in his or her own soul. This explains the star being recognized as distant and intimate. The unfolding of the meaning present in the soul occurs in the realizing action of the person. Whether this happens or not is dependent on man's character, that is, his daimon.[93] Through the realizing person, meaning is objectified in the actions of the person in the world.[94] These actions express the spirit, and the whole is a witness to the primal being; the primal being is the source of the meaning. The lived life, the expressions of the human person over a period of time—illuminated by meaning—become a mirror in which the symbol of primal being appears and is known. Only in this way does the "unknowable" become known.

Buber compares this knowledge with that of myth-creating primitive man. The address on "Myth in Judaism," which I examined, is relevant here. The primitive person who encounters the hero is faced with a power that he is unable to interpret. He considers the event as an expression of the unutterable, unthinkable meaning of the world. He assigns such events to the world of the absolute, thus he "mythicizes" them. The life of the hero is not "knowable" to primitive man. This "unknowable" is preserved in consciousness as something precious and "consecrated in itself, adorned with the pride of all the spheres and elevated as a meaningful constellation in the heaven of inward existence," wherein it becomes a myth bearing the sign of history and the seal of a world-spirit. In a similar way, through the act of realization, the person forms an inner awareness of meaning. Meaning is then defined as "the mythical truth of the unconstrained knower who relates to each event in its content alone and thus shapes it to be a sign of the eternal" [75]{94–95}. A mythical truth is also presented by Socrates in the *Republic*. As in the Platonic myth of the cave, the sun gives the power of sight and is seen by the sight it causes, here the insight or illumination of the understanding, in the experience of realization, enables the person to appreciate the power that activated the creative force in his or her own soul. The reference to primal being and the eternal is an acknowledgment by Buber that the power is an outside power. It is this power that assigns the meaning to the soul. Hence the truth that the wanderer appreciates is also a revelation. It reveals the source of the creative power and of meaning. Voegelin comments that in Plato's writings the divine Beyond—the formative *Nous* or "'this God' as it is called in the *Laws*, is not one of the being things, it is, then, experienced as present in all of them (*pareinai*) as their creatively formative force."[95] Buber posits the external power, but it is not understood as a presence in the person; the power in the person is only a potentiality, that which, when awakened, must be realized by the person. The potential is present, but the person realizes God and all reality.

This conception is directly based on Boehme's understanding of the Godhead—the eternal groundless will—that manifests itself in all reality in order to reveal itself to itself. The world is the necessary self-objectification of the Godhead, just as one's lived experiences are the objectification of one's own choices and meaning. Through the realization by the person of himself or herself and all reality, the manifestation of the Godhead becomes present in the totality of the world.

In the world of orientation, the realizing person appears to have no concept of the world, but in fact he has one "as immediate as Veronica's handkerchief: in his life" [77]{95}. It is in the different events and happenings on the journey through life that the unknowable is confirmed:

> The unknowable [*Unwissbare*] is authenticated for him as something living in him and through him [*als ein in ihm und durch ihn Lebendes*]. For like the primitive man, who has in magic his essential deed, in myth his essential knowledge, and celebrates them as both covenant with and festival of the mystery in which he conquers separateness and unites himself with the God, so he who has direction and meaning celebrates an ever-new mystery in his realising: the experience of realising God in all things. For God wants to be realised, and all reality is God's reality, and there is no reality except through the man who realises himself and all being. [77]{95}

The unknowable is only known through the action of the realizing person. The will of the person is realized in action. This will unfolds the potential of the person to become God. The will of the person is identical to the striving of the potential to be actualised, that is, the God-potential wants to become actual. This is the awakened power that replaces the dreamlike power of the child [81–82]{97}. The choice of giving the power to realization or orientation lies in front of Reinold. Daniel describes Reinold as standing irresolute and lost in thought as though he listened to a distant call. This is a suggestion of the call to realize unity. The fact that Reinold has spoken with Daniel is recognized as the first new step. Therefore, Daniel identifies himself as the Thou mentioned at the beginning of the dialogue.[96] Daniel says to Reinold: "Meaning appeared to you to be burst, Reinold. That is because it wanted to renew itself. In the dreaming heart a daring heart was enclosed that wants now to arise, wants to awaken from its larva to a winged life." Reinold has to descend into the abyss and in the "swinging tensions and streaming reciprocity" recognize the symbol of the primal being (*die Zeichen des Urwesens*) [82]{98}. The meaning comes from the abyss. The abyss represents the mystical Nothingness out of which everything comes into being. Some traditions of Jewish mysticism maintain that in each transformation of reality, every time the form or status of a thing is changed, the abyss of Nothingness is crossed and for a brief mystical moment becomes visible.[97] This is the region of pure absolute Being that is called Nothing. Reinold's task is to create unity out of all reality and to establish this fulfilled unity in the world. This unity is "the realised countenance of God" and its realization is an endless task. The task involves the transformation of the person into one who holds the tensions of the world in himself or herself. This is the subject of the next dialogue.

Part IV: On Polarity: Dialogue after the Theater

In this dialogue, Buber returns to the issue of polarity. The dialogue takes place after a visit to the theater by Daniel and his friend Leonhard. This dialogue is a discussion of the polarity of being and counterbeing. The abyss creates a polarity that is present in oneself, between oneself and another, and between one group and another group. In the theater, Buber claims to find himself as the unity embodying the polarity represented by the two actors on stage. The polarity is also recognized as existing between the audience and the actors, but the audience was able to identify with both sides of the opposition presented by the actors. How does one attain unity when one finds duality present in oneself? Buber's answer is through a transformation in which the tension of both poles is held in oneself. In this transformation that Buber calls "inclusion" (*Umfassung*), duality can be overcome and unity can become creative. The image of the counterbeing becomes creative when it is made present in oneself and completed. The unity that is realized is the image of the unknowable.

BEING AND COUNTERBEING

Coming from the theater with a friend, Leonhard, Daniel says that he has seen the theater itself clearly for the first time [85]{101}. He explains, using the example of seeing a familiar face in a new light and being struck by wonder. In this face one may recognize an unfathomable, significant secret—the fundamental measure (*Grundmass*) and fundamental relation (*Grundverhältnis*) of life. Daniel speaks of experiencing the play without its spatial context except for a single connection with what was in front of him. It was also a moment detached from the course of time, fulfilled in itself, without a before and after. It was a moment of realization. Even the imaginary story before or after the immediate event on the stage did not exist for Daniel [88]{103}. Daniel says the players announced to him nothing other than their presence: "Rather, when they appeared to me, they came from the edge of being, and when they went, they died away into the void, as a tone dies away. They announced to me nothing other than their presence. And they did this with the precision of a shadow" [88]{103}. Pointing to the shadow of a branch on the ground, he asks, "Have you ever seen in the upper world of the trees a branch so outlined, so clear, so abstract as here? Is that not the simple branchness of the branch [*die ledige Zweighaftigkeit des zweiges*]?" [88]{103}.[98]

In this moment of realization, the presence of the actors revealed to Daniel not the polarity of good and evil, but the "primal duality of being and counter-being [*Wesen and Gegenwesen*], opposed to each other and bound to each other as pole to pole: polar opposition and polar association—the free polarity of the human spirit." In the world outside, Daniel comments, it is difficult to see the polarity clearly, as the two poles are enveloped by mediacy and thus unrecognizable. In the theater, however, they were laid bare. Between the two poles was the "I of the spirit whose primal secret duality they revealed" [90]{104–5}. The two actors, claims Daniel, had made a *daimon*, which was magnified by the *daimon* of the theater. Buber is using the principle established by Plato in the *Republic* that "the polis [in this case the theater] is man written large." Out of the dialogue of the players resounded the antiphony of "*ananke*"—irrational, irreducible necessity. The pair of players, like Creon and Antigone, had neither right nor wrong, neither guilt nor innocence, had nothing but their being, their polarity, their destiny. Daniel, though, felt "world-great" in comparison to them: "as though I were the I of the spirit whose primal secret duality they revealed" [91]{105}. Daniel suffers an "elemental happening" in which he suddenly experiences his "I" expanded to the "world-I," which he identifies with the spirit whose duality is revealed in the polarity of being and counterbeing.

This touches on an episode in Buber's life, again when he was twenty-four. At the Sixth Zionist Congress in 1902, the leader, Theodor Herzl, had insulted his friend, David Trietsch. Buber went to point out to Herzl, whom he had opposed, but continued to have faith in as a man, the untenable nature of his, Herzl's, accusations. However, Buber found that when he entered the room that Herzl was "like a caged lion," and that it was impossible for Buber himself to remain inwardly the representative of one side. Through this event, which was "perhaps the first time that I set foot on the soil of tragedy," he learned that in the tragic situation there is no longer such a thing as being in the right.[99] The attitude of the audience to tragedy is apparent to Daniel in the next act.

INCLUSION—EMBRACING

During the interval, Daniel took notice of the audience. Although they may have interpreted the play differently, they were all bound in participation. Referring to the Eleusinian mystery religion, Daniel compares the multitude of the audience to "Eleusis which had represented the marriage of heaven and earth and the birth of God's son [*Geburt des Gottes-sohnes*]" [93]{107}. This image suggests that the unity created by the audience is a representation of the birth of God's son. This is the enlarged image. Buber then moves to the individual situation in which Daniel experienced himself as a member of the community of the audience, but the whole of the audience became present to him as a single being, "so unitedly present as a single being is present to himself in his consciousness" [94]{107}. Buber is indicating a personal experience of the unity of oneself and numerous others. Daniel has here identified with the audience: his experience is of a single self, which he calls— "my We-I." This self exists in a polarity with the unity of being on the stage, which has formed out of the polarity of the two actors [94]{107}.

The multiplicity of the opposing beings was held together in its contradiction, just as the audience, in the "We-I" consciousness of the person, was held together in its agreement. This is an expression of Boehme's two forces of conflict and love. It is love that moves the being toward a "born-again" unity of power in Boehme's writings. This explains Buber's earlier reference to the image of the audience as representing the marriage of heaven and earth and giving birth to God's son.

The relationship of being and counterbeing now existed between the audience and the stage. Each side persevered in its own task, the actors in the happening on stage, the audience in awareness of them. The audience, however, was not composed of merely neutral observers; it took on itself the opposing position, and in some way the audience expressed and confirmed the whole reality over against it.[100] The audience confirmed the contradiction, the destiny, and the decision: "Therefore it sided with no party; it was, as it were, itself a party which met those two [actors] as a unity." Buber contrasts this confirmation by the audience with the example of a drawing, on an early Greek vase, in which Hermes is shown weighing the souls of two heroes fighting in front of him: "he does not take sides but his will follows the decisions of the scales; he wills what must happen, and his will is a fanfare." The One whose primal duality was revealed is the will present in both sides of the *agon*. Buber is implying that the person also experiences this oneness, and the same will is present in him or her.

In the play, Daniel notices that the audience not only wills what is taking place, but also seems to experience what is happening to both sides of that other being on the stage:

> Yes, when on the stage the murdering knife is raised, the heart of this dark being, the audience, palpitates in the knife's point; but it quivers at the same time in the flesh that receives the blow. It joins with the fate that guides the hand of Oedipus, and it lives in the blinded eyes. It swings along with that wave that drives Lear to his madness; it circles in the pain of the king, mad like him. [96–97]{109}

The audience also possessed a single heart: "they became one in the act of inclusion [*in dem Akt der Umfassung*]" [97]{109}. The implication here is that the person also unites the duality in himself or herself in the act of inclusion. The German word for "inclusion" may also be translated as "embracing." As we have discussed, the embracing love previously outlined by Buber was one in which the embracer becomes one with all that is embraced. This love includes no relation: "the love of the perfected man rests upon unity with all things."[101] The notion of inclusion will gain importance in Buber's philosophy of dialogue, but it will then also maintain the relation between the two parties.[102] Buber gives an initial explanation of this key concept:

> For thus one may perhaps name what happened here. One being stands over against his counter-being; it expresses, accompanying the impact of fate, his polarity; but at the same time he throws himself across into the opposite pole and suffers its life with it. How shall one name this remaining with oneself and setting out, this desire to attack and rejoice in sacrifice, this bipolar living? I say inclusion and know that I say too little. [97]{109–10}

Daniel says that although "inclusion" says too little, when he utters it he has another polarity in mind: that of the loving person who has a living experience not only of his or her own struggling desire, but also of the blossoming beloved, and embraces what is opposite him as his very own (*Ureigenste*). This embracing love holds the tension between the poles; it unites them in itself. However, as we have discovered, this implies that love is a unity in oneself rather than a mutual relation between two beings.[103]

Daniel was struck by his insight into the nature of the theater: "I had known all along and yet had not known: that most self-evident [*Selbstverständlichste*],[104] most inclusive, most trivial reality which this theatre was" [98–99]{110–11}. Everything that had taken place was the "fictitious life of an evening and the part that had now come to pass was the real life of the generations." I take it that Buber is referring here to his understanding of the theater as a whole as the representation of real life. Having been familiar with the theater for years, only now was Daniel aware of its true nature. However, it was suddenly no longer trivial to Daniel, but thought provoking. Many questions occurred to him regarding the nature of the theater—the power that attracted audience and players and the performance itself. These questions remained with Daniel as the third act began.

TRANSFORMATION

During this act, Daniel is drawn into considering how a person represents a goddess in a play or God in a street procession. Daniel asks whether the consciousness of the person representing the goddess is moved: "It represents the goddess. To be sure, it does not 'act' it. But is it not in its inactive feeling somehow moved? Is not its sleep affected by an incomprehensible breath of transformation?" [102]{112–13}. Buber draws attention here to the inactive element of consciousness. This is the part of the person that has the potential to be moved. He suggests that the person is awakened from sleep, as Reinold was awakened from his naive sense of meaning. What is the transformation? Another event that Daniel visualizes draws him closer to an answer: a Swedish procession in which the statue of Freyr and of the virgin who is the most beautiful better half of the God (*[der dem Gotte angetrauten allerschönsten Jungfrau*) are carried through the streets.[105] During the procession, an outlaw from Norway—Gunnar Helming—breaks through the crowd and approaches the carriage. He is similar to the God in shape, bearing, and dress and receives from the people the sacrificial offering. Daniel adds: "He—played the God" [103]{113}.

A third event was visualized by Daniel: the old Dionysian play that represented the *Thiasos*—the procession in honour of Bacchus—and the nuptials, the passion and the resurrection of the God, and the souls flung into unending movement. Daniel saw the transformations in the eyes of the young man who was prepared to sacrifice his body for the body of the savior:

> I recognised with holy heart the hero of souls. And he, the youth
> . . . what was it that happened to him: what was it that happened
> in him? Did not the mystery of magic rest on him, to which all
> virginal peoples are devoted: he who transforms himself into the
> God, lives the life, does the deed, does the work of God? Did he
> not realise the God in and with his soul as in and with his body?
> [104–5]{114–15}

The primal power or force that affects the primitive man rests on this young man who transforms himself into God. Buber has referred to this power in discussing the myth. In *I and Thou*, he names this power "*Mana*."[106] This youth realized God in transforming both body and soul into God. Daniel then looked at one of the actors, but "something veiled his being from me."[107] Suddenly, in this veiled being's place, Daniel saw clearly two beings standing in two different lights—one an unearthly white light, and the other a bluish weak light. Both beings resembled the one actor. Here Daniel says he saw being and counterbeing in a new form, and he was so aware of them that the hero could not be nearer his heart than the actor.

Buber then considers the situation of a person who only engages in a partial realization: "who lives only the soul's [psychological] part of it, who feels that nameless spark, that *kinesis* through which the deed from being the life-experience of an individual becomes a happening given to all: is he not similar to the actor and yet above all his adversary [*Widerpart*]?" [106] {116}. Buber remarks that the partial realization takes on the autonomy of the whole: it creates the illusion of a wholeness because it satisfies his feeling, although first it was to him in its incompleteness a phantom and a terror, now it becomes for him the bread of life. Instead of being partial, it becomes the representation, the "simulacrum," of the deed. Whereas the deed points toward a way, "it stands like a sign on the crossroads of the world"; the image or appearance has no existential meaning: "it comes and vanishes on the plains of the soul." There are people in whom the desire for realization is of such strength that no illusion lasts for them. These people may be torn apart by the contradiction in their lives or the image may become creative. They act the *kinesis*; they free themselves in their acting. However, they can only do this when they transform themselves [107]{116}.

Buber's idea of the image becoming creative is comparable to a disciple following the way of a master through the actions of his life rather than merely knowing how to do so or creating the mere appearance of doing so. Buber advocates a real imitation or transformation. In the first dialogue, Daniel remarked to the woman: "And is not this, our way, a passionate image of that free remaining in the One that is denied us?" This way of return to a metaphysical unity, besides confirming the lack of relation, cannot be attained as a permanent state by human beings. It is not something that is achieved once in a lifetime, but as Daniel argued at the end of the last dialogue, it is an endless task.[108]

The actor witnesses to the true transformation that is possible. The great and genuine actor, according to Daniel, stands over against the hero "as the image the deed, as the possible the actual, as the ambiguous the simple, as the [aimless] wandering the direct proceeding: polar" [108]{116–17}. The actor does not try to weaken the opposition by mimicking the hero: "rather confirming the distance between the poles he stands over against the hero and transforms himself into him" [108]{117}. Daniel claims that this is the paradox of the great actor. Freed, purified, transformed, he realizes the hero in a unique way with his soul as with his body.[109] In the act of transformation, the actor does not pretend to be the hero; he actualizes the potential in himself to be the hero and so becomes the hero. Thus Daniel comments that the great actor does not wear masks. When he decisively lives his role, he penetrates—transforming himself, surrendering his soul and winning it back again—into the center of his hero to obtain from him the secret of his personal *kinesis*, the union of meaning and act particular to him.[110] The actor then incarnates (*einverleibt*) in himself this union of meaning and deed [110]{118}.

In the experience of this union, the person experiences the excitement or arousal (*Erregung*) of his soul. This excitement is above desire and pain and dearer to the soul than these two states. All such excitement has its origin in a polarity that is experienced and realized. There are many ways in which this may occur. Buber has mentioned three ways. First is the way of struggle: "that is the conflict that is borne by genuinely faithful people on account of their desire for unity; bearing is acting—speaking—or keeping silent." Second is the way of inclusion: that is the love in which a genuinely present person embraces beings, so that he may live persisting in perfect power. Third is the way of transformation that which Buber calls the way of knowledge: "as the actor transformed himself in the Bacchus play into God and realised him, so the knower transforms himself into the world and realises it." This is the knowledge that is attained when one is united with the world and realizes it.[111] The mystery of the world cannot be perceived by the senses nor be inquired into by thought; it can only be penetrated through the transformation of the person:

> Transformed, he accomplishes with the movements of his existence the secret movement of the world: he lives the life of the world, he does its deed, he works its work—and so he knows it. For the mystery of the world is the *kinesis* of the infinite, the union of meaning and being, and no one comes near it who reflects upon it: only he comes near it who does it; and he is the knower. He carries out the polarity in which he stands by realising its opposite pole: through "finding" the meaning, as the Bacchic youth finds Dionysus and the actor finds the hero; the image that becomes creative in him is the imitation [*Nachahmung*] of the unknown God—which is realisation. Thus through knowledge, as through struggle and through love,[112] because a duality is fulfilled, unity is established out of it. [111]{119}

Buber identifies the infinite with the world. The youth transformed himself into the god Dionysus and realized him with body and soul through his life and action. Each person can transform himself or herself into the world, that is, he or she becomes the unity of the all. The meaning of the mystery that lies in the world is then found; this is the cosmic power of actualization, the power to unite meaning and being. This is the power of the infinite present in the world. It is the result of realization—the union of meaning and being that is God. The person who achieves this union has transformed himself or herself into God. This is the new birth and resurrection referred to earlier.

In the light of his own thankfulness for his transformation in which he received the meaning, Daniel searches for the recipient of his thanks. It is the author of the play. It was his word that the actors spoke, his bidding that their gestures followed. Was it, though, really his word or had the work been transposed into another order? It seemed to Daniel that the work was a fulfillment of the poet's primal deep intentions, but within it, there were tendencies so mature that this art was no longer sufficient to encompass them and they must seek or awaken another. Daniel then left, since if he had stayed he would now be listening for the "essential spoken word of the poem" behind the word of the actor, and behind the word of this poem, the infinite word of the eternal poet would rustle for him. However, just then he could only seek and will this infinite word, "although not behind the forms, but in the solitary spirit." This infinite word is the word of the cosmic spirit, that is, the eternal poet, the One that gives birth to all multiplicity. This word is not to be found by looking "behind the forms," that is, away from the world of multiplicity, but "in solitary spirit." In order to be able to do this, Daniel goes into the garden.

He thinks of the poet, Enoch, who is said to have walked with Elohim.[113] Daniel recognizes the unity in Enoch, of whom it was said that he had become one of the angels who was all eyes and wings. He is wholly in one thing that he experiences (*erlebt*) and is already in all others at the same time. Considering the action of the poet in writing a poem, Daniel realizes that all human action is a mixture of creation and destruction, and every doer must "knowingly or unknowingly, reject the many that might arise through him for the sake of the one thing he chooses" [117]{122}. However, the poet whom Plato calls the messenger of the "beyond polarity," that is, unified, God (*überpolaren Gottes*), is also the messenger of the polar earth. In the previous dialogue,

Buber rejected the attempts to deny the division experienced as an abyss in oneself. Unlike those consulted earlier, the poet experiences the polarity of being and counterbeing. In him, as in all living things, the duality is present; in him also are all the tensions, and every blunt opposition is intensified in him to polarity:

> He knows the pole of exuberant strength and that of weakness, that of freedom and that of dependence, that of concentration and that of abandon, that of guilt and that of purity, that of form and that of formlessness: he recognises them all in the world because he knows them in himself. [118]{123}

The poet's heart, Daniel claims, is the hub into which the spokes of polarities converge in union and fruitfulness.[114] The poet is said to bear the contradictions of the spirit, and in him they are fruitful. He has a twofold great love: the love of the world—in which everything that he experiences as extreme and contradictory flowers in a wonderful reconciliation—and the love of the word: "which born out of the deep tension of earlier human dreams, shaped into the deep tension of seeking human generations, can redeem and unify all tensions." Thus we can argue that in the love of the poet, world and word, which represent being and meaning, unite. The poet, in embracing the contradictions in himself, brings forth the unity of word and life: "To speak the world: that builds the rainbow bridge from pole to pole" [119]{124}. This unity of word and life is the insight into the fundamental meaning and fundamental relation mentioned at the beginning of the dialogue. The unfathomable significant secret is the unity of meaning and being that is God. "To speak the world" is a reference to the Word expressed by God. The Word according to Buber is the symbol of primal existence; it is unity before any separation into divinity and humanity. The potentiality for this unity is present in each person. The polarity that the person experiences can be overcome, and unity can be attained. However, this unity has to be created through our action. Unity is the subject of the fifth and last dialogue.

Part V: On Unity: Dialogue by the Sea

In our examination of this dialogue, we must remember that as late as 1917 Buber advised his readers to refer to it for his understanding of unity rather than to that given in "Ecstasy and Confession."[115] The unity discussed in that essay was the unity experienced in ecstasy. This dialogue accepts the essential duality of the person and his or her life in the multiplicity of the world. Overcoming or annihilating the tension between the polarities, in this case of life and death, is not the way to reality. The tension must be held or embraced in the person and united in himself or herself. Unity can be realized by the person through the awakening of the "I" that holds the tension. In achieving this, the person realizes the unity of the world in the unity of his or her own soul. This "I" is the "I" of the world; it is the unconditioned. What is unconditioned is without any conditions; it depends on nothing else for its meaning. It is the ultimate truth. Uniting this ultimate meaning and being in the form of a person is a claim that the person is God. The dialogue takes place by the sea, which is the symbol of the "mother of all beings"[116] who in turn gives life to all multiplicity and is the unity to which they return.

THE "MOTHER OF ALL BEINGS"

In this dialogue a friend, Lukas, tells Buber of the grief that he experienced following the drowning of an acquaintance, Elias. The night before this event, Elias, while gazing tenderly at the sea, said to Lukas: "Now the mother is free and no longer the maid of sun and heaven and may be allowed to carry her own colours" This acquaintance always addressed the sea as "mother." Buber is expressing the insight that the world of nature is not simply at the service of the Platonic form of the good or the transcendent heavens, but may be seen as one that gives birth and nurtures offspring itself. This is the God who has become nature, according to Spinoza. In the first dialogue, Buber wrote that one comes to the mother only through the son. The mother there was described as the "boundless into which we must dive from the shore of limits in order not to perish in contradiction"[15]{55}. The mother rests around the child as the earth around the seed; the child grows in the womb of the mother and through realization the child can know the unity to be found there [18]{57}.

Buber, in the statement that the "mother is free and no longer the maid of the sun," may also be referring to the questions put by Nietzsche in the section in *The Gay Science*, where the madman proclaims the death of God:

What were we doing when we unchained this earth from its sun? Where is it moving to now? Where are we moving to? Away from all suns? Are we not continually falling? And backwards, sidewards, forwards, in all directions? Is there still an up and a down? Aren't we straying as though through an infinite nothing? Isn't empty space breathing at us?[117]

An onlooker, Kajetan, who saw the drowning of Elias, thought of Empedocles[118] when he saw Elias stroking the water with his two hands: "like the limbs of a beloved being." Lukas tells Daniel that after this death he had a new experience. He did not feel grief at Elias's death or a desire that he should remain alive: "rather his dying appeared to me right and well done" [127]{129}. Lukas thought that "up till now he had been absent somewhere and now filled his place. The reality [*Wesenheit*] out of which he was once broken in order that he might be formed [conceived] through the action of two human bodies remained incomplete until this moment when he returned; and now he stepped into it again and completed its existence. Completed? No: fulfilled" [127–28]{129}. This person was transformed and was summoned back to transform the mother herself. Buber is indicating here that it is through the transformed person that unity is brought to the world. Lukas claims that out of this moment the old mystery shuddered through him [128]{129}. Lukas asks if life was a ripening and death the entrance into a sphere of divine action before which mortality stood only as an allegory. However, this could only be the case for the completed person. Drawing on the example of the cells of the human body, most of which die, but those which are generative persist, Lukas wonders whether it is the case that some people perish and others ripen to eternity [128]{129}. These thoughts, though, were pride and unholy fantasy.

Thinking of Elias entering the bottomless "There" [*Dort*], Lukas said to himself:

There . . . and out of my own words the contradiction flashed. How could there be a There if it was not also here? How could I come to [know] death if I had not already suffered it? My existence was no rolling ball that I could think of as stopping somewhere or preferably being thrown further. It was the bed into which two streams, coming from opposite directions, flowed and mingled with each other. [129]{130}

Buber is pointing toward the movement from the point of birth to the point of death or beyond and the counter-movement that is the apparent approach of death. Existence itself is composed of these two forces. Each moment that Lukas experienced as a living man grew out of a mixture of the two streams, the downward and the upward; they mixed with each other like man and woman and created his being: "What I *knew* was the stream coursing downward alone; but what I *was* comprehended both downward and upward streams in one" [130]{130}. The force bearing him toward death he called time, but of the other, Lukas says: "but in my face blew a strange wind, and I did not know what name to give its flight" [130]{130}. The coming to be and passing away did not alternate with each other, but lay together in the unity of an endless embrace at each moment. Buber points out that it "was foolish to limit death to any particular moments of ceasing to be or of transformation; it was an ever-present power and the mother of being" [130]{131}. Buber distinguishes life as the "father" of being and death as the "mother" who receives and bears it. Life and death are essential as "parents" of being. Buber asserts that the certainty expressed here was not an unholy fantasy; it was not a feeling of security, "but the unarmed trust in the infinite" (*sondern das ungerüftete Vertrauen zum Unendlichen*) [131]{131}. This is faith in the cosmic spirit. It reminds us of the "leap of faith" explained by Kierkegaard. Moving beyond any certainty, the person holds the tension in himself or herself and resists the temptation to "let it go." However, according to Kierkegaard, before one chooses oneself, one must choose despair.

Lukas now finds that rather than life and death being "primally distant" from each other, they are close to each other as companions. Imagining that he is carried in Elias's boat, Lukas finds that he now journeys uneasily with life and death. Once it was enough to know of their existence, but now that they are familiar to him, they have become immense and disturbing. He asks: "what sort of a sea is it on which we travel, they and I, what sort of a sea has given birth to us, them and me. I know that in some way I am myself this sea, but I cannot reach there where I am it" [131–32]{131}. However, Elias reached there, that is, the unity. Is what we call death perhaps the way to it? Lukas, though, says that to think this is senseless, and that what life has not accomplished will not be accomplished by death either. "Elias was *reached*; as he died, he spoke only of that which exists, of being [*das Seiende*].

But I? He does not exist for me; how can I begin to live for him?" [132]{132}.

PHILOSOPHICAL ANTHROPOLOGY AND AUTOBIOGRAPHY

Lukas tells Daniel that once he was satisfied with the notion of the duality of life and death, "it was easy and good to wander from life to death, and their duality was an ultimate existence behind which I had no desire to look because it was the end and the consecration [*Weihe*] of my world" [132]{132}. This outlook has since changed. Lukas now considers these two not as boundaries, but as existing in each other and not ruling over him, but in him. His perception of them as an alternating movement no longer satisfies him. He is now driven by them to penetrate into the supporting Unity (*sie treibt mich, hinter sie in die tragende Einheit zu dringen*) [133]{132}. As death and life work in him and through him, Lukas says "I listen, I am aware, I ask: what is the command?" This is the action of the person who performs the "non-action" in Tao. The command is unity. "But the Unity that commands and leads this creation, that which bears life and death in right and left hand, that holy sea I want to know. I do not wish to grasp what is outside me, but I long to behold what I am."[119] This is *the* question for philosophical anthropology; here "man himself is given to man in the most precise sense as a subject."[120] In his later writings, Buber states the position of the philosophical anthropologist:

> But the philosophical anthropologist must stake nothing less than his real wholeness, his concrete self. And more; it is not enough for him to stake his self as an *object* of knowledge. He can know the *wholeness* of the person and through it the wholeness of *man* only when he does not leave his *subjectivity* out and does not remain an untouched observer. He must enter, completely and in reality, into the act of self-reflection, in order to become aware of human wholeness.[121]

Buber began the first dialogue of *Daniel* by articulating his own experience of the transformative event. In this last dialogue, Buber reflects on his own lived-experiences that have led to his understanding of man. The argument in this dialogue elucidates the personal transformation in the first dialogue. The whole book is an exploration of and a reflection on Buber's own experience. The idea of presenting one's story as an argument is, of course, not new. Socrates, in the *Phaedo*, gives an account of his experiences, since he cannot appeal to the criteria of rationality inherent in the earlier mechanistic methodology or to his own new method.[122] In this situation, an argument may be made from the experience of life:

> As a philosophical argument, an autobiography relates how the narrator was able to chart his way across the unfamiliar terrain, and implies that if the reader is also disoriented and follows the narrator's path, the reader too shall feel oriented, or better oriented. As such, an autobiography may be seen as an argument but obviously not an argument in a rigorous, logical, deductive sense. It is not an argument in any empirical or inductive sense either. Considered as an argument, an autobiography attempts to appeal to the experiences and values of the reader and attempts to show the reader how the narrator was able to find meaning and coherence in his intellectual struggles by approaching them in a new way.[123]

Buber approaches an explanation through his own story; he trusts that his own life-experience will evoke the glimmer of "knowing" in Lukas. The fact of this personal experience cannot be questioned, but the implication of Buber's understanding of it leads us to an appreciation of the final dimension of Buber's concept of God.

AN AUTOBIOGRAPHICAL EXPERIENCE

When he was seventeen, Buber saw his uncle fall from a horse and die.[124] Considering how this experience is described, it must have had a profound effect on Buber at the time:

> I was seventeen years old when a man died whom I had loved. Death laid itself about my neck like a lasso. It seized me as the Christian God seizes a sinner who must atone in God's place. That there was dying in the world had become my sin for which I had to do penance. Because of my isolation I could take no sleep and because of my disgust with living I could tolerate no nourishment; I believed that this happened as a penance. My family, strengthened by friends and physicians, regarded me fussily and helplessly as a changeling. Only my father met me with a calm,

collected glance that was so strong that he reached my heart, inaccessible to all other perceptions. It was also this man, silent but
united with the future, who soon came to the special decision
through which I was saved: he sent me all alone into a secluded
mountain place. I believe that the great time that I lived through
there will return once more in the images of my dying hour.
[133–34]{133}

This sojourn in the mountains is significant, as Buber experiences during this time contact with what he calls an "effective divine power"
(*eine wirkende Gottesmacht*)—which he describes as breath (*Luft*)
[135]{133}. The presence of this power is critical in our discussion, as
it indicates the actual power that awakens the potential to realize unity
that is latent in the person. This is the presence of the spirit that I will
discuss in my conclusion.

Although Buber had experienced the separation from his mother
when he was three years old, the recognition of separation came to him
following the death of his uncle: "Just now I recognised, that I was cut
off; just now I found myself before the eternal wall" [135]{133}. At
the same time, Buber knew that he could not meet his deceased rela-
tives, not even through death, and the dead could not meet him, not
even through birth, because he claims that he saw the actions of the
world from a different viewpoint than that of the proclaimed truths. He
did not believe that he would be reunited with his uncle after death or
even through reincarnation. In the light of this knowledge, Daniel no
longer lost himself, but won himself through despair: "For despair,
Lukas, is the highest of God's messengers; it makes us into spirits, who
can create and decide" [135]{133–34}. Daniel resigned himself to the
loss of his uncle. In the previous dialogue, Buber mentioned that the
poet, according to Plato, was one of God's messengers; here he goes
further and claims, like Kierkegaard, that despair is the highest messenger because it opens us to the possibility of a new life.[125]

Daniel then outlines an experience in which he felt himself at home
in the unity of nothingness. He climbed an alp that overlooked a small
lake. Gazing at the lake, he felt weakened, as everything in himself was
going into the lake: "finally it drew even the living power of grief, my
orphaned state, out of me—I was as little orphaned now as a newborn
child whose mother is dead" [136]{134}. Not only the grief over the
death of his uncle, but also the deep grief over the absence of his mother

seems to be included in this description of self-emptying. Then Daniel fell asleep, and even his glance over the deep disappeared before the consuming nothingness [136]{134}. He slept in timelessness while in the world of time his hours were counted. Buber describes here the movement into the "Nothing of the Unconditioned," which is "the power before creation and is called chaos" and in which no creature can exist. This dying into nothingness is essential for the rebirth to a new life.[126]

When he woke, Daniel's glance could not individuate things—everything was joined together in a cloudy image, an unformed world. His body felt like an island in a tide where everything blended together. His solid being rested in the middle of the chaos—yet his existence was shaken and distorted [137]{134}. This experience is the glimpse of the abyss of nothingness. It signifies Daniel's rebirth or transformation. Then in place of the simplicity of the lived human image, Daniel found a duality in himself: "One half of me was life, the other had become death; in both I found not states but powers, here the command of the surging blood, there the compulsion of death" [137]{134}. Daniel experienced the movement of formation and the convulsion of decomposition. Both of these forces were intensified to such an extreme (*ins Äusserste*) that Daniel's feeling "lay like an anvil and suffered the two-fold hammer blows." There, at this most extreme point, stood his soul in him. This is not that deceptive-soul (*Scheinseele*) that plans preservation, but the genuine watchman who wills completion [137]{135}.[127] The soul trembled violently due to its abhorrence of Daniel's division and longed to go into the world in order to bring him unity. In the world, however, it found only mixture and confusion, not unity.

Although the soul could not bring unity to Daniel, his body could—by a simple gesture:

> my two arms raised themselves, my hands bent to each other, my fingers entwined, and over all horror there arched the god-power-ful bridge [*gottesgewaltige Brücke*]. Then my body united itself, the world united itself to me, my glance returned to me unbur-dened: free and unencumbered I lay and looked at the lake, which looked at me. And in this doubly united gaze of giving and re-ceiving I learned that I was no longer divided. I had torn down the eternal wall, the wall within me. From life to death—from the living to the dead flowed the deep unity. I could not come to my

dead, nor he [the uncle] to me, but we were united like the eye and the lake: because I was united in myself. [138]{135}

Buber claims that the person as an incarnated being is united as the One from which all things come and to which they all return after death. Because Daniel took on himself the tension of life and death, his soul awakened. He later calls soul the "I" of the tension. Through this awakening, one is united in oneself, and everything is united in oneself. This is the reborn or transformed soul. It was at that hour, Daniel says, that the teaching of the "one thing needful" came to him: "it came to me mute and concealed, like the grain of seed in the earth; it laid itself on my breast and remained with me. I had it from that time on, but I did not know it. On all mistaken tracks I felt its presence, but I did not grasp it and had to go on from every track into a new one" [138–39]{135–36}. It was later, when he remembered the experience, and one moment joined itself to another, that he understood.

In 1895, Buber was seventeen years old when this event occurred. It was not until fifteen years later, in 1910, when he was thirty-two years old, that he understood what he had learned at that traumatic time.[128] Before explaining the event through which the teaching ripened in him, Buber outlines some of the mistaken tracks that he journeyed on.

REJECTED WAYS

Daniel explains that what he understood was that one "who genuinely experiences [*erlebt*] the world, experiences it as duality" [139]{136}. Daniel claims that all wisdom of the ages has this duality of the world as its subject; its starting point is to know it and its goal is to overcome (*überwinden*) it. Whether the two forces are called spirit and matter, form and material, being and becoming, reason and will, positive and negative elements, or any other pair, wisdom tries to overcome their tension, to unify their duality. Wisdom seeks this overcoming in many ways, but none of these can satisfy the person who is faithful to the totality of his or her life-experience.

> The longing for unity is the glowing ground of the soul, but he feels that he would degrade it if he surrendered something of the fullness of his life-experience to please it and that he can only in truth become obedient to it when he serves it out of his completeness, and out of his completeness strives to fulfil it, so that the

experienced duality remains undiminished in the force of its distance. Therefore, none of the ways that the wisdom of the ages takes can satisfy him. That is not the right unity for him, for the sake of which the powerful voices of duality must be silenced; the tensions which he experienced in the storm he does not desire to cancel out but to embrace [*umfassen*]. They have marked his life with the diagram of greatness; only in them, out of them, with them can he advance to the greatest.

The person does not want to "drown out the powerful voices" of duality for the sake of unity, but to embrace the tensions. Each way of the wisdom of the ages that the seeker followed, like Buber himself, became a mistaken way. Each of these ways Buber had to abandon because he knew that if not, he would himself have to abandon the mystery of his life-experience. The person who is faithful to the totality of his life-experience wanders from way to way until he comes to the "simple path of his self which is prepared for him" [141]{137}.

Buber then outlines the three ways that he himself had rejected: Hinduism, German Idealism, and Taoism.[129] The first of the wrong ways for Buber was that sublime wisdom "which commanded one to strip off the world of duality as the world of appearance 'like a snakeskin' and to enter the world of unity, or rather to recognize himself as standing in it, as being it" [141]{137}. In this connection, we remember that in his essay on Boehme, Buber wrote that his own position was very close to the Vedânta. However, this way of denying experience must be rejected:

> For the faithful person wants to find unity,[130] not as one who turns away [*als Weggewandter*], not as one torn from becoming [*als Entwordener*], he wants it as just this human being who lives through the whole oscillation of duality, who receives and bears its terrible blessing. What does it matter to him henceforth that this is the world of illusion? He has measured its depths and may no longer deny his measure. Henceforth he will not retreat before the fluctuating, raging, whirling world of division and of contradiction; he will stand steadfast therein, in the midst of it stand steadfast and dare just out of it to derive and create unity. He will not go again into the wilderness where one needs only to annihilate in order to find; he does not want to annihilate but to fulfil, and he would rather renounce salvation than exclude

Satan's kingdom from it. Not behind the world but in the world will his unity be sought. For what he seeks is not overcoming but completion, and he who completes cannot desire to obliterate anything, to weaken anything, or to resemble anything. [141–142]{137–38}

From this passage, it is clear that Buber is turned to the world. He does not seek to find unity by turning away from the fullness of everyday life. This is his "no" to Kierkegaard.[131] He agrees, however, with Kierkegaard that the tension has to be held by the person. The turning away from ecstasy confirms a decisive shift from the position in the introduction to the *Ecstatic Confessions*. Furthermore, the whole of the world, good and evil, is to be included in the unity. Salvation must encompass all. However, the unity is to be created by the person alone in the world. It is not achieved through encounter with another being, human or divine.

Yet Buber points out that this way ripened a truth in him. It confirmed in him the striving for unity. What was revealed to him in "formless depths of the abyss" existed; therefore, it must also be present in the multiplicity. What revealed itself to him in self-collectedness must prove itself true for him in the scattered totality of his life-experience.

The second wrong way for the faithful person was "that just wisdom that thought duality together into unity." Daniel explains that he means those who see the two forces as two sides of the one identity.[132] However, this way did not satisfy the faithful man either: "For if I for instance know that nature and idea are manifestations of one single being, is that being then immediately present to me as unity, present in the midst of the elemental tension of nature and idea that shatters my firm heart?" Buber does not dismiss these genuine thinkers, he wants to honor them, "as I honour those who genuinely put aside becoming, but I do not want to take their way. For their way leads away from the clattering and unruly highway on which I live and beyond which I will not accept God" [143]{138}. Buber implies that he will accept God in the world. This, however, is not the transcendent God, but the realized God. This second way confirmed for Buber that for unity to be reality, it must be lived and realized. It is not sufficient to have an intellectual knowledge of unity.

Buber, as the faithful person, could not avail of the third way either: "that innermost wisdom which proclaims that the awakened man neutralises all opposites and all antinomies in himself." [143]{138}. This is his rejection of the neutralizing of the opposites present in the teaching of the Tao. However, this neutralizing of the tension of duality cannot be unity for him. For his place is not in compromise, but in bearing the tension [144]{139}. This way undertakes to realize the unity; in his own being, all duality was tested, and in his whole manner of life in the world, unity was sought. However, because the search took place not in the living of the tension, but in indifference to it, what was won was not unity, filled by "all-being" (*Allsein*), but the "independence of nothing" (*die Unabhängigkeit des Nullpunkts*) [145–6]{140}. This awakened person is independent of all, not at one with all. For Buber, the genuine, filled unity can be nothing but the human being, all of whose tension is united, and in whom the "world unifies all its tension" [146]{140}. The human being is therefore one with "all-being."

CREATING UNITY

Buber then explains how the teaching ripened in him, although he says that there is very little to tell. One morning while walking, he picked up a piece of mica. He looked at it for a long time. Suddenly, raising his eyes from it, he realized that while he had been looking, he had not been conscious of "subject" and "object": "in my looking the mica and 'I' were one; in my looking I had tasted unity"[146]{140}. Looking again, the unity did not return. Then Buber closed his eyes, gathered all his strength, and joined himself with the object: "I raised the mica into the kingdom of existence [*das Reich des Seienden*]" [146]{140}. Buber continues: "And there, Lukas, I first felt: I; there first was I. The one who looked had not yet been I; first this man here, this unified man bore the name like a crown" [147]{141}. The first unity had been "as the marble statue may perceive the block out of which it is chiselled; it was the undifferentiated, I was the unification."

In the first experience, Buber was looking at the mica. It was immediately present to him as an object that is sensed. He was not simultaneously adverting to his own action of looking at it. He was conscious of it, but was not also conscious of himself looking at it. It was an undifferentiated unity. This was an immediate experience of unity in which the mica and Buber participated before any reflection took place. This Buber describes as a "taste of unity." He looked again at the mica, but the unity did not return, although he wanted it to, and he felt that it burned in him "as though to create." This moment is related to the discussion regarding life-experience calling the person who is ready to realize it. This call is emerging from the experience of unity, that is, unity of lived-experience (*Erlebnis*), in which the person and the mica participated, and not only from the mica. This experience, as Buber stressed earlier, when broken in two, such as into subject and object, is injured in its core. This core is unity, and it is this that issues the call to create unity. After his reflection, Buber closed his eyes and "joined himself" to the mica. In order to create unity, Buber now had to unite the totality of his being in order to realize the experience. The power in him awakens, and he creates unity. The "I," who is not simply a grammatical fact or a useful expedient, is realized. The person constitutes himself or herself as the "I" in the act of realization.

The call of the unity of the lived-experience to the person misleads Buber. The call is to realize the life-experience. In order to do this, the creative power, which exists in the person as a potential, must be awakened. In the first dialogue, Buber stated that how a soul withstands the whirlpool of happenings decides its nature. The preparation consists in concentrating oneself into a whole. This concentration of the whole being was discussed in the second dialogue in relation to the examples of the wrestler, the ball-player, and the runner. Then the power of the directed soul to realize or create is awakened. Therefore, Buber asserts that the person can concentrate his whole being through his own agency. The call is not recognized by Buber as a call from the other being to unify himself in relation to it; to become an "I" in relation to the unity of the other being as a "Thou." It is at a later time, in "The Religion as Presence Lectures," that Buber recognizes this development of the "I." Indeed, he argues for it in *I and Thou*: "Concentration and fusion into the whole being can never take place through my agency, nor can it ever take place without me. I become through my relation to the Thou; as I become I, I say Thou."[133] The call from the other being preserves the relation, whereas if the call is perceived as a call to unity, relation is destroyed and the "I" is absolutized.

Buber is still speaking here about an experience of realization that each person may have in himself or herself. However, he is turned toward the act of this person in the world. In *I and Thou*, Buber refers to this event: "O fragment of mica, looking on which I once learned, for the first time, that I is not something 'in me'—with you I was nevertheless only bound up in myself; at that time the event took place only in me, not between me and you."[134]

Buber, in the dialogue, adds that he did not fully understand the experience with the mica until he remembered the time fifteen years earlier when he had raised his arms, and his entwined fingers united life and death to "I." He then understands that true unity cannot be found, it can only be achieved through action: "he who does it realises the unity of the world in the unity of his soul" [147]{141}. The "I" is not something in him, but is a task that must be completed. Thus he must first live through the tension of the world in the tension of his own soul. Buber claims that whenever the soul experiences itself, it experiences itself as a duality. It neither experiences unity nor multiplicity: "in all its movement, in all its perceptions, it experiences itself as duality, tension, task." Knowing and feeling, acting and valuing, the human stands in the "protean phenomenon of the inner polarity in which the one pole is always immediate to him, the other mediately present, the one possessed by him, the other is known. Thus in him the particular tension is present which he will expand into the tension of all [*zur Allspannung*]" [148]{141}. That is, he will take on the tension of the world. The inner polarity is a microcosm capable of expansion into the macrocosm: "The inner polarity is the vessel that becomes full with the smallest content and yet can contain the infinite: with this it is filled, by him who wants to effect unity" [148]{141}.

Buber recognizes the tension of existence as the human condition. The person takes on himself the tension of the world, so that it is lived by the soul as its own. The polarities that are present in all being become those of his own self. For example, he takes on himself the tension of spirit and matter, and "the soul experiences the world-tension as its own freedom and bondage, its own spontaneity and its own being conditioned, its own bearing and its own being borne." It is no longer the case that the one pole is immediately present, the other only mediately present, but in the soul, the full polarity occurs simultaneously in "undiminished brilliance and power." The person also takes on the tension of matter and form, and the soul experiences the tension of the world as its "own wildness and its own taming, its own fullness and its own shape, its own chaos and its own cosmos." It understands in itself action and suffering (passivity) at once, and the stream between both, which flows through it, is the stream of the eternal powers. The eternal power to create is active, but in awaiting the response of the person, it is passive.[135] The human being takes the tension of being and becoming on itself, and the soul experiences fully its own stillness and its own movement, its own rigidity and its own whirl, its own constancy and its own transformation. "The two aspects of the great nature stand with each other in the outstretched heaven of the living soul." The stillness is the stillness of the primal being; the movement is the stirring of the will of the primal being to manifest itself. Both are united in the person in the moment of transformation: "Thus the world lives its duality from within the man who wills to create unity." Unity is created through the person bringing together the polarities of the tension; this is the point at which the cosmic spirit awakens the spirit of the person: the "I" of this tension. "There is truly no I other than that I of a tension in which it brings itself together. No pole, no force, no thing—only polarity, only stream, only unification can become I" [149]{142}. Buber/Daniel explains through an example:

> Look before you, Lukas, it is ebb tide. Can the ebb tide say I? Or the flood tide? But imagine the sea to have a spirit that embraces in itself the unity of ebb and flood: it could say I. The mica could not say it, he who looked at it could not say it; and the undifferentiated of its first look was only material. But then when its tension had been brought together, the unified could say it . . . the I of the tension is work and reality. [149–50]{142–43}

Buber claims that one has the qualities of an "I" to an increasing extent as one realizes ever greater tension in oneself. This implies that one becomes more and more real. The highest test is to live the tension of the whole world. Joining the polarities, for example, constancy and transformation, that is, being and becoming, in the "all-present" (*Allgegenwart*), the soul awakens the I that possesses constancy and transformation as its gestures [150–51]{143}. This is the "I" of the primal being; the unity of the primal being is lived by the human being. This person at the point of realization is the intersection of timeless with time. In death, the person is no longer constrained by time, but is timeless, as expressed in the following summary, which I will discuss in the conclusion:

> This I is the I of the world. In it unity fulfills itself. This I is the unconditioned [*Dieses Ich ist das Unbedingte*].[136] And this I is set in a human life. Human life cannot dispense with the conditioned. But the unconditioned is written indelibly in the heart of the world.

The sum of a life is the sum of its unconditionality. The power of a life is the power of its unity. He who dies in the completed unity of his life, speaks out the I, which is not inserted: which is the naked eternity. [151]{143–44}

Finally, Daniel replies to Lukas:

We spoke of death, my friend Lukas; we have all the time spoken of nothing else. You wish to know the holy sea, the unity which bears up life and death in right and left hand. You cannot know it otherwise than when you take to yourself and live through the life and death of the world as your life and death. Then the I of this tension is awakened in you, the unconditioned, the unity of life and death. [151–52]{144}

CONCLUSION

At the end of the last dialogue, Buber is attempting to articulate the paradox of the birth of God in the soul as encapsulated in the saying from Scotus Eriugena placed at the beginning of the book. There is no distinction between the "I" of the person and the "I" of the world. The "I" of the world is the cosmic spirit. The "I" of the world is captured in the image of the sea as the "mother of all beings" and the one to whom all beings return. The "I" is therefore the unity of being and becoming. Unity that gives rise to multiplicity can return to unity through the realizing acts of the person. The power to attain this unity is the potentiality present in the person; it is the creative power of the One. It is this potential that has been awakened and brought to fulfillment. Through realization, reality is attained; this reality is the reality of God, according to the discussion in the third dialogue. It is God who has been brought to realization. Without realization there is no God. In the act of realization, the person is identical with God; therefore, it is not possible to relate to this God as another being. The person is thus both unconditioned and conditioned. The person is God, insofar as he or she is unconditioned.[137] As there is no purely realizing person, there is no fully unconditioned person. Realizing hours are followed by hours of orienting, of integrating the experience in one's life. At the moments of realization, one is the unconditioned. After death, as Buber argued in the first dialogue, we attain immortality. The person is then identical to God, as he or she is no longer conditioned.

Buber stated that he would not accept God outside of the "clattering highway" on which he lives. This is the way of life of the human being in all its multiplicity and becoming. Here Buber accepts God as a potentiality present in each thing. This understanding of divine immanence can be related to the Hasidic-Kabbalistic teaching that God is the "soul of the soul."[138] Buber argues that God is a potentiality in the soul that may be realized by the person through his or her own act or may be realized in the things of the world by the act of the person. This potential then becomes the being—the reality of the person. When the potential in each thing is realized, God is the reality of the whole world. The principle involved here is the responsibility of man for the fate of God in the world. In this understanding, elements of the teaching of Meister Eckhart and Hasidism are joined. In order to appreciate this position, we have to address an issue that I touched on earlier: the question of who or what awakens the creative power in the person. This power is "inborn" or innate in each person; it is present as a potentiality. If Aristotle's argument on *kinesis* is followed, we discover that the power to awaken the creative power in the soul must come from outside the person. Buber commented on this power in his essay on Boehme when he wrote, "God opens our spirit with his spirit." How do we understand this spirit of God that opens or awakens the spirit of realization in us? In the second dialogue, Buber identified spirit as realization and adds that the spirit, which is common to all, fulfills itself without constraint in the creative person. However, the power to awaken the spirit cannot be identical with the spirit that fulfills itself. The former must be actual, while the latter is potential. Buber may consider the paradox contained in the motto from Scotus Eriugena sufficient to answer this problem, but I will examine this question further.

In the fourth dialogue, Buber mentioned "Enoch[139] who walked with Elohim." Enoch was compared to the poet. The poet reminded Buber of the eternal poet, and this memory occasioned the mention of Elohim. Of the poet and thus also of the eternal poet, it is said: "He is wholly in the one thing that he experiences, and is already and still in all the others at the same time" [116]{122}. This pantheistic expression implied that the divine is present in all things, and in each thing fully. Buber also refers to the legend of Enoch in both *Hasidism and Modern Man* and *On the Bible*. It is, however, "Elohim" that I wish to discuss. Kohn mentions in a footnote that Buber's inner attachment to Judaism grew stronger during the period of withdrawal when he studied the Hasidic texts. He mentions a letter written by Buber in strange and unusually large handwriting, immediately after the Pogroms of Bialystok (December 1906). Buber wrote: "I write now an account which is my answer to Bialystok: I mean: Adonai . . . I am in the first real work period of my life. You are my friend and understand me: I have a *new answer* to give to all. Now only have I found the form for my answer. It is a trilogy of stories: Elohim, Adonai and JHWH. I cannot speak more of it now and [to speak] of something different is not right. I am growing into my Heaven—my life begins. I experience nameless suffering and nameless grace."[140] Buber's interest in the conception of God continued until he arrived at an understanding of the presence of God as the eternal Thou.

In *The Legend of the Baal-Shem* (1908), Buber gave an explanation of the Hasidic understanding of the concept of God: "God has fallen into duality through the created world and its deed: into the being of God, Elohim, which is withdrawn from the creatures, and the presence of God, the Shekina, which dwells in things, wandering, straying, scattered. Only redemption will unite the two in eternity."[141] The human being can bring about the redemption that will unite the *Shekina* with its source. Scholem explains: "The glory of God, the *Kavod*, i.e. that aspect of God which He reveals to Man, is to the Hasidim not the Creator but the First Creation."[142] God, who remains infinite and unknown also in the role of Creator, has produced the glory as the first of all creations. This creation is the *Shekina* and it is identical with the "*ruah ha-kodesh*, the 'holy spirit,' out of whom there speaks the voice and word of God."[143] This explanation, if applied to Buber's writings, would imply that the divine present in all things, the *Shekina*, is for Buber the potentiality that is to be realized by man. The spirit is the cosmic spirit, and this spirit is actual. Therefore, out of the spirit, the voice or word of God could open or awaken the creative power, the potential, present in each person. This happens when the person has concentrated his or her whole being and is ready to realize. This spirit is the grace that appeared to Daniel, as mentioned in the first dialogue. The mistress, referred to at the end of that dialogue, who can only be said in deeds, and brings Daniel to God in the evening, is the *Shekina*, who is usually referred to as a feminine presence. In the deeds of the person who realizes God in all things, the mystery of the realization of the unknown is accomplished [77]{95}.

In a much later essay, Buber returns to the discussion of God and the Soul.[144] This later text gives us an insight into the position that he adopted in 1913. He argues that at times, mysticism is considered as the return to the primal being before creation, to the unity beyond all duality. Here mystics dare to deal with "God as he is in Himself, that is, outside His relationship to man, indeed outside his relationship to the created world."[145] Buber claims that mystics know, as Eckhart put it, that "no one can say of God what He is." But the mystics' conception of the absolute unity is "so strong that even the highest conception of the person must yield before it. The unity that is related to something other than itself is not the perfect unity; the perfect unity can no longer be personal."[146] Buber then recognizes that the distinction may be placed in the divine itself. He quotes Eckhart: "God and Godhead are different as heaven and earth. . . . God becomes and ceases to be." Buber explains that the divine is called "God," insofar as it has made itself in creation and revelation into the One facing the world and thereby into the partaker in its becoming and ceasing to be. "For 'God' only exists for a world, by the divine becoming just its God, the world's; when world becomes, God becomes, and if there is no world, God ceases to be, and again there is only Godhead."[147] This conception of God, in the form acceptable to Buber in 1913, that is, that God wills to be realized, but only becomes a reality in the world through the human being's act of realization, fits his position in *Daniel*. There is no reality—there is therefore no God—without realization, as Buber argued in the third dialogue. Buber's conception changes by the time that he is preparing the "Religion as Presence" lectures. Then God is the One facing the world—God is the "Confronter."

Buber's concept of God in *Daniel* retains the Godhead, which he calls the primal being, but Buber explains a further conception in which it is possible to appreciate how the Godhead may be understood as one with God. In Hasidism, we are led to this further significant point in which it is the limitless primal Godhead itself whose act establishes the world. Here the paradox is reached between "the original Godhead designated by the Tetragrammaton, that wants to impart Himself directly, and in order to do this accomplishes the limitation to Elohim, the creation, and this other, Elohim, who in the entire fullness of nature in the widest sense, in all worlds, works what is worked, creates, animates, inspirits."[148] Buber adds that Elohim is the impersonal figure of God that may be compared to Spinoza's *natura naturans*. This is the creative active force of God present in all things and is wholly present in each thing according to Buber's interpretation of Boehme. Schopenhauer expresses the same understanding: "the operating, original force, the *natura naturans*, is *immediately present whole and undivided* in each of its innumerable works, in the smallest as in the largest, in the last as in the first."[149]

In his pre-1913 essay, "Renewal of Judaism," Buber recognizes the conception of Spinoza as a peak in the Judaic spiritual process. Buber recognizes that the process had reached a point where transcendent unity became immanent—"the unity of the world-permeating, world-animating, world-being God: *deus sive natura*."[150] In his later essay, "God and the Soul," which we have been considering, the more mature Buber points out that in the Hasidic conception, "before and above Elohim"—*natura naturans*—there remains the limitless primal Godhead—the "Being." It is not the self-limitation (*tzimtzum*) that speaks the "I" of revelation, but the limitless original Godhead itself.

Buber's conception of the divine in 1913 is based on Jacob Boehme's writings. I will summarize Boehme's conception and then outline that of Buber. My summary of Boehme's conception of the divine is drawn from Hans Martensen's book and our initial consideration of Boehme.[151] Boehme posits the primal being as the Godhead or "abyss." The will of the abyss desires to manifest itself and so fashions a mirror. In this mirror, everything that will become on heaven and earth becomes manifest. This mirror is the eternal Idea, also called the feminine Wisdom. The Godhead desires to realize all, including the Trinity, which is revealed in the mirror. The eternal Nature is summoned out of nonexistence. This eternal nature is a spiritual potency; it is the will that has separated itself from unity and pours itself into the particularities of the infinity of wills. Nature by itself is "an unsatisfied hunger, and an anxiously eager restlessness." There is a dialectic of contraction and expansion in nature, which results in tension, conflict, and anguish. "Nature's inmost essence is need of God and His grace—a hunger and restlessness, which can only be stilled, satisfied, and calmed by freedom. On the other hand, freedom yearns after Nature, in order that, through Nature, it may manifest itself."[152] This is indicated in Boehme's statement that the higher yearns after the lower and the lower after the higher, which we encountered in Buber's essay on Boehme.

A conquest then takes place in which the Spirit lets its light stream into the darkness and confusion of Nature, and a tremor or shock passes through the whole of Nature. The light or "Lightning," which is the first contact of Spirit and Nature, breaks forth as simultaneously a joyous and appalling surprise. The lightning consumes what is gross, dark, and selfish in the desire of Nature. Nature's properties accept the will of the light, surrender to it, and become as those who have no power of their own and desire only the light. Here, Martensen comments that we "notice a doctrine which pervades Boehme's writings and is full of very profound practical applications, viz.: That every life must be born twice in order that nature may traverse the path to the light and to freedom through the lightning or kindled fire."[153] Finally, the image, which the Godhead beheld in the mirror, is realized. This is the "Kingdom," which possesses unspeakable beauty. It is also important to remember that this process takes place not in time, but in eternity. In eternity, everything is "in 'circular' movement; nothing is first, nothing last in point of time; but everything is simultaneous. . . . And in eternity one thing does not stand outside another, as in our relation of material space, but the one thing is in the other, and yet is different from it (v. *Aurora*, x., 40)."[154]

Buber combines Boehme's conception with his knowledge of Jewish, particularly Hasidic, mysticism and philosophy. *Daniel* is a work of many layers. Buber attempts to harmonize these layers into one expression of his thought. Buber accepts that there is a primal being that wills to manifest itself. In order for the primal being to manifest itself and attain again its original unity, nature or the world is brought into being. The spiritual potency, or the will to realize this unity, is present in everything as a creative force. The *Shekina* and Spinoza's *natura naturans* represent this spiritual potency. It is this potency that man realizes and in doing so realizes God. However, as we have seen, following Buber's use of Aristotle's concept of *kinesis*, man cannot unlock this potential himself; this must be achieved by a power that is actual—this power is the Holy Spirit. Now that we can recognize it, we can find it in Buber's reference in the first dialogue when he mentions that "the lightning of the heights hurled down on my head, and earthly fire mixed with heavenly fire." This reference to "lightning"—in Boehme's conception discussed above, is the first contact between the Spirit and nature. It is the moment of transformation. The contact of this Spirit and the person ready to realize the potential within his or her core results in the illumination, the "fire," of the understanding and the surrendering of the will of the person to the will of the primal being. The human being through the realization of his or her potential unites in himself or herself spirit and nature and thus attains the unity of the primal being that separated into spirit and nature. Man is therefore the manifestation of the primal being, which is God.

My inquiry into Buber's conception of God was undertaken because, as Voegelin states, whatever "the degree of elaboration or consciousness of purpose, the deformations of the human pole of the tension into a world-immanent entity are attacks on the life of reason, an *aspernatio rationis* in the Stoic sense."[155] This rejection of reason is a turning away from the humanity that is constituted by the tension toward the divine ground of existence. Rather than maintaining the tension between the divine and human poles of existence, Buber overcomes the tension in the realization of the person as God. Buber overcomes the existential *philia*, or openness toward the ground, in his conception of the person as the ground. In his quest for unity, Buber lost the meaning of genuine *philia*. Perfect unity does not permit a relation of love to exist.

Although Bergman describes Buber's approach as mystical, in an essay written in 1914, Buber denies he is a mystic, although he continues to write of realization. He writes as if in a dialogue with a monist. He claims that he is not a mystic, "for I still grant to reason a claim that the mystic must deny to it. Beyond this I lack the mystic's negation."[156] Buber writes that he is enormously concerned with this world, this painful and precious fullness of all that he sees, hears, and tastes. He cannot wish away any part of its reality.[157] Remembering that the Hebrew word "to know" also means "to embrace lovingly," we read that while the world is not comprehensible, it can nevertheless be embraced—through the embracing of one of its beings.[158] By this, Buber means that there is a way to the "great reality" that is not that of a detached reason or of the negation of the world, but rather that of love.[159] However, as we have discussed, embracing is not encountering or confronting for Buber. The person is not met as a separate unique person. In this essay, Buber mentions the active and passive nature of all things. The active part is the "confronting, the shaping, the bestowing in things." He adds that he "who truly experiences a thing so that it springs up to meet him and embraces him of itself has in that thing known the world."[160] Whether or not Buber wants to call it mystical, his thought remains focused on realization in this essay.

Recognizing God as the Confronter, whose presence has an effect, will be part of Buber's breakthrough to dialogue. There is a way that is

neither that of rationalism nor negation of the world, but Buber has not
yet found the key to it. Love has not yet moved to a position between
the I and Thou. Buber's turning in this direction only became concrete
through real encounters during the period of the First World War. The
decisive transformation was the movement of the realizing attitude out
of the sphere of subjectivity to the sphere of the "in-between." Buber
then recognizes his responsibility to respond to the presence and call of
the other. I will briefly consider some of Buber's writings from the period immediately after the war in order that the novelty in his position
may be appreciated. Much of the remainder of Buber's intellectual journey is well known and documented.

However, in order to summarize, I shall quote from two letters; in
the first, Hans Kohn questioned Buber's understanding of God's transcendence in a letter of November 1912. Kohn wrote:

> I think that in my last letter I did not state quite clearly what I
> mean by 'renewal.' I also think that, although we are indeed the
> ones who carry 'it' out, in a certain sense 'it' is transcendent:
>
> > Whatever you have said,
> > Another was your guide.
> > No matter where you tread,
> > He stays right by your side.
>
> I don't know where Weber found those lines, but I like them. This
> 'it' certainly can be revealed *only* in us, can develop only through
> 'us'; the fulfilment of the 'it' is, empirically speaking only the
> fulfilment of the individual—no doubt abut that. And yet this 'it'
> the way I feel it, is not identical with the individual.[161]

Buber did not refer to Kohn's statement in his reply, but in a letter written in October 1914—on the eve of the First World War—Buber wrote
to Frederik van Eeden regarding his understanding of the experience of
the Absolute. It is worthwhile quoting a significant part of this letter,
as it summarizes Buber's position:

> Rather, the experience of these times confirms me in my funda-
> mental view that our connection with the Absolute manifests it-
> self not in our knowledge but in our action. We do not experience
> [*erleben*] the Absolute in what we learn, but in what we create. It
> [the Absolute] appears in the human being not as a What, but as

a How, not as something thinkable [*Denkbares*] but as something liveable [*Lebbares*]. Therefore it is not *those* human beings who cherish the same intentions who are transcendentally close and allied with one another, but those who realise their—however diverse—intentions in the same way; not those who profess the same thing, but those who translate into action what they profess with the same intensity, honesty, directness etc. What eternally distinguishes the decisive person from the drifter, is not what he believes or intends, but the fact that what he believes and intends does not remain stuck in his thoughts, but becomes an event. I call this power (according to the Aristotelian expression which indicates the transition from the potential to the actual) *kinesis*. In it the Absolute proves itself, reveals itself. Everyone is able to experience God only in his own *kinesis*, in his own actualising [*Verwirklichen*]. . . . Not in their profession, but in their dedication the divine manifests itself. They cast aside the familiar, the secure, and the conditioned, in order to throw themselves into the abyss of the unconditioned. . . . God waits [*wartet*] in all things as a seed [*Keim*] and a possibility to become [*Werdenkonnen*], he becomes realised by the fervour [*Inbrunst*] with which he is experienced [*erlebt*]; and he becomes established [*eingesetzt*] through the power [*Gewalt*] of *kinesis*.[162]

The above extract summarizes Buber's concept of God; God is no longer "the dimly glimpsed product of future evolutions."[163] According to Buber's pre-dialogical writings, each person can bring God to realization through the process of realizing himself or herself.

5. The Presence of God

Introduction

The events, which led to Buber's turning toward the presence of God, have been well documented; it is only necessary for me to mention them. Perhaps the best known is Buber's experience of not being fully present to the young man, Mehe, who came to talk to him in 1914 and met an untimely death afterward. After a morning of "religious" enthusiasm, Buber was not there with his whole being for this caller.[1] Later, Buber wrote: "When I answer the call of present being—'Where art thou?'—with 'Here I am,' but am not really there, that is, not with the truth of my whole life, then I am guilty." When this happens, Buber claims, out of the distance, out of the disappearance of the first being who calls, "comes a second cry as soft and secret as though it came from myself 'Where were you?' *That* is the cry of conscience. It is not my existence which calls to me, but the being which is not I."[2] Before this event, Buber had not recognized the call to be present that comes from another person or being. As we have discussed, he had only recognized the call to realize unity.

Another event is the meeting in Potsdam, also in 1914, of a group of representatives of several European nations under the initiative of Frederick van Eeden, to whom Buber had written of his understanding of the experience of the Absolute. The purpose of the meeting was to organize a common front that might help to avert the impending catastrophe. Buber wrote that although no agreement had been reached beforehand, all the presuppositions of genuine dialogue were in place.

There was "immediacy" and "an unheard-of unreserve" between the participants at this meeting.[3] "The conversations were marked by that unreserve, whose substance and fruitfulness I have scarcely ever experienced so strongly. It had such an effect on all who took part that the fictitious fell away and every word was an actuality."[4] One human being fully present to another has such an effect.

Again in 1914, Franz Rosenzweig wrote an article on "Atheistic Theology," "which attacked Buber without once mentioning his name."[5] Rosenzweig opposed the position that held that self-awareness and ultimate truth originate within the national consciousness and personality of the people. In contrast to this position, he "posited the polarity of God and man as the basis for an understanding of revelation; and he rejected the notion of God as a mere human projection."[6] The article, which was openly critical of mystical thinking, was rejected with Buber's knowledge by the editor of the publication to which it was submitted. However, within a year, Buber, now the editor of *Der Jude*, personally invited Rosenzweig to contribute to that journal, and thus began their long friendship and collaboration.[7]

Another event, which led to the transformation, was a letter from his close friend, Gustav Landauer, criticizing Buber's nationalistic statements about the war.[8] Buber is guilty of German chauvinism, and Landauer remarks that his statements are "painful, exceedingly repugnant and well-nigh incomprehensible." Landauer claims that Buber's attitude toward the war suffers from an aestheticism. Following this confrontation that, Mendes-Flohr argues, was a pivotal factor in Buber's turn from mysticism to the philosophy of dialogue, there are three new elements in Buber's writings.[9] These are "an explicit opposition to the war and chauvinistic nationalism; a re-evaluation of the function and meaning of *Erlebnis*; and a shift in the axis of *Gemeinschaft* from consciousness (i.e., from subjective-cosmic *Erlebnis*) to the realm of interpersonal relations."[10]

Of lasting significance was the meeting between Buber and his friend, the Reverend William Hechler in 1914. Buber describes being asked by this friend: "Do you believe in God?" Buber implies in his "Autobiographical Fragments," which were not written until 1959, that the answer to this question came on the day Hechler departed on his journey. However, Rivka Horwitz has argued that in fact the answer did not emerge before 1921.[11] It is in the seventh lecture of the "Religion as Presence" series that Buber himself dates the answer to this question as occurring to him in the autumn of 1921. The answer came to him suddenly while he was on a train journey. Buber's inability to satisfy Hechler must have been repressed for seven years until the moment of inspiration on the train. "For Buber, the answer was a sudden awareness that *God must always be addressed in the second person, as the Confronted—as Thou.* The force and vitality of his future book and philosophy rest on his discovery of the new name for God."[12]

Each of these events point toward the breakthrough to presence as the key to Buber's later philosophy. Also important in this breakthrough is Buber's long involvement with Hasidism. This involvement spans most of Buber's life, both the pre-dialogical and the post-dialogical periods. It is sufficient here to add a relevant comment in which Buber describes the essence of Hasidic mysticism:

> In a time that has learned to give attention to the contribution of Judaism to human work, the Baal-Shem will probably be extolled as the founder of a realistic and active mysticism, i.e. a mysticism for which the world is not an illusion, from which man must turn away in order to reach true being, but the reality between God and him in which reciprocity manifests itself. . . . A "mysticism" that may be called such because it preserves the immediacy of the relation, guards the concreteness of the absolute and demands the involvement of the whole being; one can, to be sure, also call it religion for just the same reason. Its true English name is perhaps: presentness.[13]

In this short summary, Buber points to two elements that he himself had overlooked in his earlier writings: the immediacy of the relation and the concreteness of the absolute. The mutual presence of God and the human person, and of human beings with each other, is the lesson Buber learnt during the period of the war. Although Hasidism had a great formative influence on Buber's thought, it is a mistake to identify one with the other. Buber himself warned against this: "I beg that my interpretation of Hasidic teaching not be confused with my own thought; I can by no means in my own thinking take responsibility for Hasidic ideas, although my thinking is indebted and bound up with them."[14] In particular, he stresses his opposition to Gnostic ideas.[15]

PRESENCE AND THE BETWEEN

In a letter to Franz Werfel, dated 17 March 1917, Buber implies that he has undergone a turning around, a "change of thoughts," a *metanoia.*[16]

Buber writes that "Christian teaching hinders men, by referring them to divine grace, from making that decision which Jesus proclaimed, that *METANOEITE*" (*Jene Lehre aber, die sich die christliche nennt, hindert den Menschen, indem sie ihn auf die Gnade verweist, an der Entscheidung, die Jesus verkündete METANOEITE*). Buber adds that when he met Werfel in Leipzig in 1914,[17] he had not yet learned from bitter experience the profundity of the summons of "*metanoeite.*" In this letter, in which the emphasis is placed on each person's decision to change or "return,"[18] Buber also mentions his experience of God revealing himself. He considers that Werfel has a similar experience, and indeed raises the probability that this experience is universal. This is an indication of the change that has taken place in Buber. God is now other than oneself, and this other reveals itself to the human being. This is a change in Buber's way of thinking that moves him from the position of his earlier mysticism. It is a departure from Buber's position at the end of *Daniel*, where he asserts that one realizes oneself as the unconditioned. This *metanoia* is confirmed by a short outline proposal for a book dated 5 February 1918.[19] In this outline, the proposed title is, "The Confronted and the Between." Examples of the confronted are God, work, and the beloved. In the "Religion as Presence" lectures and in *I and Thou*, Buber repeats these examples. In *I and Thou*, "the confronted" will be called the Thou, and God as the confronted is the basis for Buber's development of a concept of God as Eternal Thou.[20] In the outline, Buber proposes to write on the relations between oneself and what is confronted. The concept of the "between" as the "place or bearer" of these relations emerges later. Already present in this outline is the notion of the between as an obstacle in the way of the encounter.

What is clear is that a change is taking place in Buber's understanding of "the one thing needful." By considering the obstacles to the encounter with the confronted in a negative light, Buber points toward the encounter itself as something to be valued. This change is evident in two addresses written immediately after the war. The first, "The Holy Way: A Word to the Jews and to the Nations,"[21] was delivered in May 1918 and was subsequently dedicated to Buber's friend Gustav Landauer who was assassinated in May 1919. This address was greatly influenced by Landauer's social thought.[22] Landauer had argued that the (nation-) state is a specific pattern of relations between human beings. The problem was to alter these relations from those of force used by the state to those of the spirit (*Geist*) as found in the bond of communities. Spirit is identified with humanity's "pristine drive for fraternal communion"; it is connection and freedom; it is the bond of humanity.[23] Landauer was a pacifist who suffered a brutal death; he believed that the state (as an oppressive force) could be destroyed by the contraction of other relations by human beings, that is, by behavior governed by the spirit. Buber adopts this perspective in his address. He wrote that Jesus was an anarchist (in Landauer's sense). Jesus preached that evil should be resisted by doing good. Buber gives his interpretation: "do not attack the reign of evil but unhesitatingly band together for the reign of the good—and the time will come when evil can no longer resist you, not because you have conquered it, but because you have redeemed it."[24] Buber's philosophy is tending toward an examination of the relations between human beings and the formation of community: "To bring about a true transformation of society, a true renaissance, human relationships must undergo a change."[25]

Furthermore, Buber now changes his understanding of Judaism's "disposition toward realisation." He stresses that this disposition means "that true human life is conceived to be a life lived in the presence of God."[26] This is the key to Buber's philosophy. It is confirmed later, when Buber writes: "Being true to the being in which and before which I am placed is the one thing that is needful."[27] Later in *I and Thou*, Buber argued that "the one thing needful" is the full acceptance of presence (*die vollkommene Akzeptation der Gegenwart*). Buber's philosophy of dialogue is an attempt to work out the implications of this acceptance, which means authentic human living in the presence of God.

"THE HOLY WAY"

In "The Holy Way," Buber begins by writing that for Judaism "God is not a Kantian idea but an elementally present spiritual reality."[28] God, he continues, is not something conceived by pure reason or something postulated by practical reason. God is the present spiritual reality "emanating from the immediacy of existence as such," which the religious person confronts and the non-religious person evades. Buber explains this confrontation metaphorically by calling God the sun of mankind. He claims that the meeting between God and the person does not take place when a person turns away from the world of things toward the sun. This person does not remain steadfast and live in the presence of God. She understands God to be an idea rather than a reality. Neither does the person who "breathes, walks, and bathes his self and all things in the sun's light" truly live in God's presence. For God may be "seen seminally within all things, but He must be realised between them." Buber's explanation lessens to some extent the implication that God comes to fulfillment through the actions of human beings. Buber clarifies that just as "the sun's substance has its being among the stars yet beams its light into the earthly realm, so it is granted to human creatures to behold in their midst the radiance of the ineffable's glory." The radiance of God is found dimly glowing in each person, but this manifestation is present in its full brightness only between persons:

> The Divine may come to life in individual man, may reveal itself from within individual man; but it attains its earthly[29] fullness only where, having awakened to an awareness of their universal being, individual beings open themselves to one another, disclose themselves to one another, help one another; where immediacy is established between one human being and another; where the sublime stronghold of the individual is unbolted, and man breaks free to meet other man. Where this takes place, where the eternal rises in the Between, the seemingly empty space: that true place of realisation is community, and true community is that relationship in which the Divine comes to its realisation between man and man.[30]

Buber struggles to explain his understanding of the manifestation of God using elements of Plato's simile of the sun, and even the notion of "meeting" or presence to another that corresponds to the biblical sense of the "tent of meeting."[31] He attempts to make clear both the transcendence of God and the potential of human beings to create the situation in which God can become an actual presence in the world. He continues to stress the need for an awakening to the divine presence in oneself and introduces the notion of the ability of human beings, in relation with each other, to open the space of the encounter with the divine. Buber is concerned with the role of human choice and action in creating an authentic human life. Holiness, he adds, is "true community with God and true community with human beings, both in one."[32]

This is a radical change from Buber's earlier conception of realization as taking place within the individual. Buber's conception of the one thing necessary has taken a major step forward. The true place of realization, Buber claims in 1919, is not within the individual, but in the "immediacy" established between one person and another—this is community. The "Between"[33] becomes the locus of the manifestation of the Divine. There is already here a distinction between God as a transcendent being and God's manifestation in the world.

This distinction is clarified further in an address delivered in 1919, "Herut: On Youth and Religion." Here Buber speaks clearly of the impact of the unconditional. He writes that "Man's mind thus experiences the unconditional as that great something that is counterposed against it, as the Thou as such."[34] In the creation of symbols, the human mind comprehends "what is in itself incomprehensible; thus, in symbol and adage, the illimitable God reveals Himself to the human mind, which gathers the flowing universal currents into the receptacle of an affirmation that declares the Lord reigns in this and in no other way." These symbols change over time, but Buber insists that it "is not God who changes, only theophany—the manifestation of the Divine in man's symbol-creating mind—until no symbol is adequate any longer, and none is needed; and life itself, in the miracle of man's being with man, becomes a symbol—until God is truly present when one man clasps the hand of another."[35]

Buber explains the impact of the unconditional on the human being: "The unconditional affects a person when he lets his whole being be gripped by it, be utterly shaken and transformed by it and when he responds to it with his whole being: with his mind, by perceiving the symbols of the Divine; with his soul, by his love of the All; with his will by his standing the test of active life."[36] Here we notice the evident change in Buber's use of the phrase, "his love of the All." This is the existential *philia* that was impossible if one is the All. The willingness to confront the impact of the unconditional is the latent religion present in each person. This deep wellspring within each person can be unlocked, and truer knowledge pours forth from it than that from the "shallow wavelets of his private experiences."[37] It is a perversion when a person imagines that he has surrendered to the unconditional when in fact he has evaded it. Like Buber before his *metanoia*, this person then interprets the fact of having been affected by the unconditioned as having had an "experience" (*Erlebnis*). But his being is unchanged, he "does not know the response; he knows only a 'mood' (*Stimmung*). He has 'psychologised' God."[38]

"PSYCHOLOGIZING GOD"

Buber explains the concept of "psychologizing" in notes for an informal lecture in 1923. These notes both correct Buber's pre-1923 position and help to explain some aspects of *I and Thou*. Buber writes that psychologizing disturbs what is essential in human life—the relation between the I and the world and between the I and "the Being that does not manifest itself in the world." These fundamental relations cease to be relations between I and a Thou. Buber then defines the psychologizing of the world:

> "Psychologizing of the world" thus means abstraction, attempt at a complete detachment of the soul from its basic character of relationship. This derives from the fact that the spirit in its condition of highest differentiation is inclined to bend back on itself, i.e., that the spirit to the extent of its individuation is inclined to forget, to deny that it does not exist *in* man (in I), but between man and what is not man (what is not world). Then Being is psychologized, installed within the soul of man. The world no longer confronts the soul. That is the soul-madness of the spirit.[39]

The tension between the tendency to "psychologize" God and to discover that God is present when one person meets another in community, "whether its name be love, friendship, companionship or fellowship,"[40] is the basis of the "Religion as Presence" lectures.[41] The change in Buber's thinking was recognized with astonishment by Franz Rosenzweig, who asked Buber to give these lectures. In 1914, Rosenzweig had been critical of "atheistic theology," such as Buber's, which failed to take revelation seriously.[42] However, when he met Buber in December 1921, he asked him to give a course of lectures at the Frankfurt Lehrhaus. Buber wrote to Rosenzweig agreeing to lecture on a subject to be called "Religion as Presence," which he described as "the prolegomena" to a work that he was engaged on.[43] Rosenzweig replied that when he visited Buber, he realized with "joyful astonishment" that the lectures called "Religion as Presence" would deal with "God's

Presence." In his letter, Rosenzweig notes the shift in Buber's position by citing Goethe's epigram: "When people think I am still in Ossmann-stedt, I am already in Jena."[44]

"RELIGION AS PRESENCE" LECTURES

These eight lectures,[45] but particularly the fourth, fifth, sixth, and eighth, formed the basis for *I and Thou*. It is in these four lectures that Buber expresses his understanding of presence. However, this under-standing is expressed in opposition to other philosophical thinking on religion. In the first three lectures, Buber clears the way for his own expression through his criticism of the understanding of religion as a function of, or being dependent on, various spheres of human life. In doing so, Buber is also critical of his own earlier thinking. He invites his audience, and his readers, to proceed with him through this clearing process in order that we may together arrive at an appreciation of pres-ence. The core change in Buber's thought between 1914 and 1918 is on the question of presence. The audience may not be aware of the change in Buber's way of thinking, as before these lectures it was only publicly indicated in two articles I have mentioned, "The Holy Way" and "Herut: On Youth and Religion." Buber expands the question he and the audience are concerned with, that is, "the extent to which there is religion as presence" by adding "religion not as remembrance and hope but as lived presence" (*als gelebte Gegenwart*).[46] Buber stresses that the question that must be asked is: In what way is religion absolute presence, which can never become past and must become presence and be presence in every time and for every time? As the two senses of the word *Gegenwart*, presence and the present (as distinct from the past or the future) are not distinguished in the German language, some confu-sion can arise.[47] Buber separates this question into three parts, perhaps as a way of distinguishing these elements. The first question to be ad-dressed, and Buber's immediate explanation of it, is as follows:

> In what way is religion absolute presence that cannot become past? . . . All presence, as we know it, must, by the very fact that it is present, become the past in the next moment, the next pres-ent. This occurs because all presence is a concept of the soul; every presence is a moment of the human soul that is followed by another moment. An absolute present that did not become past

would have to be one that did not merely exist in man as a moment of his soul, but one in which man stood, something in which man lived, yet which he could fulfil only in his inner being, by the dedication of his entire being.[48]

The second question Buber asks is:

To what extent is religion a presence that cannot be limited by any other and that therefore cannot be superseded by any other?

To what extent is religion unconditional actuality that nevertheless does not border on anything actual, does not stand out against anything actual, cannot be corrected by anything actual—but that is unconditionally actual of itself, in itself?

For all actuality that we know is actual because it stands out against other actual things. It is precisely because of the borderlines that divide it from other things that it preserves its own actuality, which is conditioned thus and not otherwise. But here we are concerned with something that does not have its place beside other actual things as one of the component parts of a collective actuality, with something that is purely and simply actual, that cannot be corrected, superseded, by other actual things. We are concerned, then, with something absolutely actual.[49]

Buber's third question is:

In what way is religion presence for everyone? To what extent is it something that is there for everyone?

Presence in this sense must be for all. It cannot be intended that somewhere one part of humanity, one division of spiritual beings, possesses this actuality, lays claim to it, as it were, has a monopoly on it by virtue of its chosenness, by virtue of its greater participation in the spirit. Rather, the meaning of an absolute presence requires that it be everywhere there is spirit—not that men find it out of some special spiritual talent but that every man can unlock for himself the power of the phenomenon, "spirit" in which he himself is.[50]

Buber is considering religion as a universal phenomenon present in "spirit," which is common to all human beings and forms the basis of the invisible bond of humanity. In *Daniel*, Buber had already argued that the spirit is common to all.[51] The spirit was called "that genuine iron ore" present in every, even the most miserable, human soul. Now each person can unlock this power for himself or herself. Buber does not explain, just yet, how this occurs. Buber finishes the outline of his subject by stressing that because "religion is unlocked for all," it is "a phenomenon upon which an invisible humanity is founded. . . . For this is the only way and the only possibility of conceiving of humanity, that the phenomenon of the spirit in which humanity stands expresses itself in an absolute actuality and presence that is in each of us and that can be unlocked in each of us."[52] The "phenomenon of the spirit" is something that we participate in and it is also present in each person.

Distinguishing between "relativization," which attempts to make everything that is unconditioned conditioned, and "functionalization," Buber considers the prevailing attitude to be the latter: "all religion is grasped, or an attempt is made to grasp it, not as an independent quantity but as something dependent on another quantity, increasing or decreasing along with it." It is a "tendency to undermine the independence of the religious sphere" and "making it into a dependent function of another sphere, one of the spheres of the cosmos." These spheres, which Buber proceeds to examine in turn are: evolution, social/national, culture and religion, art, ethics, science, and psychology. Buber is his own best critic. In discussing these spheres, he repeatedly criticizes views that he had previously held himself. I will only point to a few of the indications of Buber's change in thought that are relevant to our discussion.

In the second lecture, Buber begins with the notion of the aesthetic way of looking at things. Being critical of his former self, he says that it is a peculiarity of a certain philosophical style to let "worldviews and religions pass before one like landscapes, like works of art, like plays."[53] That is, to look at them as a surface, to fail to enter "the very dimension that is their own peculiar and decisive dimension, to leave their mystery uncontemplated."[54] This manner of observation corresponds to the consideration of religious concepts as "free creations of the human spirit."[55] However, this expression, "free creation," does an injustice to art and a greater injustice to religion: "Probably both religion and art are action under a mandate. But art, artistic creation, originates in the mandate of something that strives to come into being, something formlike [*Gestalthaften*] that is not yet actual, that is still dormant and latent in the actual, and that wants to be brought to life, to be actualised. I repeat: It is the mandate of a thing that strives to come into being."[56]

The idea of an encounter with God begins to emerge here. Buber introduces the notion that both religion and art are probably action under a mandate or on an instruction (*ein Tun in einem Auftrag*). The artistic creation begins in the mandate of something that strives to come into being. The similarity to Buber's notion of the realization of God in *Daniel* is evident here. Buber adds, however, the beginning of the religious concept differs to that of the work of art. Whereas the artistic creation is the result of the relationship between the artist and a potentiality that strives to come into being, the religious concept emerges from the relationship between the human being and *the* Being. In this significant change in his thought from his position in *Daniel*, Buber now acknowledges God as Being rather than as a potential to be actualized. It is worth quoting Buber's explanation, as it indicates his struggle to express the notion of the divine-human encounter:

> So different is this mandate that here we can no longer speak of a creation in the human sense, let alone of a free creation in the all too human sense. For this is a mandate of a Being [*eines Seienden*], the mandate of *the* Being [*des Seienden*]. All religious concepts rest on a foundation of a bond of being [*einer Seinsbindung*], a tie to the Being [*an das Seiende*], and without this foundation, without this relationship [*ohne diese Bindung*][57] religious concepts are not that, they are nothing.[58]

Buber explains that this "bond of being"—the tie to the Being—is often incorrectly called faith. Faith implies a certain kind of duality; there is something that is believed and someone who believes it to be true. This is not the case with this relationship to the Being. Here Buber is emphasizing that it is out of this bond that religious concepts arise. Without this relationship or "bond to the Being," religious concepts would be an objectionable subspecies of art. Nevertheless, one can appreciate the artistic in religious forms, but this appreciation fails to explore their real, decisive dimension. For example, if prayer is considered to be an artistic form, it is less than a poem. If a religious celebration is considered to be an artistic form, it is less than a performance in a theater. All these things get their decisive meaning (*Sinn*) and existence (*Bestand*) through the relationship to the Being, through the fact that they originate in the demand of that Being that is.[59]

His earlier idea of a "becoming God" is rejected again by Buber: "And therefore it is one of the greatest or perhaps the very greatest foolishness and carelessness of our time to drivel about a becoming God." The criticism then continues:

> But: *God* becomes, that which is becomes. It is the mischief and libertinism of our time to overstrain itself on this mystery by saying that man, the human spirit, has at some time and some place to bring forth God. Obviously this tendency originated in certain scientific theories, then took on a form through the tremendous spiritual passion of Nietzsche, and finally degenerated into—I cannot change the name I have given it—a highly unpleasant kind of claptrap [*Gefasel*].[60]

This repeated rejection of his former position[61] may have come as a great shock to those members of the audience who were not aware of the profound change in Buber's thinking. Having moved from being the advocate of "atheistic theology" to a theistic position, he is now arguing for this new position in which the key element is his acceptance of the presence of God to human beings. According to Buber, the multiplicity of religious concepts are provisional: "each religious concept exists in the will toward a universality, toward a completed universality of religion that is in the process of perfecting itself, in which the multiplicity of religious concepts is annulled/superseded [*aufgehoben*]."[62] Religion, according to Buber, stands "at the edge of form and of the realm of form, pointing to what is formless [*hindeutend auf das Ungestaltete*] and, despite all the eternal attempts at formation, nonformable [*Ungestaltbare*]."[63] Buber is aware of the difficulty of speaking about God.[64] He is above all calling attention to the human being's relation to God. It is in this relationship that religious concepts, and thus also anything Buber says about God, is anchored. Using concepts to speak of what is formless is paradoxical, but it is one of the ways in which human beings attempt to communicate with each other. Each of the religious concepts arises out of a relationship with God whose nature cannot be limited to any concept.

GOOD AND EVIL

In this discussion, Buber confirms what he has discovered in Hasidism and from his friend, Landauer. Buber argues that the religious sanction, or the moral law as something demanded by God, does not strengthen a decision. In fact, Buber claims: "What is valid is not what the representatives of the philosophy of fiction think. What is valid is not: Act as if there were a God. But I might almost say—I think I can't make it clearer to you in any other way than by saying: Act as if there was no God."[65] It is because the religious sanction is not one of the elements of decision that the decision of the person who is religiously opened is based on freedom. Appearing to step out of the religious sphere, this person "remains most deeply within it and thus assures it of autonomy." In this way, through freedom, the person who decides touches the sphere of religious being, touches divine freedom, which is above all unself-consciousness [*Unbefangenheit*].[66] This freedom, however, cannot be achieved through speculation or impulse.[67] One may point to a person who seems instinctively to do the right thing without the tension of decision. Buber says it is a misunderstanding to interpret an apparently impulsive action in this way. In fact, this person "is one in whom the decision takes place in those elemental depths of the soul that are closed to reflection and inaccessible to analysis. That is a person of pure, ultimate unreservedness of decision and of the ultimate (in the sense of which I have spoken), the innermost unconsciousness of God as one who makes demands."[68]

However, when the decision is knowingly made, there is no good or evil. One does not decide for *the* good or for *the* evil. Instead, "there is only, if one can say it in a specific sense, the just and the unjust, that is, the directed—directed by decision and choice—and the undirected." Direction, as Buber explained in *Daniel*, "is that primal tension of the human soul which moves it to choose and act to realise this and no other out of the infinity of possibilities" [18–19]{56}. Later he adds that behind good and evil as the criteria of the ethical stand direction and the absence of direction.[69] Good and evil are not a pair of opposites like right and left or above and beneath. "Good" is the movement in the direction of home, "evil" is the "aimless whirl of human potentialities without which nothing can be achieved and by which, if they take no direction but remain trapped in themselves, everything goes awry."[70]

Buber distinguishes between the level of decision, where there is only the actual—which is done and the nonactual—which is not decided upon and hence not done and the level of moral judgment in which there are two kinds of reality—good and evil. Having made a moral judgment and affirmed one course of action as good, one may not implement it. The willingness to decide to act in accordance with the judgment of what is of value is religious openness for Buber. It could also be described as religious conversion. If the religious is understood as a function of morality, then this duality of good and evil is raised to an absolute. Then the negation of evil and the affirmation of good becomes something rigid and inhuman. "Because God is not opened up in immediacy but through the good, because God is nothing more than the hypostatization of the good, the raising of it to a substance, not only the human soul falls apart, but the whole."[71] The whole world falls into evil and good parts. The stronger this duality becomes, however, the stronger is the demand for an overarching, unifying deity. For the person who remains in the moral sphere, affirmation of good and negation of evil, reception of good and rejection of evil, are valid. However, for the person who has been opened up to religion, who acts out of his or her religiosity, "what is valid is precisely love for evil, living with evil, being with evil."[72] This is the beginning of the transformation of evil.

Buber's conviction that evil is transformed stems from his acquaintance with Hasidism and indeed with Landauer's social thought. We have noted the latter in the address, "The Holy Way." What Buber considers of most importance in Hasidism "is the powerful tendency, preserved in personal as well as in communal existence, to overcome the fundamental separation between the sacred and the profane."[73] The hallowing of the everyday is the manner in which the demonic is overcome through being transformed.[74] In order to appreciate Buber's meaning, it is worth quoting the following lengthy, seemingly autobiographical, passage from *I and Thou*:

> The fiery stuff of all my ability to will seethes tremendously, all that I might do circles around me, still without actuality in the world, flung together and seemingly inseparable, alluring glimpses of powers flicker from all the uttermost bounds: the universe is my temptation, and I achieve being in an instant, with both hands plunged deep in the fire, where the single deed is hidden, the deed which aims at me—now is the moment! Already the menace of the abyss is removed, the centreless Many no longer plays in the iridescent sameness of its pretensions; but only two alternatives are set side by side—the other the vain idea, and the one, the charge laid on me. But now realisation begins in me. For it is not

decision to do the one and leave the other a lifeless mass, depos-
ited layer upon layer as dross in my soul. But he alone who directs
the whole strength of the alternative into the doing of the charge,
who lets the abundant passion of what is rejected invade the
growth to reality of what is chosen—he alone who "serves God
with the evil impulse" makes decision, decides the event. If this
is understood, it is also known that this which has been set up,
towards which direction is set and decision made, is to be given
the name of upright; and if there were a devil it would not be one
who decided against God, but one who, in eternity, came to no
decision.[75]

SOUL AS RELATION

In the third lecture, Buber treats the sphere that he claims underlies the
other spheres of the personal spirit. Here Buber goes to the root of his
own misunderstanding: the concept of lived-experience (*Erlebnis*). The
psychological sphere, Buber states, is based on the concept of soul.
What, though, is the meaning of the term "soul" as used in this sphere?
First, Buber says it may be helpful to clarify in what sense one does not
speak of soul in this sphere:

> For if soul, as it seems to me, means nothing other than the rela-
> tion of the human being to the world, to things, to nature, to hu-
> mans, to the Being [*zu dem Sein*], to oneself, then soul is this
> relation, insofar as it is known to humans in an unmediated way,
> insofar as the human has knowledge of it without having to ask
> others, insofar as soul means simply this relation. In other words,
> it is something into which the human being is inserted, which es-
> tablishes itself again and again between the human and all being,
> and which the human being, as person, knows in this unmediated
> way. If soul means this bridgelike being between human and
> world, insofar as the human knows of it in an unmediated way,
> then, of course, we do not need to "defend" religion—if I may
> use that expression—against dependence on it.[76]

Buber argues that soul, in the above sense, forms an essential prerequi-
site of the religious, but this soul is not the object of psychology. The
latter is concerned with the human being isolated from relation to the
world. This part of the human being is considered as if it existed in

itself, as a process in a self-enclosed domain with which one is ac-
quainted. The same holds for other isolated parts of the world, which
are contemplated in isolation such as thought, emotions, will, and so
forth. These are interesting and significant for science, but are not of
immediate importance in these considerations. However, it is on the
soul in the psychological sense that people want to make religion dependent. Different groups of phenomena are distinguished within the
soul, and the attempt is made to assign religion to one of these groups,
for example, the feelings.

An illustration of such a theory is one in which the religious is conceived as "the absolute feeling of dependence" (*schlechthinnige Ab-
hängigkeitsgefühl*). This is an implicit reference to Schleiermacher,
who bases the religious category on a form of self-consciousness,
which is the feeling of one's dependence.[77] Buber also mentions the
different formula proposed by Rudolf Otto: "creature-feeling" (*Kreaturge-
fühl*). In every such definition, only a small part of the extent of the
religious is included. One could even emphasize instead the feeling of
absolute independence. Buber stresses how dangerous and impoverish-
ing it is to make "a feeling, a specific feeling, the essence of religion."[78]
As feelings exist in a polar tension, one is clarified by its opposite, for
example, pain by pleasure. In the attempt to assign the religious to one
of these feelings, a feeling is taken out of such polarity.

Buber then asks what does feeling really mean for this psychology.
He claims it can be defined only negatively: "It constitutes the aspect
of a psychic phenomenon that cannot be grasped as an external." An
objection that this feeling of dependence is meant metapsychologically,
as something that transcends individual difference, Buber claims, is
without foundation. Feelings exist "within a plurality of feelings and
other things"; they border each other, limit each other, and so forth.
Buber adds with disbelief: "And now in this world of feelings there is
supposed to be something that has the religious as its essence or its
object." However, this religious feeling, which Buber was previously
familiar with, remains a feeling that "does not really happen to and
with the human being but that allegedly takes place in the human being,
that is squeezed into this happening inside the human—delimited by
his compartments, circumscribed and confined on all sides by his other
processes. And that is supposed to be the religious. That is supposed to
comprise the relation to the absolute?"[79]

Buber argues that the psychological attitude has been carried to extremes by a concept of "living experience." He explains that he is "somewhat accustomed to the hell that the misuse of this word signifies." This was a hell, as we have discussed, that he had experienced himself. Buber then comments on his more mature understanding of *Erlebnis*:

> Experience [*Erleben*], yes, the word "experience" no doubt had and has even now its justification: when it is a matter of emphasizing subjectivity in life, in the course of life; of pointing out that confronting our life, or we should rather say within this life, there are moments when we feel our relation to our I particularly strongly. . . . And this relation to the I sometimes crystallizes around single events, so that we can no longer say: I live, but rather: I am living this experience, I am pulling this out of myself as something that now vibrates as utter subjectivity.[80]

These experiences are considered as "gems of the soul" and religion is one of these gems. Here, though, religion is transient, unconnected, and occurs in disjointed moments of the soul: "Of all the fictions into which religion has been converted this is the most fictive." It is the annihilation of the religious. However, some people have become aware of this and have reacted against it. Buber refers to Max Scheler's attempt to grasp the religious in its essential process as an act. Max Scheler was introduced to Buber and his friends in Berlin when Scheler settled there in 1912.[81] In the following year, Scheler published *The Nature of Sympathy*.[82] Buber, at the time, was undoubtedly aware of Scheler's views, as they collaborated together on a journal in 1914.[83] Although Scheler's attempt to overcome the psychologizing of religion remains a psychological attempt, according to Buber, it is a very interesting psychological attempt.[84] This view assumes that "all psychic phenomena, whether processes, feelings, or strivings of the will can be either religious or non-religious acts." Scheler, however, claims that every human being really performs the religious act. This act relates either to God or an idol. "The idol may have one of many names: power, possession, woman, money, or anything else." According to Scheler, it would suffice to indicate to the person that the act could be directed to God rather than to an idol,[85] but precisely this, claims Buber, shows that the division is not ultimately serious. Consequently, if the "religious act is not necessarily founded in the one absolute bond of being but can relate, although falsely, to an empirical object, then there are not two kinds of act. But in actuality, the religious act is simply a certain heightened psychic act."[86]

Buber concludes that all these conceptions have in common and necessarily in common, is that "the religious occurs *within* the human being, that is, in this being-cut-off that psychology calls soul, in this encapsulation within the human being that it calls soul." Here, Buber insists, the religious does not occur, "as it occurs in truth, to the human being, *with* the human being. Seen psychologically, it clings to him as a rightful or unrightful experience [*unrechtmässige Erfahrung*], but it is not in him as in a presence, in an actuality." Buber asserts that this is the most dangerous of all presuppositions, as aside from everything else, "it is this most of all that leads to the real perdition of our age, namely mixture—here, to the mixture of the religious occurrence with illusory and hallucinatory psychological and psychopathological processes."[87]

THOU-EXPERIENCES

In the fourth lecture, Buber begins to express his new understanding of experience. He states that what is to be discussed is so simple, "that a certain conceptuality, a certain philosophical terminology that has become firmly set in most people's heads, conflicts with it." Buber asks that people refrain from juxtaposing what he has to say with ready-made, traditional formulations and instead juxtapose it only with your self-experience, with what you know from yourself about these things and forget other formulations.

Buber states that he once read the following phrase in a book: "And since our conscious life consists of experiences [*Erfahrungen*]...." He asks if it means that our conscious life consists of events in which we experience something. "Experiences would then be events in which something, some thing, an object is experienced." Originally, *Erfahrung* meant that which one acquires when one travels, when one goes over the surface of things. "One experiences things and in so doing extracts experience from them; one extracts a knowledge of things, so to speak, out of things, and this knowledge then has things as its object." Thus Buber claims the statement he read means: "Our conscious life consists of events in which we experience something knowable and assertible about the condition of things, that is of outer and inner things."

Is this, however, all our conscious life consists in? Buber now integrates the distinction drawn in *Daniel* between realization and orientation:

> And now the basic question with which we will start is this: Does our conscious life indeed consist of such events? . . . What is the case with this? If you reflect on yourselves, not under the influence of any conceptuality but in a completely unbiased manner, does your memory indeed reflect your conscious life back to you as a series of experiences and nothing else? Or are there things, moments, events in your life that you cannot designate as experience? Are there events in your life in which what is brought to you is not something, the condition of something, something knowable and sayable, but in which you confront something or other, a so-called inner or a so-called outer thing, differently from the way you would confront [*gegenüberstehen*] an experienceable object, an object about whose condition I can know and say something, about which it is given to me to know and say something?[88]

Buber defines "It-experiences" (*Es-Erfahrungen*) as experiences in which one always experiences something, a content, an object, something that is situated as an It in the world of things, inner and outer. However, are there other types of experiences? "Are there only It-experiences? Are there only such events in which things are brought to us as an It, as a something in the world of things? Or are there events in which a thing or being of the outer or inner world confronts [*entgegentritt*] us in a different manner?"[89] In a discussion with Buber, a member of the audience then arrives at the answer that there are experiences of I and Thou. Buber confirms that "this is indeed the perfectly simple matter that is different in kind from an experience, that we can at first, just for a moment, call Thou-experience. That is the simple fact of being confronted by a Thou [*Gegenübertretens eines Du*]." Buber then proceeds to outline four examples of such encounters: with a beloved human being, with nature, with a work of art, and with a decision. These are examples that Buber has to an extent already touched on in *Daniel* and that he repeats in *I and Thou*.

A review in lecture five allows Buber to conclude what it is that is significant about such "Thou-experiences":

> It suffices to answer that it is true if each one makes present to himself what his life contains in the way of, let us say for now,

just moments which he himself has felt and preserved as decisive, authentic, as the substance of life. If he questions himself with ultimate honesty, he will be able to understand all these moments not as moments of experience, for they have a peculiar quality of their own. They all have the peculiarity that what is experienced is not something, something that is composed of qualities and that can be pointed to as having these qualities. It is rather that in these moments the human being stood in relation to a Thou, and this was precisely the essential character of this relationship, which, as long as it lasted, left no room for an I and manifested [*kundgab*] this Thou only as Thou, but not as It, not as He, nor as She.[90]

This extract indicates the continuity of Buber's thought with the position that he outlined on the moments of lived-experience in *Daniel*. Now, though, the locus of meaning has moved from an internal experience to a happening between one being and another in which the other being's intrinsic value is appreciated. Buber's theory until now understood other human beings in terms of their use: they were necessary as means toward one's own unification. Only now does he begin to recognize the other person's intrinsic nature as a good in itself.

Following this recognition, Buber recognizes two qualitatively different states in life. "There are two modalities of world: there is the It-world and there is the Thou-world, the world of relation." These two worlds are different in the way of proximity and distance—they lead toward a position that can be designated as "nearness to God [*Gottnähe*] and distance from God." What does Buber mean by nearness to God? Here, at last, Buber redefines realization. It is no longer an event that occurs in the person alone, but is intrinsically linked to relation. What one experiences is not an "aggregate of qualities"; it is not an object. One enters with one's whole being into an encounter with another whole being, not as a sum of qualities, but as a being of intrinsic meaning:

If you have followed me, to this point, then in this moment you already understand what I meant by calling these lectures "Religion as Presence." Now at last we have arrived at the first meaning of these words. There is presence in life to the extent and only to the extent that there is relation, that there is Thou, that there is relation to a Thou. From such relation, from it alone, presence [*Gegenwart*] arises. When something confronts us and becomes

our confronter, our exclusive confronter, by the fact that something becomes present to us, presence arises, and only on the
strength of this is there presence.[91]

However, are these Thou-moments similar to the moments of lived-
experience in *Daniel*, are they only unconnected moments? Buber answers that every Thou, because of its finiteness as a thing or its being
delimited as a thing cannot remain a Thou, but must become an It. As
a result, the relations are therefore necessarily moments of life, which
come and go, between which there is no continuity. How, though, is a
"world of Thou," a world of immediate truth, to be built up when necessarily it is unconnected moments, transient moments that alone enter
our life?

In another general criticism of his previous position, Buber then
mentions attempts to make the "world as a whole, the It-world, independent, to detach it from relation, to know it as what exists, to fathom
its secret." Buber, however, recognizes now that "all these attempts are
in vain, this world is nothing other than a creation which has run away
from God." Buber's new conception of God is bound up with relation:

> God is the absolute Thou, who by his nature can no longer be-
> come an It. When we address as Thou not any limitable thing that
> by its nature must become an object but the unconditional—
> Being itself—then the continuity of the Thou-world is opened up.
> The human being's sense of Thou, of every innate Thou, that is
> latent in him and unfolds in the relationship, which must again
> and again experience the disappointment of the Thou becoming
> It, strives beyond all of them towards its adequate Thou. There is
> in truth no God-seeking; rather one discovers something, beyond
> all obstacles, that was with one from the very beginning.
>
> It is not a seeking but a finding. It is a finding without seeking:
> It is a discovery of what is the most primal and most immediate.
> The human being's Thou-sense, which is insatiable until it finds
> the Thou-in-itself [*an sich*], had this Thou present in itself from
> the beginning, and needed only to bring out this presence and
> make it wholly actual.[92]

Buber's desire for presence, the desire for a Thou that overcomes all
absence and the disappointment of the necessary change of all other
Thou-relations to It-relations, has at last found fulfillment. The openness of one's whole being to others is recognized as an intrinsic part of

human nature; we are relational beings. In *I and Thou*, Buber calls this the "*a priori* of relation": "In the beginning is relation—as category of being, readiness, grasping form, mould for the soul; it is the *a priori* of relation, *the inborn Thou*."[93] The origin of this notion is in the "inborn direction" that was discussed by Buber in the first dialogue in *Daniel*. In these lectures and also in *I and Thou*, Buber explains this notion of the "inborn Thou" through his understanding of the development of the primitive person and specifically the development in the child of the consciousness of himself or herself. Buber summarizes his understanding in *I and Thou*: "The 'I' emerges as a single element out of the primal experiences, out of the vital primal words *I—affecting—Thou* and *Thou—affecting—I*, only after they have been split asunder and the participle has been given eminence as an object."[94] In this new position, the human being becomes "I" in relation to a Thou.

REVELATION

Finally, in the last lecture, Buber comes to an understanding of revelation. As we have seen, when Buber was elaborating his earlier view of realization, he did not invoke revelation. I have argued that the earlier concept of God did not allow a relation in which God was present to the person. Buber now asks: "What is the primal phenomenon, the eternal, omnipresent primal phenomenon present in the here and now, of what we call revelation?"[95] Buber answers: "that the human being does not emerge from the moment of pure relation as the same person who entered into it." As we have discussed, Buber's understanding of love implied in the concept of realization could not appreciate the other being as affecting oneself. Now Buber can recognize that the moment of relation to the absolute Thou "is a real event, in which something happens to the human being." What the human being receives "is not a content, but a presence, a presence as strength." This content includes three elements. In outlining these three elements, Buber indicates his real transformation:

> First it includes the whole fullness of actual reciprocity, a state in which one is no longer cut off, no longer thrown back on oneself, no longer abandoned, although one cannot tell what it is to which one is linked, with which one is associated, or what its character is. Second, it includes—it is really the same thing only contemplated from another angle—the confirmation of the meaning.

There is undeniably a meaning, not a meaning that can be pointed out and asserted, but a meaning that is thus confirmed and guaranteed to oneself, a meaning that one cannot translate. And third, this presence and this strength include a call to the human being to put this meaning to the proof in his life through his actions. This meaning whose guarantee he has received, does not remain locked up in the human being, but it rather steps out into the world as reality and that is put to the proof in the world, by the world. The meaning can be received but it cannot be known. It cannot be known, but it can be done, can be received and put into action; it cannot be known, pointed out or stated in words. These three qualities are inherent in the strength that the human being receives. These three qualities in unison act as actual strength upon the life of this human being.[96]

This means the liberation of the heart, but the person has to be vulnerable in his or her openness to receive. Here meaning is found that transcends yet includes oneself. One is no longer abandoned.

Buber's understanding of Boehme misled him. Buber later asks: "Why has the limitless Godhead, from being an absolute Person, whom nothing stands over against, become one faced by a recipient?" The answer, according to Hasidism, is: "From longing for the recipient upon whom It, the Godhead, could bestow its light. . . . The actuality of God's way is to be understood from the actuality of His will to show love."[97] Love is the key to relation that Buber finally came to appreciate. Central to love is the one thing needful—"the full acceptance of presence."[98]

Notes

CHAPTER 1: CHILDHOOD

1. Martin Buber, "Autobiographical Fragments," in *The Philosophy of Martin Buber* (La Salle, Ill.: Open Court, 1967), 3.

2. Maurice Friedman, *Martin Buber's Life and Work,* vol. 1: *The Early Years, 1878–1923* (Detroit: Wayne State University Press, 1988), 4.

3. Haim Gordon, *The Other Martin Buber: Recollections of his Contemporaries* (Ohio: Ohio University Press, 1988), 50.

4. Buber, "Autobiographical Fragments," 3.

5. Ibid., 22.

6. Haim Gordon, *Martin Buber: A Centenary Volume* (Jersey City, N.J.: KTAV, 1984), 28.

7. Martin Buber, *The Letters of Martin Buber: A Life of Dialogue* (New York: Syracuse University Press, 1991), 672.

8. Ibid., letter, 2 June 1909, 122.

9. Ibid., letter, 5 February 1928, 357–59.

10. Friedman, *Martin Buber's Life and Work,* 1, 232–33.

11. Letter addressed to me from Margot Cohn, 30 June 1999.

12. I am indebted to Mr. Reinhard Schmidt-Supprian, Director of the Goethe Institute in Dublin, for his help in deciphering and translating these letters.

13. Buber, "Autobiographical Fragments," 4.

14. Ibid., 3.

15. Ibid., 4.

16. Gordon, *The Other Martin Buber,* 17. This book is a collection of interviews with family members and other contemporaries of Buber. I have been in correspondence with Buber's granddaughter, Dr. Judith Buber-Agassi, who lives in Israel, and she has advised me that she was not happy with the manner of publication of the interviews she gave for this book.

17. Ibid., 133.

18. Buber, *The Letters of Martin Buber,* 269.

19. Buber, "Autobiographical Fragments," 3–4.

20. Aubrey Hodes, *Encounter with Martin Buber* (London: Penguin, 1972), 55.

21. Grete Schaeder, *The Hebrew Humanism of Martin Buber* (Detroit: Wayne State University Press, 1973), 27.

22. Ibid.

23. Buber, "Autobiographical Fragments," 4–5.

24. Ibid., 19–20.

25. Martin Buber, "Reminiscence," in *A Believing Humanism: My Testament, 1902–1965* (New York: Simon and Schuster, 1967), 29.

26. Buber, "Autobiographical Fragments," 5.

27. Ibid.

28. Schaeder, *The Hebrew Humanism of Martin Buber*, 25.

29. Buber, *The Letters of Martin Buber*, 69.

30. Ibid., 115 and 122.

31. Gordon, *Martin Buber: A Centenary Volume*, 30.

32. Buber, *The Letters of Martin Buber*, 148.

33. Buber, "Autobiographical Fragments," 4.

34. Buber, *The Letters of Martin Buber*, 70.

35. Hodes, *Encounter with Martin Buber*, 56.

36. Buber, "Autobiographical Fragments," 6–7.

37. Ibid., 7.

38. Ibid.

39. Ibid., 23.

40. Ibid., 10.

41. Ibid.

42. Friedman, *Martin Buber's Life and Work*, 1, 8.

43. Buber, "Autobiographical Fragments," 5–6.

44. Schaeder, *The Hebrew Humanism of Martin Buber*, 25–26. Schaeder notes that Goethe conceived a novel in which various members of a family, in different parts of the world, exchanged impressions in the languages of their respective countries.

45. Ibid., 26.

46. Buber, "Autobiographical Fragments," 22–23.

47. Ibid., 9.

48. Hodes, *Encounter with Martin Buber*, 82.

49. Ibid.

50. Buber, "Autobiographical Fragments," 9.

51. Ibid., 9–10.

52. Ibid., 10.

53. Schaeder, *The Hebrew Humanism of Martin Buber*, 27.

54. Martin Buber, "The Way of Man according to the Teachings of Hasidism," in *Hasidism and Modern Man* (New Jersey: Humanities Press, 1988), 148–49.

55. Martin Buber, "What is Man?" in *Between Man and Man* (New York: Collier Books, 1965), 136.

56. Buber, "Autobiographical Fragments," 11–12.

57. Ibid., 12.

58. Buber, *Between Man and Man*, 136–37.

59. Buber, "Autobiographical Fragments," 12.
60. Ibid., 13.
61. Martin Buber, *Daniel Dialogues on Realization* (New York: Holt, Rinehart and Winston, 1964). Friedman uses the American spelling of "Realization."
62. Ibid., 132–33.
63. Maurice Friedman, *Martin Buber's Life and Work*, 1, 156.
64. Hodes, *Encounter with Martin Buber*, 55.
65. Buber, *Hasidism and Modern Man*, 48.
66. Hodes, *Encounter with Martin Buber*, 56.
67. Buber, "Autobiographical Fragments," 31–32.
68. Ibid., 32–33.
69. Ibid., 33.
70. Ibid.
71. Buber, *The Letters of Martin Buber*, 290.
72. Ibid.
73. Schaeder, *The Hebrew Humanism of Martin Buber*, 30. I have obtained a copy of his address from the Archives.
74. Buber, *Between Man and Man*, 184.
75. Buber, "Autobiographical Fragments," 19.
76. Buber, *Hasidism and Modern Man*, 171.
77. Buber, "Autobiographical Fragments," 19–20.
78. Ibid., 20.
79. Ibid.
80. Buber, *Hasidism and Modern Man*, 45–46.
81. Ibid., 49.
82. Hans Kohn, *Martin Buber: Sein Werk und Seine Zeit* (Köln: Joseph Melzer Verlag, 1961), 19.
83. Schaeder, *The Hebrew Humanism of Martin Buber*, 20.
84. Ibid., 20–21.
85. Rudiger Safranski, *Martin Heidegger Between Good and Evil* (Cambridge, Mass.: Harvard University Press, 1998), 20.
86. Ibid.
87. Carl Schorske, *Fin-de-Siècle Vienna Politics and Culture* (New York: Knopf, 1980), 8–9, quoted in Steven Kepnes, *The Text as Thou Martin Buber's Dialogical Hermeneutics and Narrative Theology* (Bloomington: Indiana University Press, 1992), 154, n. 16.
88. Hans Fischer-Barnicol, "'. . . und Poet dazu.' Die Einheit von Denken und Dichten bei Martin Buber," *Bulletin des Leo Baeck Instituts* 9, no. 33, 1966 (Tel Aviv: Verlag Bitaon Ltd.), pp. 4f, 11, quoted in Friedman, *Martin Buber's Life and Work*, 1, 16.
89. Buber, *A Believing Humanism*, 30.
90. Friedman, *Martin Buber's Life and Work*, 1, 17.
91. Buber, *A Believing Humanism*, 30.
92. Buber, "Autobiographical Fragments," 14.
93. Buber, *Between Man and Man*, 98.
94. Ibid., 203.
95. Buber, "Autobiographical Fragments," 14.
96. Buber, *A Believing Humanism*, 30.

97. Buber, "Autobiographical Fragments," 14.

98. Martin Buber, "Replies to my Critics," in *The Philosophy of Martin Buber*, 696–97.

99. Paula Winkler, "Betrachtungen einer Philozionistin," in *Die Welt*, 6 September 1901, no. 36, 4–6.

100. Grete Schaeder, "Martin Buber: A Biographical Sketch," in *The Letters of Martin Buber*, 9.

101. Kohn, *Sein Werk und Seine Zeit*, 292, n. 26.

102. Schaeder, "Martin Buber: A Biographical Sketch," 12.

103. Ibid., 10.

104. Friedman, *Martin Buber's Life and Work*, 1, 337.

105. Ibid., 337–38.

106. Gordon, *The Other Martin Buber*, 31.

107. Ibid., 19.

108. Ibid., 3.

109. Ibid., 41 and 44.

110. Buber, *The Letters of Martin Buber*, 688.

111. Gordon, *The Other Martin Buber*, 42.

112. Buber, *The Letters of Martin Buber*, 573–74.

113. Buber, "Autobiographical Fragments," 3.

114. Published in English as *The Philosophy of Martin Buber*, vol. XII of *The Library of Living Philosophers* (La Salle, Ill.: Open Court, 1967).

115. Buber, "Autobiographical Fragments," 37–38.

116. Buber, *The Letters of Martin Buber*, 269–70.

117. Martin Buber, *Daniel:Dialogues on Realization*, 138.

CHAPTER 2: THE BECOMING GOD

1. Kohn, *Martin Buber: Sein Werk und Seine Zeit*, 23.

2. Ibid.

3. Ernst Benz, *Les sources mystiques de la philosophie romantique allemande* (Paris: J. Vrin, 1968), 8.

4. Kohn, *Martin Buber: Sein Werk und Seine Zeit*, 23.

5. Buber, *Hasidism and Modern Man*, 171.

6. Ibid., 51.

7. Buber, *Between Man and Man*, 126.

8. Schaeder, *The Hebrew Humanism of Martin Buber*, 44.

9. Martin Buber, "Ein Wort über Nietzsche und die Lebenswerte," *Die Kunst im Leben* 1, no. 2 (December 1900), 13. The translations are my own, but I wish to thank Dr. Gesa Thiessen for her advice.

10. H. P. Rickman, *W. Dilthey Selected Writings* (Cambridge: Cambridge University Press, 1976), 107–121.

11. Paul Mendes-Flohr, *From Mysticism to Dialogue: Martin Buber's Transformation of German Social Thought* (Detroit: Wayne State University Press, 1989), 49.

12. Dilthey means by this term the source of the world. See Rickman, *W. Dilthey Selected Writings*, 144.

13. Rickman, *W. Dilthey Selected Writings*, 112.

14. Ibid.

15. Ibid., 113.
16. Ibid., 114.
17. Ibid., 115.
18. Ibid., 116.
19. Ibid., 118.
20. Ibid., 120.
21. Ibid., 121.
22. Cited by Rickman in *Wilhelm Dilthey: Pioneer of the Human Studies* (Berkeley: University of California Press, 1979), 54.
23. Rickman, *W. Dilthey: Selected Writings*, 175.
24. Ibid., 176.
25. Ibid., 208.
26. Ibid., 154.
27. Rickman, *Wilhelm Dilthey: Pioneer of the Human Studies*, 41.
28. Rickman, *W. Dilthey: Selected Writings*, 162.
29. Mendes-Flohr, *From Mysticism to Dialogue*, 17.
30. Rickman, *W. Dilthey: Selected Writings*, 29.
31. Ibid.
32. Mendes-Flohr, *From Mysticism to Dialogue*, 17.
33. Martin Buber, "Religion as Presence Lectures," in Rivka Horwitz, *Buber's Way to I and Thou*, 49. That Buber means an aversion to *Erlebnis* rather than *Erfahrung* is confirmed by the published German typewritten copies of the lectures in Rivka Horwitz, *Buber's Way to I and Thou: An Historical Analysis and the First Publication of Martin Buber's Lectures "Religion als Gegenwart"* (Heidelberg: Verlag Lambert Schneider, 1978), 76.
34. Hans-Georg Gadamer, *Truth and Method*, 2nd ed. (London: Sheed and Ward, 1993), 60.
35. Ibid., 61.
36. Ibid.
37. Ibid.
38. Ibid.
39. Ibid., 62.
40. Ibid., 62–63. It is interesting that Derrida mentions Rousseau as his model of interiority. Derrida's acclaim of the aesthetic may be compared to the effect of the concept of *Erlebnis* on Buber. The danger of the "totalization of the aesthetic," as St. Amour phrases it, is what Buber escaped from in his discovery of presence. Paul St. Amour, "Presence and Differentiation: A Response to Elizabeth Morelli's "Oversight of Insight and the Critique of the Metaphysics of Presence," in *Method: Journal of Lonergan Studies*, 18 (2000): 23.
41. Gadamer, *Truth and Method*, 63.
42. Kohn, *Martin Buber: Sein Werk und Seine Zeit*, 21.
43. Some of those listed by Gadamer are: *Akt des Lebens* ("act of life"), *Moment* ("initial element"), *eigenes Gefühl* ("one's own feeling"), *Einwirkung* ("influence"), *Regung als freie Selbstbestimmung des Gemüts* ("feeling as the free self-determination of the heart"), *das ursprünglich Innerliche* ("the original inwardness"). It would be interesting to trace the influence of some of these synonyms in Buber's writings.
44. Ibid., 64.

45. Buber, "Replies to my Critics," in *The Philosophy of Martin Buber*, 711–12.

46. Kohn, *Martin Buber: Sein Werk und Seine Zeit*, 64.

47. Mendes-Flohr, *From Mysticism to Dialogue*, 54.

48. Kohn, *Martin Buber: Sein Werk und Seine Zeit*, 28.

49. Mendes-Flohr, *From Mysticism to Dialogue*, 50.

50. Ibid.

51. Martin Buber, "Alte und neue Gemeinschaft," a handwritten, much-corrected manuscript obtained in the Martin Buber Archives, ref. 47/B.

52. Mendes-Flohr, *From Mysticism to Dialogue*, 58.

53. Ibid., 5.

54. Buber, "Alte und neue Gemeinschaft," 6.

55. Mendes-Flohr, *From Mysticism to Dialogue*, 58.

56. Buber, "Alte und neue Gemeinschaft," 6.

57. Friedman, *Martin Buber's Life and Work*, vol. 1, 77.

58. Kohn, *Martin Buber: Sein Werk und Seine Zeit*, 30.

59. Schaeder, *The Hebrew Humanism of Martin Buber*, 90.

60. Ibid.

61. Mauthner is mentioned by Schaeder in connection with the mysticism of the period (see page 51); Friedman mentions Mauthner's close friendship with Landauer, (see vol. 1, 236–37, 246, 252–55). Mendes-Flohr briefly outlines Mauthner's influence on the conception of mysticism in the "Editor's Introduction" to *Ecstatic Confessions* (New York: Syracuse University Press, 1996).

62. Martin Buber, *Briefwechsel aus sieben Jahrzehnten, Band 1: 1897–1918*, ed. Grete Schaeder (Heidelberg: Verlag Lambert Schneider, 1972), 238.

63. Ibid.

64. Mendes-Flohr, "Editor's Introduction" to *Ecstatic Confessions*, xiv.

65. Ibid.

66. Cited by Mendes-Flohr, xv.

67. Ludwig Wittgenstein, *Tractatus Logico-Philosophicus* (London: Routledge & Kegan Paul, 1994), 74. Cited by Mendes-Flohr, "Editor's Introduction" to *Ecstatic Confessions*, xv–xvi.

68. I will examine Buber's introduction in Chapter 3.

69. Buber, *Between Man and Man*, 184. Angelus Silesius was a pseudonym of Johann Scheffler (1624–77), a Protestant physician who became a Catholic priest. He was a mystical poet who transcribed the mystical theology of Eckhart and Johannes Tauler of Strasburg (1300–61), one of Eckhart's immediate disciples, into epigrams. He also was a great admirer of Jacob Boehme's teachings and many of the couplets of his book, *Cherubic Wanderer*, bear the traces of Boehme's teachings. See Hans L. Martensen, *Jacob Boehme (1575–1624)*, 3; Ernst Benz, *Les sources mystiques de la philosophie romantique allemande*, 21; and F. Ueberweg, *A History of Philosophy*, 484.

70. Kohn, *Martin Buber: Sein Werk und Seine Zeit*, 29.

71. Mendes-Flohr, *From Mysticism to Dialogue*, 154, n. 107 and 155, n. 113.

72. I will adopt the convention of referring to Boehme as Jacob Boehme in the text and where this is the manner in which his name is spelt as author or in the English title of a book, and I will retain Jakob Boehme or Böhme

where these are used by Buber in the German titles of his essay and dissertation.

73. Martensen, *Jacob Boehme*, 3.

74. David Walsh, *The Mysticism of Innerworldly Fulfillment: A Study of Jacob Boehme* (Gainesville: University Presses of Florida, 1983), 10. I am indebted to Walsh's discussion of Boehme's texts.

75. Ibid., 125.

76. Ibid., 7.

77. Ibid., 11–12.

78. Ibid., 116, n. 15.

79. Ibid., 14–15.

80. Eric Voegelin, *Anamnesis* (Columbia: University of Missouri Press, 1990), 96.

81. Ibid., 96.

82. Ibid., 103.

83. Ibid., 95.

84. Eric Voegelin, *The Collected Works of Eric Voegelin, Vol. 28: What is History? And Other Late Unpublished Writings* (Baton Rouge: Louisiana State University Press, 1990), 6 and 21.

85. Ibid., 5.

86. Ibid., 6.

87. Ibid., 81.

88. Friedman, *Martin Buber's Life and Work*, vol. 1, 32.

89. Martin Buber, *Pointing the Way: Collected Essays* (New York: Humanity Books, 1999), x.

90. Martensen, *Jacob Boehme*, 3.

91. See Mendes-Flohr, *From Mysticism to Dialogue*, 60–62; Schaeder, *The Hebrew Humanism of Martin Buber*, 60–61; Friedman, *Martin Buber's Life and Work: The Early Years, 1878–1923*, 77–79.

92. Martin Buber, "Über Jakob Boehme," *Wiener Rundschau*, vol. 5, no. 12 (15 June 1901): 251. See Appendix.

93. Martin Buber, "My Way to Hasidism," in *Hasidism and Modern Man* (New Jersey: Humanities Press, 1988), 49.

94. Buber, *Between Man and Man*, 167.

95. Ibid.

96. Friedrich Nietzsche, letter to Franz Overbeck, dated 2 July 1885, quoted in Emil L. Fackenheim, *God's Presence in History: Jewish Affirmations and Philosophical Reflections* (New Jersey: Jason Aronson, 1997), 64.

97. W. Windelband, *A History of Philosophy with Especial Reference to the Formation and Development of its Problems and Conceptions* (New York: Macmillan, 1910), 367. Although Buber gives no references or bibliography with this essay, I have discovered from archival material that Windelband's history was one of the sources that he listed for his dissertation.

98. In his *Book of Prayers*, Boehme writes that he will describe how man shall perform all his work *with* God—just as the tree's branch bears its twigs and its fruits with the life force that flows from its roots, how a man shall create with the power springing from God's fountain, and how he shall thank his Creator for every gift. See Martensen, *Jacob Boehme*, 14.

99. Jacob Boehme, *Mysterium Magnum* (Montana: Kessinger, 2000), ch. 4: ss. 1 and 7.

100. Walsh, *The Mysticism of Innerworldly Fulfillment*, 56.

101. Martin Buber, "Zur Geschichte des Individuationsproblems (Nicolaus von Cues und Jakob Böhme)," unpublished and unbound typewritten pages, Martin Buber Archive, Jerusalem, ref. 350/2–1c, 34.

102. Boehme, *Mysterium Magnum*, ch. 52, ss. 3 and 7.

103. Buber, "Über Jakob Boehme," 251. Buber omits all references to Boehme's writings.

104. Walsh, *The Mysticism of Innerworldly Fulfillment*, 69.

105. Ibid., 16.

106. Ibid., 16–17.

107. Buber, "Über Jakob Boehme," 251.

108. Walsh, *The Mysticism of Innerworldly Fulfillment*, 54.

109. Boehme, *Mysterium Magnum*, ch. 5, s. 7. The principle that we come to know only in terms of oppositions is present in Paracelsus's teachings (see Frederick Copleston, *A History of Philosophy*, vol. 3 (Tunbridge Wells, U.K.: Paulist Press, 1950), 267). Boehme had read some works of Paracelsus (see Martensen, 21 n. 10).

110. Walsh, *The Mysticism of Innerworldly Fulfillment*, 50.

111. Boehme, *Mysterium Magnum*, ch. 5, s. 10.

112. Walsh, *The Mysticism of Innerworldly Fulfillment*, 55. This is the same point that Plotinus made concerning the One: "If there is a reality that is the simplest of all it will have no self-knowledge." See Etienne Gilson, *Being and Some Philosophers*, 23.

113. Walsh, *The Mysticism of Innerworldly Fulfillment*, 32.

114. Buber, "Über Jakob Boehme," 251.

115. Windelband, *A History of Philosophy*, 365–66.

116. Ibid., 367.

117. Copleston, *A History of Philosophy*, vol. 3, 269.

118. Windelband, *A History of Philosophy*, 370.

119. Ibid.

120. Friedrich Ueberweg, *A History of Philosophy, From Thales to the Present Time*, vol. 1: *History of the Ancient and Mediaeval Philosophy*, 2nd ed. (London: Hodder & Stoughton, 1875), 476.

121. Windelband, *A History of Philosophy*, 370.

122. Ibid.

123. Ueberweg, *A History of Philosophy*, 473.

124. Ibid.

125. Buber, "Ein Wort über Nietzsche und die Lebenswerte," 13.

126. Martin Buber, "Über Jakob Boehme," 251.

127. Gustav Landauer, "Durch Absonderung zur Gemeinschaft," *Das Reich der Erlösung*, 2 (1901): 65, quoted in Mendes-Flohr, *From Mysticism to Dialogue*, 57.

128. Julius Hart, "Der neue Mensch, *Das Reich des Erfüllung*," 2 (1901): 27, quoted in Mendes-Flohr, *From Mysticism to Dialogue*, 57.

129. Mendes Flohr, *From Mysticism to Dialogue*, 57.

130. Ibid.

131. Empedocles: see Fragment 17; G. S. Kirk, J. E. Raven, and M. Schofield, *The Presocratic Philosophers*, 2nd ed. (Cambridge: Cambridge University Press, 1991), 287.

132. Buber, "Über Jakob Boehme," 252.

133. Jacob Boehme, *The Clavis or Key*, s. 199.

134. Martin Buber, "Distance and Relation," in *The Knowledge of Man*, 49–50.

135. Buber, "My Way to Hasidism," in *Hasidism and Modern Man*, 51.

136. On this point, see Gershom G. Scholem, *Major Trends in Jewish Mysticism* (New York: Schocken Books, 1974), 237f. Scholem comments that "Boehme, more than any other Christian mystic, shows the closest affinity to Kabbalism precisely where he is most original. He has, as it were, discovered the world of Sefiroth all over again." Ibid., 237.

137. Buber, "Über Jakob Boehme," 252.

138. Boehme, *Mysterium Magnum*, ch. 40, s. 8.

139. Ibid., ch. 1, s. 2.

140. Buber, "Über Jakob Boehme," 252. Note that Schopenhauer, whose influence on Buber will be considered later, identified a similarity between St. Francis and the Buddha Sakya Muni in their turning from prosperity to poverty. He adds, "In fact, it is worth mentioning that his relationship with the Indian spirit also appears in his great love for animals, and his frequent association with them, when he always calls them his sisters and brothers; and his beautiful *Cantico* is evidence of his inborn Indian spirit through the praise of the sun, moon, stars, wind, water, fire and earth." Arthur Schopenhauer, *The World as Will and Representation*, vol. 2 (New York: Dover, 1966), 614.

141. Ludwig Feuerbach, *Principles of the Philosophy of the Future* (Indianapolis: Bobbs-Merrill, 1966), 71.

142. Ludwig Feuerbach, *The Essence of Christianity* (New York: Harper & Bros., 1957), 13.

143. Buber, *Between Man and Man*, 147.

144. Feuerbach, *Principles of the Philosophy of the Future*, 71.

145. Buber, *Between Man and Man*, 148.

146. Buber, "Über Jakob Boehme," 252.

147. Friedman, *Martin Buber's Life and Work*, vol. 1, 78.

148. Buber, "Über Jakob Boehme," 252. Again, notice the similarity in this sentence with Buber's later views, particularly the emphasis not on union but on relation.

149. Detail from Buber's College Book in the Martin Buber Archives, ref. 350/6.

150. Schopenhauer, *The World as Will and Representation*, vol. 1, 353, par. 63.

151. Ibid., 102, par. 18.

152. Patrick Gardiner, *Schopenhauer* (Harmondsworth, U.K.: Penguin, 1967), 58.

153. Schopenhauer, *The World as Will and Representation*, vol. 2, 202.

154. Ibid., vol. 1, 110, par. 21.

155. Ibid., 162, par. 29

156. Ibid., 113, par. 23.

157. Buber, "Über Jakob Boehme," 252.

158. Ibid., 253.

159. Boehme, *Mysterium Magnum*, ch. 2, s. 6. This example is very similar to an event mentioned by Buber in *Daniel*, when a piece of mica is picked up and unity is experienced.

160. Ibid., ch. 6, s. 22.

161. Walsh, *The Mysticism of Innerworldly Fulfillment*, 115, n. 4.

162. Ibid.

163. Martin Buber, "Über Jakob Boehme," 253.

164. Ibid.

165. Schaeder, *The Hebrew Humanism of Martin Buber*, 62.

166. Ibid.

167. Friedman, *Martin Buber's Life and Work*, vol. 1, 79.

168. Buber, "Über Jakob Boehme," 253.

169. Ibid.

170. Martin Buber, *The Letters of Martin Buber*, 79.

171. Hans Urs von Balthasar, *The Glory of The Lord: A Theological Aesthetics*, vol. 4: *The Realm of Metaphysics in Antiquity* (Edinburgh: T. & T. Clark, 1989), 244.

172. His notes on Boehme and this essay were undoubtedly part of the basis for this work because he mentions the dissertation to Paula in a letter in August 1900. "For the present, I find the doctoral dissertation impossible, like something stiff. I am no good at drudgery." See *Letters*, 79.

173. Martin Buber, "Zur Geschichte des Individuationsproblems," ref. Arc. Ms. Var. 350/2–1c. This dissertation, including the introduction, extends to thirty-eight pages.

174. Ibid., Foreword, 2.

175. Ibid., 9–10.

176. Ibid., 12.

177. Ibid., 13.

178. See von Balthasar, *The Glory of the Lord*, 280f.

179. Martin Buber, "Zur Geschichte des Individuationsproblems," 29.

180. Ibid.

181. Franz Rosenzweig, "Aus Bubers Dissertation," *Aus Unbekannten Schriften: Festgabe für Martin Buber zum 50. Geburtstag* (Berlin: Verlag Lambert Schneider, 1928), 244.

182. Schopenhauer, *The World as Will and Representation*, vol. 1, 124.

CHAPTER 3: THE ONE THING NEEDFUL

1. Buber, "My Way to Hasidism," in *Hasidism and Modern Man*," 51–52.

2. Buber, "Foreword," in *Pointing the Way*, ix.

3. Buber, *On Judaism* (New York: Schocken Books, 1995).

4. Buber, "Judaism and Mankind," ibid., 32.

5. Buber, "Foreword," in *Pointing the Way*, x.

6. Martin Buber, "Foreword,'" in *Ecstatic Confessions*, xxxi.

7. Ibid.

8. Voegelin, "Experience and Symbolization in History," in *The Collected Works of Eric Voegelin, Vol. 12*, 124.

9. Joseph Maréchal, S.J., *Studies in the Psychology of the Mystics* (London: Burns Oates & Washbourne, 1927), 102.

10. Ibid., 102–3.

11. Bernard Lonergan, S.J., *Method in Theology* (London: Darton, Longman & Todd, 1972), 29.

12. Voegelin, "Reason: The Classic Experience," in *Anamnesis*, 96.

13. Evelyn Underhill, *Mysticism: A Study in the Nature and Development of Man's Spiritual Consciousness* (London: Methuen, 1949), 72.

14. Voegelin, "Reason: The Classic Experience," 94–95.

15. Buber, "Dialogue," in *Between Man and Man*, 13.

16. Buber, "Foreword," in *Pointing the Way*, ix.

17. Ibid.

18. Buber, "Ecstasy and Confession," in *Ecstatic Confessions*, 1.

19. Ibid.

20. Buber, "Über Jakob Boehme," 253.

21. Boehme, *The Clavis or Key*, s. 199.

22. Ibid., s. 204. This precept that each person should seek God in himself or herself was also used by Eckhart; see Schopenhauer, *The World as Will and Representation*, vol. 2 (Indian Hills, Colo.: Falcon's Wing Press, 1958), 612.

23. Martin Buber, "Ecstasy and Confession," 1.

24. Buber maintains the ideas of the concentration of the whole being and grace in both *Daniel* and *I and Thou*: Buber, *Daniel*, 10; *Daniel Dialogues on Realization* (New York: Holt, Rinehart and Winston, 1964), 51; *I and Thou*, 20 and 24.

25. Martin Buber, "Ecstasy and Confession," 2.

26. Martin Buber, "Zur Geschichte des Individuationsproblems," ref. Arc. Ms. Var. 350/2–1c, 38.

27. Martin Buber, "Ecstasy and Confession," 2.

28. Ibid., 3.

29. Martin Buber, "Dialogue," in *Between Man and Man*, 25.

30. Fritz Mauthner, *Wörterbuch der Philosophie, neue Beiträge zu einer Kritik der Sprache*, 2nd ed. (Munich and Leipzig: 1920), 2:131–32. Cited in P. Mendes-Flohr, "Editor's Introduction," in *Ecstatic Confessions*, xv. Wittgenstein was interested in Mauthner's theories. Note the idea of language games present in this quote.

31. Etienne Gilson, *Being and Some Philosophers*, 2nd ed. (Toronto: Pontifical Institute of Mediaeval Studies, 1961), 208.

32. Ibid.

33. Martin Buber, "Zur Geschichte des Individuationsproblems," 30.

34. Schopenhauer remarks that what is described in the *Veda* as "reunion with *Brahma*" (which is the union with the primal self, in Buber's terms) is described negatively by the Buddhists as *Nirvana*, which is the negation of this world, or of *Samsara*. "If *Nirvana* is defined as nothing, this means only that *Samsara* contains no single element that could serve to define or construct *Nirvana*," in *The World as Will and Representation*, vol. 2, 608.

35. Gilson, *Being and Some Philosophers*, 208.

36. Martin Buber, "From the tract 'Sister Katrei,'" in *Ecstatic Confessions*, 154.

37. Schopenhauer, *The World as Will and Representation*, vol. 2, 612.

38. Ibid., 613.

39. Voegelin, "Reason: The Classic Experience," 108.

40. Ibid., 96.

41. For the qualities of the Godhead, see Martin Buber, "Zur Geschichte des Individuationsproblems," 30. Eckhart's idea of the birth of God in the soul is implicit in Boehme's conception and is also relevant here. See Voegelin's discussion of Plato's *Timaeus* and the *anima mundi* in "Experience and Symbolization in History," 126–27.

42. Buber, "Ecstasy and Confession," 2.

43. Ibid., 2–3.

44. Ibid., 3.

45. Ibid.

46. Ibid.

47. Schopenhauer, *The World as Will and Representation*, vol. 2, 611. Schopenhauer remarks in a footnote that whoever has grasped that in this sphere all knowledge ceases will no longer regard it as excessively extravagant "that in many a passage of the *Upanishad* guidance is given to sink oneself, silently and inwardly uttering the mysterious *Om*, into the depths of one's own being, where subject and object and all knowledge vanish."

48. Buber, "What Is Common to All," in *The Knowledge of Man*, 87.

49. See "The Teaching of the Tao": "but in the Upanishads, too, the significance of the teaching of the Atman does not lie in the fact that a statement is made thereby about the unity of being, but that what one calls being is nothing other than the unity of the self and that the unified one thereby encounters the world as being, as unity, as his self," in Buber, "The Teaching of the Tao," in *Pointing the Way*, 37. "Brahman" is a mystical concept used in the Upanishads to express the source from which all phenomenal existents spring and to which they all in the end return. See Gardiner, *Schopenhauer*, 294.

50. Buber, "Ecstasy and Confession," 3.

51. Ibid., 4.

52. Ibid., 8.

53. John of the Cross, "The Ascent of Mount Carmel," book 2, ch. 5, in *The Collected Works of Saint John of the Cross* (Washington D.C.: ICS, 1991), 165.

54. Vernon Gregson, *Lonergan, Spirituality, and the Meeting of Religions* (Lanham, Md.: University Press of America, 1985) 82.

55. Buber, "Foreword," in *Pointing the Way*, ix.

56. See Hans Kohn's comment on this: "*Er hat das ekstatische Erlebnis und damit Welt und Gott völlig in das Ich, verlegt, hat es, das doch nur ein Pol des Geschehens, ein Pfeiler der Spannung ist, verabsolutiert.*" Kohn, *Martin Buber: Sein Werk und Seine Zeit*, 116. See also Kohn's disagreement with Buber regarding the transcendent in a letter to Buber, 14 November 1912.

57. Gregson, *Lonergan, Spirituality, and The Meeting of Religions*, 85.

58. Buber, "Ecstasy and Confession," 4.

59. Buber, "From the Mahabharatam," in *Ecstatic Confessions*, 143.

60. Ibid., 144. Note Buber's understanding of *Mana* (effective force/power) that leads the way to the Brahman, in *I and Thou*, 34–35. The primal experience of Mana is "that which effects," from which come the primal words I–affecting–Thou and Thou–affecting–I.

61. Buber, "Über Jakob Boehme," 253.

62. Buber, "Ecstasy and Confession," 6.

63. Ibid., 6.

64. Ibid., 9.

65. Ibid.

66. Ibid., 6. Buber will return to the understanding of knowledge as the coordinate system of space, time, and causality in *Daniel*.

67. Ibid., 7.

68. Buber will refer to the star as the source of meaning and illumination in *Daniel*.

69. Buber, "Ecstasy and Confession," 7.

70. Ibid., 10.

71. In the "Foreword," xxxii, to *Ecstatic Confessions*, Buber mentions that he speaks not of words that are beautifully put together, but of the Word: "This is another beauty than that of the aesthetic: the voice of the human being sounding in my ears . . . those who dared to tell of that abyss. I live with them; I hear their voices, their voice: the voice of the human being."

72. Ibid., 4.

73. Ibid., 7–8.

74. Ibid.

75. Ibid., 8.

76. Ibid., 10.

77. Martin Buber, "Introduction" to *The Legend of the Baal-Shem* (Princeton: Princeton University Press, 1995), 11.

78. Martin Buber, "Myth in Judaism," in *On Judaism*, 104. Note that Buber reinterprets the original definition that he gives from Plato: a narrative of some divine event described as corporeal reality; see 95.

79. Buber, "Ecstasy and Confession," 10.

80. Ibid., 10–11.

81. Ibid., 11.

82. Kohn, *Martin Buber: Sein Werk und Seine Zeit*, 305, note to p. 71.

83. Buber, "Introduction" to *The Legend of the Baal-Shem*, 13.

84. Buber expresses the call in this way in "What is Man?" in *Between Man and Man*, 166.

85. The "Word," according to Eckhart, is uttered by God in the ground of the soul: it is the birth of God in the soul. The "Word" may also be considered as an insight into the process of reality.

86. Buber, "Afterword," in *Between Man and Man*, 213.

87. Martin Buber, "The Spirit of the Orient and Judaism," in *On Judaism*, 57.

88. Ibid., 62.

89. Ibid., 69.

90. Ibid., 60–61.

91. Ibid., 62.

92. Ibid., 45.

93. Martin Buber, "The Teaching of the Tao," 42–43.

94. Ibid., 44–45.

95. Ibid., 58.

96. Heraclitus, "Fragment 50," in *The Presocratic Philosophers*, 187.

97. Ibid.

98. Ibid., 190, Fragment 67.

99. Kirk, Raven, and Schofield, *The Presocratic Philosophers*, 191.

100. Ibid., 203, Fragment 32.

101. Martin Buber, "The Teaching of the Tao," 45–46.

102. Ibid., 46. Buber refers to Lao-tzu as L.

103. Ibid. 49.

104. Ibid., 48.

105. Ibid., 49–50.

106. Jonathan Herman, "I and Tao, Buber's Chuang Tzu and the Comparative Study of Mysticism," in *Martin Buber and the Human Sciences* (State University of New York Press, 1996), 125.

107. Buber, *I and Thou*, 24.

108. Robert Wood, "Oriental Themes in Buber's Work," in *Martin Buber: A Centenary Volume*, 333.

109. Martin Buber, "The Teaching of the Tao," 47.

110. Ibid., 48.

111. Ibid., 51–52.

112. Ibid., 50.

113. Ibid.

114. Ibid., 49.

115. Ibid., 50.

116. Ibid.

117. Ibid., 56.

118. Eric Voegelin, *Order and History, Volume 2: The World of the Polis*, (Baton Rouge: Louisiana State University Press, 1991), 235.

119. Martin Buber, "The Spirit of the Orient and Judaism," 60.

120. Voegelin, *Order and History, Volume 2: The World of the Polis*, 226.

121. Martin Buber, "The Teaching of the Tao," 52.

122. Ibid., 53.

123. Ibid., 54. Note the emergence here of Buber's movement toward the distinction between orientation and realization present in *Daniel*. Buber expands on this understanding in his essay "Productivity and Existence," [1914] in *Pointing the Way*, 5–10.

124. Note Wood's comment that for the ancient roots of the Western tradition, "My most private acts affect the totality, not simply in terms of the direct or indirect effects of my overt acts, but in terms of what has been called 'winning God's blessing for the world,' the deepest theological rationale for the contemplative life." Wood, "Oriental Themes in Buber's Work," 333.

125. Buber, "The Teaching of the Tao," 54–55.

126. Ibid., 55.

127. Ibid., 40

128. Ibid.

129. Ibid.

130. Note the relation of this prelinguistic position to Buber's comment regarding the undivided word in *I and Thou*: "Only silence before the *Thou*—silence of all tongues, silent patience in the undivided word that precedes the formed and vocal response—leaves the *Thou* free, and permits man to take his stand with it in the reserve where the spirit is not manifest, but *is*." See *I*

and Thou, 58. The spirit is an ontological presence; what is present is not merely a manifestation.

131. Jonathan Herman finds "proto-dialogical" thought in the fact that the parable does not arise directly from the oneness, but is mediated through the existential multiplicities in which oneness inheres. This "develops a concept of unity that is compatible with and actually demands a world of individuated phenomena in genuine relation with one another." See Herman, "I and Tao, Buber's Chuang Tzu and the Comparative Study of Mysticism," in *Martin Buber and the Human Sciences*, 119.

132. Martin Buber, "The Teaching of the Tao," 35.

133. See Buber's example in *I and Thou*, 60.

134. Martin Buber, "The Teaching of the Tao," 36. See also *I and Thou*, 148 and 151f.

135. Martin Buber, "The Teaching of the Tao," 37.

136. Ibid., 37.

137. Ibid., 44.

138. This is the One for Plotinus: the first principle that is above being. Also note that for Plotinus, "To be and to know are one and the same thing." One is not the being of all things as it is no being, no thing. See Gilson, *Being and Some Philosophers*, 25.

139. Boehme, *The Clavis or Key*, 9, ss. 17–26.

140. This unity is Spinoza's concept of substance, i.e., God.

141. Gilson, *Being and Some Philosophers*, 28.

142. Schaeder, *The Hebrew Humanism of Martin Buber*, 50.

143. Buber, "Jewish Religiosity," in *On Judaism*, 80.

144. Ibid., 86.

145. Buber, "Jewish Religiosity," 94: "For God does not want to be believed in, to be debated and defended by us, but simply to be realised through us." I use Bergman's translation of this phrase as he used the original text in which this address was first published: *Vom Geist des Judentums*. Hugo Bergman, "Martin Buber and Mysticism," in *The Philosophy of Martin Buber*, 301.

146. Buber, "Judaism and the Jews," in *On Judaism*, 12. This reference to "the absolute" was subsequently changed to "the unconditioned" (*zum Unbedingten*), see Mendes-Flohr, *From Mysticism to Dialogue*, 164, n. 298.

147. Buber, "Judaism and the Jews," in *On Judaism*, 12.

148. Ibid., 13–14.

149. Ibid., 14.

150. Ibid., 15.

151. Ibid. In his "Introduction" to *On Judaism*, xiii, Rodger Kamenetz comments: "Writing within the dominant discourse of his time with its emphasis on racial stereotypes, he [Buber] treads dangerously close to racial theories that in the hands of nazis like Alfred Rosenberg proved disastrous to the Jewish people. But one has to see his purpose. Buber was seeking a basis in blood—in genetics—for an abiding mystery that he sensed but could not yet explain: the continuing spiritual quest of the Jewish people that has survived centuries of defeat and persecution."

152. Ibid., 15–16.

153. Mendes-Flohr, *From Mysticism to Dialogue*, 165–66, n. 321.

154. "*Denn wie die Juden der Urväterzeit, um sich aus der Entzweiung ihrer Seele . . . zu befreien, sich ganz an den nichtentzweiten, den einen einheitlichen Gott hingaben, so sollen wir, die wir in einer besonderen Zweiheit stehen, uns daraus befreien, nicht durch Hingabe an einen Gott, den wir nicht mehr wirklich zu machen vermögen*, sondern durch Hingabe an den Grund unseres Wesens, an die Einheit der Substanz in uns." Cited by Mendes-Flohr, ibid., 166. (Emphasis added by Mendes-Flohr.)

155. Buber, "Judaism and the Jews," in *On Judaism*, 15.

156. Ibid.

157. Buber later recognized this and wrote: "But when . . . something is taking place between heaven and earth, one misses everything when one insists on discovering within earthly thought the power that unveils the mystery. He who refuses to submit himself to the effective reality of the transcendence as such—our *vis-à-vis*—contributes to the human responsibility for the eclipse." Martin Buber, "Religion and Reality," in *Eclipse of God: Studies in the Relation between Religion and Philosophy* (New York: Humanity Books, 1999), 23.

158. Buber, "Judaism and the Jews," 19–20.

159. Ibid., 20.

160. Ibid., 21.

161. Buber, "Jewish Religiosity," 80.

162. Voegelin, "The Eclipse of Reality," in *The Collected Works of Eric Voegelin, Vol. 28: What is History? And Other Late Unpublished Writings*, 126. Friedrich Schiller, *Historischen Schriften* (Weimar, 1970), 370. Cited by Voegelin, 128.

163. Ibid.

164. Ibid., 129–130.

165. Martin Buber, "Judaism and Mankind," in *On Judaism*, 23.

166. Ibid., 25.

167. Ibid., 26–27.

168. Ibid., 27.

169. Immanuel Kant, *Critique of Pure Reason*, A 574–80 [B 602–8] (London: Macmillan, 1964). See also Kant's Introduction to *Lectures on Philosophical Theology* (London: Cornell University Press, 1978).

170. Martin Buber, "Renewal of Judaism," in *On Judaism*, 40.

171. Ibid.

172. Ibid., 41. Fackenheim refers to this passage when he makes the comment: "Had Buber retained the standpoint indicated in this passage he could without doubt have mustered, as a historian, the imagination necessary in order to understand the Biblical belief in revelation; but he would have at the same time asserted, as a philosopher, that what was to Biblical man a dialogue with God was in fact a form of human self-realisation and nothing else; that is a disguised monologue." Emil L. Fackenheim, "Martin Buber's Concept of Revelation," in *The Philosophy of Martin Buber*, 278.

173. Buber, "Judaism and Mankind," 32.

174. Buber, "Renewal of Judaism," 42.

175. Ibid.

176. Kant, *Critique of Pure Reason*, A 333, B 390.

177. Buber, "Renewal of Judaism," 42.

178. Ibid., 32.
179. Buber, *The Letters of Martin Buber*, letter to Landauer, 9 August 1913, 150. Buber again refers to this, saying so in a letter to Rosenzweig in 1922, see *Letters*, 275. Then he writes that the *est* sounds tremendously pagan.
180. Buber, "Judaism and Mankind," 32.
181. Ibid., 33.
182. Buber, "Preface to the 1923 Edition," in *On Judaism*, 8.
183. Ibid., 8–9.
184. Martin Buber, "Myth in Judaism," 101.
185. Martin Buber, "Zur Geschichte des Individuationsproblems," 31.
186. Martin Buber, "Myth in Judaism," 101.
187. Ibid., 102.
188. Ibid., 103.
189. Ibid., 103.
190. Ibid., 104. See Buber's discussion in *I and Thou*, 33–37.
191. Martin Buber, "Myth in Judaism," 104.
192. Ibid.
193. Martin Buber, *I and Thou*, 33.
194. Martin Buber, "Myth in Judaism," 106.
195. Martin Buber, "With a Monist," in *Pointing the Way*, 28.
196. Bergman, "Martin Buber and Mysticism," in *The Philosophy of Martin Buber*, 298.
197. Gershom Scholem, *Major Trends in Jewish Mysticism* (New York: Schocken Books, 1974), 12.
198. Buber, "My Way to Hasidism," in *Hasidism and Modern Man*, 41.

CHAPTER 4: REALIZATION

1. Gustav Landauer's letter to Martin Buber, 9 September 1912, *Letters of Martin Buber*, 136–37.
2. Ibid.
3. Buber, *Daniel*, ix. Friedman wrote the required introduction. Although Friedman mentions that *Insel Verlag* first published *Daniel* in 1913, he does not explicitly state that it is the first edition that he translated.
4. Buber, *Daniel: Gespräche von der Verwirklichung*, title page.
5. Kohn, *Martin Buber: Sein Werk und Seine Zeit*, 124.
6. Copleston, *A History of Philosophy*, 2:117.
7. Buber, *Between Man and Man*, 184–85.
8. Oliver Davies, trans. introduction to *Meister Eckhart: Selected Writings* (London: Penguin, 1994), xxiv.
9. Ibid. See "On the Noble Man"; Sermon 13 of "Selected German Sermons"; and Sermon 2 of "Selected Latin Sermons." In his essay on "The Altar," in which Buber writes of the triptych painted by Matthias Grünewald: "But it is more powerful than any church, like the sermons of Meister Eckhart who preached two centuries before in the same Alsatian cloisters. These two, Eckhart and Matthias are brothers and their teachings are fraternally related." See "The Altar," [1914] in Buber, *Pointing the Way*, 16.
10. Davies, "Introduction" to *Meister Eckhart: Selected Writings*, xxviii.

11. Ibid., xxvi.

12. Ibid.

13. Ibid., xxix

14. Ibid., xxxi.

15. Kohn, *Martin Buber: Sein Werk und seine Zeit*, 124.

16. Sydney Rome and Beatrice Rome, eds. *Philosophical Interrogations* (New York: Holt, Rinehart and Winston, 1964), 21.

17. Buber, *Daniel: Gespräche von der Verwirklichung*, 151.

18. I will refer to pages in the 1919 Leipzig edition throughout by the use of brackets [ ] in my text. References to Friedman's translation will immediately follow the German references in braces { }. Although this method is cumbersome, I consider it essential, as the early German edition is not easily available.

19. What Buber called Nietzsche's pseudo-mystery of the "eternal return of the same" may underlie this position. See "Autobiographical Fragments," 13.

20. I suggest this is a reference to Kant's discussion of the conditions of knowledge in the *Critique of Pure Reason* [A24 B38]: "we can never represent to ourselves the absence of space, though we can quite well think it as empty of objects." See Buber's autobiographical fragment on the "Philosophers," in which he recalls trying to imagine the edge of space as a teenager. His liberation at that time came from reading Kant.

21. See the image in the story "Revelation," in *The Legend of the Baal-Shem*, 71–72.

22. Martin Buber, "Ecstasy and Confession," 4.

23. Aristotle, *Physics*, 257b2–13.

24. Davies, "Meister Eckhart: An Introduction to his Life and Thought," in *Meister Eckhart: Selected Writings*, xxviii.

25. Ibid.

26. Meister Eckhart, "Sermon 30," in *Meister Eckhart: Selected Writings*, 249.

27. The full sentence is: *'Denn was ist es, dass wir uns ausgeliefert fühlen, da doch die Macht unseres Lebens bestätigt ist mit unsterblichen Siegeln?'*

28. This example may have been suggested by Buber's attempt to understand the moment when his mother made the decision to leave their house in Vienna. This house was over the Danube canal, and Buber recalls looking at the canal with a feeling of certainty that nothing could happen to him. Buber, "Autobiographical Fragments," 4.

29. I suggest this is a reference to Buber's own way, particularly that time in his journey when he began university in Vienna and "his spirit was in steady and multiple movement, in an alternation of tension and release, determined by manifold influences, taking ever new shape, but without centre and without growing substance: it was really the '*Olam-ha-Tohu*,' the 'World of Confusion,' the mythical dwelling place of the wandering souls." Martin Buber, "My Way to Hasidism," 48–49.

30. This example may be compared with the knowledge of a tree in *I and Thou*, 19–20.

31. The second sentence in this passage is omitted by Friedman: *"Nicht mit der Richtung des aufnehmenden Geistes allein—die könnte dir nur den*

Sinn der lebenden gestaltung eröffnen: viel, nicht alles." Together with the previous sentence, it indicates that Buber is attempting to move beyond Kant's epistemology. The omission of this sentence and the phrase noted below obscures Kant's influence on Buber.

32. This account can be compared to Schopenhauer's elaboration of aesthetic consciousness and his description of the aesthetic experience of a tree, in which "its pure significance, its innermost being" is disclosed to the subject of knowing. See *The World as Will and Representation*, vol. 1, 209–210. Buber attended a seminar on Schopenhauer's *The World as Will and Representation* with Prof. Dr. Paul Barth at the University of Leipzig from 1897 to 1898. See Buber's Collegien-Buch, No.1292, Martin Buber Archives, Ms.350/6. Buber refers the reader of his doctoral dissertation to *The World as Will and Representation*.

33. This I believe to be a reference to the often-cited phrase from Kant's *Critique of Pure Reason*: "Thoughts without content are empty, intuitions without content are blind." *Critique of Pure Reason*, trans. N. Kemp Smith (London: Macmillan, 1964), 93.

34. In appreciating Kant's influence, it is helpful to note the following comment by Buber regarding the impossibility of liberating himself from this influence: "That I have not been able to do so probably lies in the fact that no one has yet been able to explain to me what, for example, the hardness in the bark of a lime tree means independently of my perception of the hardness. I simply do not succeed in understanding the existing lime tree as the sum of my perceptions of it. Even the otherwise useful symbols of the physicist are incapable of helping me here." Rome and Rome, *Philosophical Interrogations*, 21.

35. A similar movement is the love in which the other person is loved for the lover's sake and not for his or her own sake. This comparison is appropriate when Buber's misguided notion of "embracing love" is considered.

36. Schopenhauer wrote that music "gives the innermost kernel preceding all form, of the heart of things . . . music expresses in an exceedingly universal language, in a homogeneous material, that is, in mere tones, and with the greatest distinctness and truth, the inner being, the in-itself, of the world, which we think of under the concept of will, according to its most distinct manifestation." *The World as Will and Representation*, vol. 1, 263–64.

37. Schopenhauer remarks that "melody alone has significant and intentional connexion from beginning to end." It is this significant and intentional connection that is expressed by the action of the inborn direction of the person according to Buber. As will become evident later, Buber agrees with Schopenhauer when he continues: "Consequently, it [the melody] relates the story of the intellectually enlightened will, the copy or impression whereof in actual life is the series of its deeds." Ibid., 259.

38. Immortality, freedom of the soul, and the One are the key Kantian themes with which Buber is concerned.

39. The third part of the sentence beginning, "It surrenders itself" is omitted by Friedman: *'die ihren Willen erziehn, statt dem Wirbel einem geordneten System der Ursächlichkeiten und Zweckhaftigkeiten zu begegnen und sich ihm einzuordnen,'* i.e., from "which educate its will" to "fit into it."

40. Meister Eckhart's statement that "the soul receives nothing from God nor from creatures, since she it is who contains herself and receives all things from herself" is relevant here. However, as the "soul and the Godhead are one," it is the power of God that is present in the soul and which makes the movement. Eckhart explains that the person in spiritual death—in which all desire, images, understanding, and form is stripped away—cannot move herself, just as a corpse cannot move itself, it is the Godhead who lives as no one other than itself. See "Sermon 30," *Selected Writings*, 248–49. This notion of spiritual death is connected to Buber's notion of the movement into the Nothingness that we will meet later.

41. Friedman omits the last phrase, i.e., "*und sie entsetzten sich über die Notwendigkeit.*" The reference here may be to Hume's critique of causality and Kant's response to it.

42. Schopenhauer argued that the same will is recognized in men and animals in the force by which the crystal is formed, the force that shoots and vegetates in the plant and the force that turns the magnet to the North Pole. See *The World as Will and Representation*, vol. 1, 110. Buber makes a distinction between that which must obey, as each magnet needle must point north, and that which commands and chooses its unique direction.

43. I disagree with Friedman's translation {58} of this passage. The German text reads: "*Aber sie läst sich ja nur in Taten, nicht in Worten sagen, und sie bekundet sich nur durch ihr Werk: sie, die mich am Morgen emporreisst und in die Wüste treibt, die mich am Mittag heimsucht und zu den lebendigen schickt, die am Abend meine hand fasst und mich zu Gott geleitet: die hohe Herrin meiner All-Einsamkeit*" [21–22]. *Herrin* is clearly mistress rather than Lord and refers to direction and not God.

44. Martensen, *Jacob Boehme*, 6.

45. Friedman, 63, omits "*auf die braune Bank unter dem Ahorn,*" on "the brown bench under the maple tree."

46. This is also the key to Husserl's problem of intersubjectivity. Buber's later correction of this position is the reason that his dialogical thought can make a contribution to this issue. See "Fifth Meditation," in Edmund Husserl, *Cartesian Meditations: An Introduction to Phenomenology*, trans. D. Cairns (The Hague: Martinus Nijhoff, 1960), 89–157. See also Alfred Schutz, "The Problem of Transcendental Intersubjectivity in Husserl" in *Alfred Schutz: Collected Papers III, Studies in Phenomenological Philosophy* (The Hague: Martinus Nijhoff, 1970), 51–91. See also the significant point that Simone de Beauvoir makes in her *Ethics of Ambiguity*: "the me-other relationship is as indissoluble as the subject-object relationship"; see discussion and citation of this phrase in Jo-Ann Pilardi, *Simone de Beauvoir Writing the Self: Philosophy becomes Autobiography* (Westport, Conn.: Praeger, 1999), 16.

47. Kant notes the twofold relation of the human being to him- or herself: "Firstly, we can regard ourselves as belonging to the 'world of sense' and subject to the universal laws of nature; secondly, we can regard ourselves as belonging to the 'intelligible world' where the only laws to which we are subject are those founded on and prescribed by 'reason.'" As the latter, we can consider ourselves to be "things-in themselves," or *noumena*, and as such to be free. Gardiner remarks that Schopenhauer considered this to be the point at which Kant's philosophy led to his. Gardiner, *Schopenhauer*, 57.

48. This is the foundation for the twofold attitude of the human being to the world in *I and Thou.*

49. Schopenhauer states that when the ordinary person who is incapable of "a consideration of things wholly disinterested in every sense" is presented with anything, "he quickly looks merely for the concept under which it is to be brought, just as the lazy man looks for a chair, which then no longer interests him." *The World as Will and Representation,* vol. 1, 187. Gardiner adds a helpful comment: "to look at objects in this manner, simply as instances of familiar concepts, is to adhere to principles of selection and comparison established solely with an eye to convenience or utility; in consequence, everything is distorted, adulterated—'in the mind of a man who is filled with his own aims the world appears as a beautiful landscape appears on the plan of a battlefield.'" The last quote is from Schopenhauer, ibid., vol. 2, 381. See Gardiner, *Schopenhauer,* 193.

50. Buber and many other young people in Vienna, in the early days of the new century, shared this opposition to orientation. It led, as I have already discussed, to his involvement with the *Neue Gemeinschaft.* In an essay published in 1914, Buber wrote: "Artifice has so much got the upper hand that the fictitious dares to usurp the place of the real. The overvaluation of productivity that is afflicting our age has so thrived and its pan-technical glance has set up a senseless exclusiveness of its own that even genuinely creative men allow their organic skills to degenerate into an autonomous growth to satisfy the demand of the day." See "Productivity and Existence," in *Pointing the Way,* 8. Note also the similarity of Buber's thought to Heraclitus's understanding that the one divine law nourishes human laws (Fragment 114). Heraclitus and Buber indicate awareness of the danger if this connection is broken, and human laws or science rule autonomously.

51. Friedman translates this phrase as "which creates out of the life-experience of reality." This translation hides the assertion that reality is created through realization and does not make sense in the light of the following question.

52. In 1917, Buber wrote to the International Institute for Philosophy in Amsterdam on creating new words: "The generation, the creation of words is for me one of the most mysterious processes of the life of the spirit. Indeed, I confess to my insight there is no *essential* difference between what I here call the creation of words and that which has been called the coming forward of the Logos. The coming into being of words is a mystery that is consummated in the enkindled, open soul of the world-producing, world-discovering man. Only such a word engendered in the spirit can become creative in man. . . . What is needed is not teaching the use of new words but fighting the misuse of the great old words." Martin Buber, *A Believing Humanism,* 31.

53. See Eric Voegelin's argument on this point in *Order and History, Vol. 5: In Search of Order* (Baton Rouge: Louisiana State University Press, 1987), 26.

54. See Buber's comment in "Ecstasy and Confession," the introduction to *Ecstatic Confessions,* 10.

55. As discussed, Buber explicitly refers to the Heraclitean logos in his essay, "The Teaching of the Tao," 45 and 58.

230 / Notes to Pages 130–135

56. Dilthey's understanding of historical consciousness is evident here.

57. This is not the end of a paragraph in the 1919 edition as it is in the English translation.

58. See section on Responsibility in "Dialogue," *Between Man and Man*, 16–17.

59. This principle is retained in *I and Thou*, see 88.

60. I have already referred to Buber's interest in the phrase, "the one thing needful." Eckhart, commenting on the verse from Luke 10:42, states, "That is why Christ says: 'Only one thing is necessary.' But what is this one thing? It is God. This is what all creatures need, for if God took back what is his, all creatures would fall into nothingness." Meister Eckhart, "Sermon 21," in *Meister Eckhart, Selected Writings*, 199.

61. The philosophical principle used here by Buber is the "*inquantum*" maxim that was also used by Eckhart: "According to Eckhart the principle which prevents the being of all creatures from collapsing into a pantheistic identity with God is the fact that properties exist in a mixed state in individual beings while they are wholly united within God. This is expressed as the *inquantum* maxim, which means 'in so far as.' Thus a man or woman who is 'good' is wholly identical with 'goodness' itself but only *in so far as* they are 'good.' In so far as we are 'just,' we are 'justice' itself, but Eckhart well knows that 'justice' is only one among many elements which constitute the human person." See Oliver Davies, introduction, in *Meister Eckhart, Selected Writings*, xxiv.

62. Judging by Buber's references to Jesus in "The Teaching of the Tao" and in *I and Thou* (90), this epithet and the whole paragraph in which it occurs could be applied to Jesus [40–41]{70–71}.

63. Buber discusses "meaning" in the next dialogue.

64. This is a reference to Ezekiel 33:1–6, in which God appoints Ezekiel as Watchman: "The Lord spoke to me. 'Mortal man,' he said, 'tell your people what happens when I bring war to a land. The people of that country choose one of their number to be a watchman. When he sees the enemy approaching, he sounds the alarm to warn everyone. If someone hears it but pays no attention and the enemy comes and kills him, then he is to blame for his own death. His death is his own fault, because he paid no attention to the warning. If he had paid attention, he could have escaped. If, however, the watchman sees the enemy coming and does not sound the alarm, the enemy will come and kill those sinners, but I will hold the watchman responsible for their death.'"

65. This analogy is used by Boehme.

66. "*Denn alles Erlebnis ist ein Traum von verbundenheit; die orientierung zerscheidet und entfondert, die Realisierung vollzieht und proklamiert sie. So ist alle Wirklichkeit erfüllte Verbundenheit; nichts Einzelnes ist in sich wirklich; alles Einzelne ist nur Voraussetzung. Die schöpferischen Stunden, handelnde und schauende, bildende und denkende, sind die verbindenden Stunden; ein verbundener ist der Held und der Weise, der Dichter und der Prophet; Kommunion heisst sein Mysterium, und er ist wirklich, weil er an dem Wirklichen teilhat weil er in den Zeiten seiner Höhe eines Wirklichen Teil ist. Nicht ist ein Etwas für ihn wirklich, sondern mit ihm; aus seinem Erleben stieg Wirklichkeit auf, die ihn umfasst.*" My translation of the last

part of this quotation differs from Friedman's. The subject of the last part of the penultimate sentence is the creative person, it is he who acts in the creative hours, he who is the hero, etc., communion names his mystery and he is real because he shares in the real, especially at those moments of intensified experience. Friedman's translation: "Communion is its mystery, and it is actual because it shares in the real, because in the times when it is highest, it is a real part." However, the "it" in this sentence could only refer to "die wesenhafte Gestalt" or "Wirklichkeit," both of which are feminine nouns. Buber's text clearly refers to "er." The paragraph as a whole is concerned with him with whom things are real and this is the point to which Buber returns at the end.

67. This is the kernel of Buber's later notion of the twofold principle of human life: distance and relation. Note the influence of Boehme's principles of struggle and love involving a tension overcome in unity. Eckhart states that when the soul moves from all multiplicity into the highest spiritual death, she can neither present an image nor a particular manner of being to anyone else, since her spirit is buried in the Godhead and the Godhead lives as no one other than itself. Thus the soul shares in the reality of God, the soul is God, and all selfhood is lost. Meister Eckhart, "Sermon 30," *Selected Writings*, 248–49.

68. On the distinction between information and revelation, see Voegelin, "The Gospel and Culture," in *The Collected Works of Eric Voegelin, Vol.12*, 202.

69. This desire recalls Nicodemus's conversation with Jesus in John 3:1–8. It reflects the desire that everyone may experience the birth of God in his or her soul as outlined by Eckhart.

70. See Walter Kaufmann's comment on "*unmittelbar*" in his translation of *I and Thou*, 62, n. 7.

71. Martin Buber, "Hasidism and Modern Man," in *Hasidism and Modern Man*, 20.

72. Ibid., 21.

73. Ibid., 23.

74. Wilhelm Dilthey, "Drafts for a Critique of Historical Reason," *W. Dilthey, Selected Writings*, 208.

75. Ibid., 213.

76. Friedman states that "Reinold's experience clearly was not Buber's," as Buber had encountered the abyss at four when he knew that his mother was not coming back, and again at twelve and at fourteen; "yet there can be no doubt that in Reinold's experience Buber created a vehicle for the communication of his own experience." Friedman, *Martin Buber's Life and Work, The Early Years, 1878–1923*, 155. However, Buber did suffer from a severe nervous illness in 1902 when he was twenty-four: see letter to Chaim Weizmann, 12 Dec. 1902. During this illness, it was very difficult for him to do any work. In a further letter on 23 January 1903, Buber states that he is an "everlasting feverish suspense" regarding obtaining enough money for his family. He ends by mentioning the abyss that no one else can understand: "At almost every moment I feel the abyss right under my feet.—But enough of this—no one else, not even one's best friend, can understand and truly sympathise in this manner." See *Letters of Martin Buber*, 86 and 89.

77. Schopenhauer writes that the person whose eyes are clouded by the veil of Maya "sees not the inner nature of things, which is one, but its phenomena as separated, detached, innumerable, very different and indeed opposed." See *The World as Will and Representation*, vol. 1, 352.

78. The references to the biblical account in Genesis of the Garden of Eden are implicit: the garden in which the dialogue takes place is a reference to the garden in Genesis 2:8; Reinold comes to visit Daniel in the morning, what he seeks is what Augustine called "morning knowledge," in which all creatures are known in God, that is without any distinctions. This "morning knowledge" of oneness is prior to the knowledge of good and evil. See Meister Eckhart, "On the Noble Man," in *Selected Writings*, 105 and note 11, 283. In his "Religion as Presence Lectures," Buber clarifies the connection between "meaning" and "good and evil," see 37.

79. Eckhart refers to the "spark of the soul" that is untouched by any createdness as "a strange land, a wilderness, being more nameless than with name, more unknown than known," *Selected Writings*, 129. That Buber is drawing on Eckhart's notion of the birth of God in the soul will be clarified in the next few pages of this chapter.

80. See Schopenhauer's account of the person sitting in a small boat in a stormy sea that is boundless in every direction. He compares this experience with the person, in the midst of a world full of suffering and misery, calmly sitting supported by and trusting the *principium individuationis*. "His vanishing person, his extensionless present, his momentary gratification, these alone have reality for him; and he does everything to maintain them so long as his eyes are not opened to a better knowledge." *The World as Will and Representation*, vol. 1, 352–53.

81. Friedman omits this sentence "*Soll ich den Sturm meiner Erkenntnis einer Formel untertan machen, dass sie ihn prüfe und verwerfe?*" The storm of knowledge is that referred to by Reinold when he says that even though he left the storm behind at sea, "it was as though I now left the last, fearful [*bangen*] hiding place of calm and entered into the harsh storm that would never end."

82. Schopenhauer states that the *principium individuationis* supports the person as long as "his eyes are not opened by a better knowledge. Till then, there lives only in the innermost depths of his consciousness the wholly obscure presentiment that all this [the boundless world full of suffering] is indeed not really so strange to him, but has a connexion with him from which the *principium individuationis* cannot protect him. From this presentiment arises that ineradicable *dread*, common to all human beings (and possibly even to the more intelligent animals) which suddenly seizes them, when by any chance they become puzzled over the *principium individuationis*, in that the principle of sufficient reason in one or other of its forms seems to undergo an exception." *The World as Will and Representation*, vol. 1, 353.

83. Schopenhauer writes of the unity of the will, which is a metaphysical unity: "Consequently, knowledge of it is transcendent; that is to say, it does not rest on the functions of our intellect, and is therefore not to be really grasped with them. The result is that this unity opens to consideration an abyss whose depth no longer grants an entirely clear and systematically connected insight, but only isolated glances that enable us to recognise this unity

in this or that relation of things, now in the subjective, now in the objective." *The World as Will and Representation*, vol. 2, 323.

84. In "The Religion as Presence Lectures," Buber retains and expands the importance of the confirmation of meaning and the call to put it into practice in one's life. However, these are the fruits of revelation.

85. See "Ecstasy and Confession," 9: "And still more arbitrary seems the content of the confession of the ecstatic, especially when he has not experienced in his own soul the tragedy that takes place when the drive for expression of the innermost and most personal meets the given language of human beings: that battle of the irrational with the rational, which ends without victory or defeat, in a scrap of paper with writing on it, which to the seeing eye bears the seal of a great suffering."

86. See *I and Thou*, 17.

87. The phrase "God cannot realise himself to man otherwise than as the innermost presence of a life-experience" encapsulates the paradox of God becoming in his creatures present in the motto from Scotus Eriugena. It translates: "*da ja Gott dem Menschen sich nicht anders verwirklichen kann, denn als die innerste Gegenwart eines Erlebnisses.*" Schaeder translates this as "God can be realised by man only as the innermost presence of a lived experience." See *The Hebrew Humanism of Martin Buber*, 114. Bergman states: "For man, God cannot become fulfilled or realised in any other way than through the innermost presence of an experience." "Martin Buber and Mysticism," in *The Philosophy of Martin Buber*, 299.

88. For Schopenhauer, the separation of the individual from the rest of the world "lies only in the phenomenon and not in the thing-in-itself; and precisely on this rests eternal justice." *The World as Will and Representation*, vol. 1, 353.

89. See Buber's statement on evolution in "Renewal of Judaism": "Man's spirit has been as greatly depressed by the sense of inescapable evolution as it had once been depressed by the sense of inescapable predestination, induced by Calvinism. The extinction of heroic, unconditional living in our time must to a great extent be ascribed to this sense." *On Judaism*, 34.

90. The wanderer may be based on Nietzsche's Zarathustra. Nietzsche's rhyme, "The Closest One," is relevant here: "The closest one from me I bar: Away and up with him, and far! How else could he become my star?" *The Gay Science with a Prelude in German Rhymes and an Appendix of Songs*, ed. B. Williams (Cambridge: Cambridge University Press, 2001), 16.

91. As mentioned earlier, Buber also referred to the illumination of one's journey by the presence of a star in "Ecstasy and Confession." Note also Buber's influence on Ira Progroff's Meditations; see, e.g., *The Star/Cross: An Entrance Meditation* (New York: Dialogue House Library, 1981). I wish to thank Dr. Bill Mathews, S.J., for bringing this influence to my attention.

92. Schopenhauer expresses a similar position: "But to become practical, to guide conduct, to transform character, are old claims which with mature insight it [philosophy] ought finally to abandon. For here, where it is a question of the worth or worthlessness of existence, of salvation or damnation, not the dead concepts of philosophy decide the matter, but the innermost nature of man himself, the daemon which guides him and has not chosen him, but has been chosen by him, as Plato would say; his intelligible character, as Kant

puts it. Virtue is as little taught as is genius; indeed, the concept is just as unfruitful for it as it is for art, and in the case of both can be only used as an instrument. We should therefore be just as foolish to expect that our moral systems and ethics would create virtuous, noble and holy men, as that our aesthetics would produce poets, painters, and musicians." *The World as Will and Representation*, vol. 1, 271.

93. Following Buber's explicit relation of his position to that of Heraclitus, the understanding of *daimon* as man's character is justified. See Fragment B119, *The Presocratic Philosophers*, 210.

94. Dilthey's correlation of experience, expression, and understanding is evident here; see Chapter 2 above.

95. Voegelin, "The Beginning of the Beginning," in *In Search of Order*, 30.

96. This represents a hint of Buber's later philosophy of dialogue.

97. Scholem, *Major Trends in Jewish Mysticism*, 217. Buber asserts this position in *The Legend of the Baal-Shem*, 40.

98. The reference to the Platonic forms is evident.

99. Martin Buber, "Autobiographical Fragments," 16.

100. Note the distinction between observing and becoming aware that Buber expands later. See "Dialogue," in *Between Man and Man*, 8–10.

101. Martin Buber, "The Teaching of the Tao," 53.

102. See "Distance and Relation," in *The Knowledge of Man: Selected Essays*, 49–61. See also the autobiographical fragment, "The Walking Stick and the Tree,'" in *The Philosophy of Martin Buber*, 22–23. Although a footnote states that this fragment is reprinted from the English translation of *Daniel*, where it appears as the "Author's Preface," it does not appear in the 1919 German edition of *Daniel*. Friedman in his introduction argues that Buber in this dialogue and in particular in the notion of "inclusion" accepts the "over-against" as the separation of subject and object as essential to the otherness and concrete uniqueness of the Thou [see 32–33]; I would comment that Buber also stresses the "becoming one": the unity of a being with a single heart and the embracing love that treats the other as oneself. Buber has not yet reached the stage of recognizing the otherness and concrete uniqueness of the Thou.

103. See Buber's understanding of the inclusiveness and exclusiveness of the relation with God in *I and Thou*, 103–4. Buber also states in *I and Thou* that the person who experiences has no share in the world: "For it is 'in him' and not between him and the world that the experience arises. The world has no share in it. It permits itself to be experienced." See 18.

104. Friedman omits this phrase from the English translation.

105. In Norse mythology, Freyr is the god of fruitfulness and crops, of sun and rain. The maiden may refer to Freya—the goddess of love, marriage, and fertility—who is the sister of Freyr.

106. Buber, *I and Thou*, 35.

107. On the veil that conceals the glory of God, see Scholem, *Major Trends in Jewish Mysticism*, 72 and 272–73.

108. In the "Religion as Presence Lectures," Buber will have to face the problem that intensity of I-Thou relations between human beings cannot continue unbroken over time. The answer, then available to him, is the continuity of God as Eternal Thou.

109. Note the similarity between this transformation of the actor into the hero and the paradox of mystical sonship contained in the motto on the title page from Scotus Eriugena. The transformation is parallel to the birth of God in the soul.

110. See Eckhart, "And so when someone wholly conforms themselves to God through love, they are stripped of images and are in-formed and transformed into the divine uniformity in which they are one with God." Davies, *Meister Eckhart: Selected Writings*, 150.

111. In this description, Buber has outlined three of the four potencies of the soul mentioned in "Man and his Image Work," i.e., faith, love, and knowledge; the fourth, art, in the form of poetry and drama, is mentioned in the next few pages. See *The Knowledge of Man*, 153. See also *I and Thou* (59–62), where knowledge, art, and love are discussed before part three which relates to faith.

112. Friedman translates this as "life."

113. I will return to the meaning of this name for God later.

114. This image of the center into which the spokes converge is maintained in *I and Thou* to describe the relation between people in a community of love, each of whom have a living relation with the center, the Eternal Thou. See 65. It is also a Plotinian image: God is the "centre of that circle whose periphery they constitute." *Enneads*, 6.8.18, cited by von Balthasar, *The Glory of God*, 299–300.

115. Martin Buber, *Die Rede, die Lehre und das Lied* (Leipzig: Insel-Verlag, 1917), 6.

116. Note that this metaphor was cited by Buber in "The Teaching of the Tao" as the original undivided state—the primal existence from which all elements spring. "The Teaching of the Tao," 49.

117. Friedrich Nietzsche, *The Gay Science*, 119–20.

118. Empedocles returned to the mother by throwing himself into the flames of the volcano. See *The Presocratic Philosophers*, 281. Eckhart argues that one should entirely abandon oneself and cast oneself into "the fathomless ocean of the Godhead in order to experience the divine death"—which is his term for the phrase, "losing oneself in order to find oneself." *Meister Eckhart: Selected Writings*, 248.

119. Schopenhauer writes of the sea as supporting life and death: "Life itself is a sea full of rocks and whirlpools that man avoids with the greatest caution and care, although he knows that, even when he succeeds with all his efforts and ingenuity in struggling through, at every step he comes nearer to the greatest, the total, the inevitable and irremediable shipwreck, indeed even steers right on to it, namely death." *The World as Will and Representation*, vol. 1, 313.

120. Buber, "What is Man?" in *Between Man and Man*, 123.

121. Ibid., 124.

122. Paul Trainor, "Autobiography as Philosophical Argument: Socrates, Descartes, and Collingwood," in *Thought* 63, No. 251 (December 1988): 379. I wish to thank Dr. Bill Mathews, S.J., for drawing my attention to this article.

123. Ibid., 381.

124. Buber, in the "Autobiographical Fragments," does not mention this event. On this point, Schaeder refers us to the fact that Adele Buber had two

sons (*The Hebrew Humanism of Martin Buber*, 118). I conclude that the uncle who died was Rafael Buber, Carl Buber's only brother.

125. For Kierkegaard, despair is a necessary step to a higher form of existence; see John Douglas Mullen, *Kierkegaard's Philosophy: Self-Deception and Cowardice in the Present Age* (Lanham, Md.: University Press of America, 1995), 59–77 and 125. As a student, Buber read and was strongly influenced by Kierkegaard's *Fear and Trembling*: see "On the Suspension of the Ethical," in *Eclipse of God*, 115; see also Buber's "Afterword: The History of the Dialogical Principle," in *Between Man and Man*, 216. See Schaeder's discussion of Kierkegaard's influence on Buber in *The Hebrew Humanism of Martin Buber*, 212–25.

126. Buber, "The Life of the Hasidim," in *The Legend of the Baal-Shem*, 40.

127. Buber refers to the creative person as the watchtower warder of the earth—to whom the inner meaning of realization is revealed—the realizing man is the genuinely real [40–41]{71}. According to Kierkegaard, the deceptive soul is the one that does not want to be what it should be. See Mullen, *Kierkegaard's Philosophy*, 71.

128. In the Foreword to *Pointing the Way*, Buber points out that his understanding of the "one thing needful" changed in 1914 from that set out in "The Teaching of the Tao," which was written in 1909, and only after a further five years did the changed understanding "ripen to expression." See "Foreword" to *Pointing the Way*, x.

129. The three ways are identified by Erich Przywara, S.J., in "Judentum und Christentum," *Stimme der Zeit* 110 (1925– 26), 87. This reference is cited in Friedman, *The Life of Dialogue*, 39.

130. Friedman omits the rest of this phrase, i.e., "not as one who turns away, not as one torn from becoming."

131. Martin Buber, "Afterword," in *Between Man and Man*, 216.

132. Kohn identifies this second way with Spinoza's arguments. For Spinoza, God is the indivisible infinite substance in which attributes though distinct are at the same time intimately related. *Martin Buber: Sein Werk und Seine Zeit*, 132.

133. Martin Buber, *I and Thou*, 24–25 and 44–45.

134. Ibid., 126–27.

135. In *I and Thou*, when the locus of meaning is in the "between," the person comes ready wholly present for the meeting with the Thou, but must await the presence of the Thou. Thus, as Buber points out, the "relation means being chosen and choosing, suffering and action in one; just as any action of the whole being . . . is bound to resemble suffering." *I and Thou*, 24.

136. Friedman omits this important sentence.

137. This is an application of the *inquantum* maxim already mentioned.

138. Scholem, *Major Trends in Jewish Mysticism*, 110.

139. Scholem comments on Enoch: "I have been unable to discover a source in the older literature for the scurrilous legend current in the Middle Ages of Enoch the shoemaker—a mythical Jacob Boehme!—who with every stitch connected the upper and lower world. The legend may or may not have grown out of Hasidic circles in Mediaeval Germany." *Major Trends in Jewish Mysticism*, 365, n. 101. This legend is repeated in "The Baal-Shen Tov's Instruction in Intercourse with God." Here the point of the story is that the deed

should be bound to the thought by the action of the person. Thus the person would unify him or herself in action. God, who rules over his creation, is considered as the "thought" who utters the word: the *Shekina*. See *Hasidism and Modern Man*, 177, 206, and 212–13.

140. Kohn, *Martin Buber: Sein Werk und Seine Zeit*, 309–10, n. 87.1.

141. Buber, "The Life of the Hasidim," in *The Legend of the Baal-Shem*, 26–27.

142. Scholem, *Major Trends in Jewish Mysticism*, 111.

143. Ibid.

144. Martin Buber, "God and the Soul," in *The Origin and Meaning of Hasidism*.

145. Ibid., 187–88.

146. Ibid., 187.

147. Ibid., 189.

148. Ibid., 195.

149. Schopenhauer, *The World as Will and Representation*, vol. 2, 322.

150. Buber, "Renewal of Judaism," in *On Judaism*, 43.

151. Martensen, *Jacob Boehme*, part 2, chs. 1 and 2.

152. Ibid., 48.

153. Ibid., 50.

154. Ibid., 50.

155. Voegelin, "Reason: The Classic Experience," in *Anamnesis*, 104.

156. Buber, "With a Monist," in *Pointing the Way*, 28.

157. Ibid.

158. Ibid., 27.

159. Ibid., 29.

160. Ibid., 27.

161. Hans Kohn letter to Martin Buber, 14 November 1912, in *Letters of Martin Buber*, 140–41.

162. Martin Buber, *Briefwechsel aus sieben Jahrzehnten, Band I: 1897–1918*, 374–80.

163. "Ein Wort über Nietzsche und die Lebenswert." See discussion in chapter 2.

CHAPTER 5: THE PRESENCE OF GOD

1. Buber, "Autobiographical Fragments," 25–26.

2. Buber, *Between Man and Man*, 166.

3. Buber, *The Knowledge of Man*, 76–77.

4. Buber, *Between Man and Man*, 5.

5. Rivka Horwitz, *Buber's Way to "I and Thou": The Development of Martin Buber's Thought and His "Religion as Presence" Lectures*, trans. E. Cameron (Philadelphia: The Jewish Publication Society, 1988), 165.

6. Ibid.

7. Ibid.

8. Mendes-Flohr, *From Mysticism to Dialogue*, 97–102.

9. Ibid., 102.

10. Ibid.

11. Horwitz, *Buber's Way to "I and Thou,"* 104.

12. Ibid., 154.

13. Buber, "The Baal-Shem Tov's Instruction in Intercourse with God," in *Hasidism and Modern Man*, 172–73.

14. Rome and Rome, *Philosophical Interrogations*, 88.

15. Ibid., 90–91.

16. Buber, letter to Franz Werfel, *The Letters of Martin Buber*, 213–14.

17. See letter from Werfel to Buber, 6 May 1914, *The Letters of Martin Buber*, 154–55.

18. Buber noted that the translation of *metanoeite* as "repent" does not capture its eschatological connotation, namely, "to return." See English translation of letter in *The Letters of Martin Buber*, 214, n. 4. See also Buber's insistence that God is the redeemer and his agreement with the prophets' demand that human beings contribute their share "in the preparation for redemption: the active readiness of the whole existence," which is designated as "the 'turning,' turning to God." Answer given by Buber, see Rome and Rome, *Philosophical Interrogations*, 101.

19. See Rivka Horwitz, *Buber's Way to I and Thou: An Historical Analysis and the First Publication of Martin Buber's Lectures "Religion als Gegenwart"* (Heidelberg, Verlag Lambert Schneider, 1978), 157–58.

20. Ibid., 159.

21. Buber, "The Holy Way: A Word to the Jews and to the Nations," in *On Judaism*, 108–48.

22. Flohr has examined this influence in *From Mysticism to Dialogue*, see p. 97–113.

23. Ibid., 176, n. 165.

24. Buber, "The Holy Way," 124–25.

25. Ibid., 147.

26. Ibid., 109.

27. Buber, "Foreword," to *Pointing the Way*, x.

28. Buber, "The Holy Way," 109.

29. Mendes-Flohr notes that the term "earthly" did not appear in the first German edition of this essay. See *From Mysticism to Dialogue*, 175, n. 158.

30. Buber, "The Holy Way," 110.

31. Buber writes of the "Tent of Meeting" as one of the three sites of revelation in the story of Moses. The true tent is characterized by Moses entering it for the sake of "meeting" the deity. See "The Burning Bush (Exodus 3)," in *On The Bible: Eighteen Studies by Martin Buber* (New York: Syracuse University Press, 2000), 47; and "Holy Event (Exodus 19–27)," ibid., 70. See also Fritz Kaufmann, "Buber's Philosophy of Religion," in *The Philosophy of Martin Buber*, 209. Buber adds, in "The Holy Way," that God speaks to us out of the burning bush of the present and out of the *"Urim* and *Tummim"* of our innermost hearts. The informative function of divine speech was taken over by the *Urim* and *Tummim*, the sacred oracle vessels of the priest. See 137.

32. Buber, "The Holy Way," 111. This is one of Buber's major insights, or as he says himself, "the central portion of my life work" is that "the I-Thou relation to God and the I-Thou relation to one's fellow man are at bottom related to each other." See *Philosophical Interrogations*, 99.

33. The "Between" as it is actualized in relation is, according to Wood, the central notion in Buber's thought. Wood, *Martin Buber's Ontology*, 41.

34. Buber, "Herut: On Youth and Religion," in *On Judaism*, 150.

35. Ibid., 151.

36. Ibid., 153.

37. Ibid., 155. A similar notion is expressed by Plotinus: "the primordial energy of all things" is a "wellspring that has no source but itself, sharing itself with all rivers, yet never exhausted in this giving but remaining at rest in the streaming forth." Balthasar, *The Glory of the Lord*, 289.

38. Ibid. (Buber, "Herut: On Youth and Religion"), 153.

39. Buber, "On the Psychologizing of the World," in *A Believing Humanism*, 144.

40. Buber, "Herut: On Youth and Religion," 159.

41. These lectures were given by Buber at the Freies Judisches Lehrhaus in Frankfurt between 15 January and 12 March 1922. A stenographer transcribed them verbatim. See Horwitz, *Buber's Way to I and Thou*, 39.

42. Ibid., 187.

43. See Martin Buber's letter to Franz Rosenszweig, 8 December 1921, in *The Letters of Martin Buber*, 262–36.

44. Ibid., 263.

45. These lectures have been published in German by Horwitz in *Buber's Way to I and Thou*; see also the English translation published by the same author: *Buber's Way to "I and Thou*. Horwitz is particularly interested in the history of the development of *I and Thou* from 1918 to its publication.

46. Horwitz, *Buber's Way to I and Thou*, 19–20 [47]. I will adopt the convention of referring in the footnotes to the English translation and giving the German page references in brackets.

47. My use of "presence" and "present" will depend on the sentence; it will not follow exactly the translation by Esther Cameron that is used by Horwitz.

48. Buber, "Religion as Presence Lectures," in Horwitz, *Buber's Way to I and Thou*, 20 [49].

49. Ibid., 20–21 [48–49].

50. Ibid., 21 [49].

51. Buber, *Daniel: Dialogues on Realization*, 39 {70}.

52. Buber, "Religion as Presence Lectures," 21 [49].

53. Ibid., 32 [58].

54. Buber retains this distinction between traveling over the surface of something and entering into relation with it as a Thou in *I and Thou*. See 17.

55. Buber, "Religion as Presence Lectures," 32 [58].

56. Ibid.

57. This phrase is omitted from the English translation of the lectures. See 32 [59].

58. Buber, "Religion as Presence Lectures," 32 [59].

59. Ibid., 33 [60].

60. Ibid.

61. Buber repeats this rejection in *I and Thou*: "what turgid and presumptuous talk that is about the 'God who becomes.'" See 108–9.

62. Buber, "Religion as Presence Lectures," 34 [60].

63. Ibid.

64. See his comments on this in the "Postscript" to *I and Thou*, 167–71.

65. Buber, "Religion as Presence Lectures," 37 [63].

66. In an essay written in 1919, "What is to be Done?" Buber writes of this unreservedness as not withholding oneself from the direct meeting with others. His answer to the question is: "You shall not withhold yourself. You, imprisoned in the shells in which society, state, church, school, economy, public opinion, and your own pride have stuck you, indirect one among indirect ones, break through your shells, become direct; man, have contact with men!" This element of unreservedness is essential for the direct relation that Buber has placed as central to religion. "What is to be Done?" in *Pointing the Way*, 109. See also "Dialogue," where Buber writes that each person is able to enter into dialogue: "There are no gifted and ungifted here, only those who give themselves and those who withhold themselves." "Dialogue," in *Between Man and Man*, 35.

67. In *I and Thou*, Buber writes that the "free man is the one who wills without arbitrary self-will. This person must sacrifice his puny, unfree will, that is controlled by things and instincts, to his grand will, which quits defined for destined being. Then he intervenes no more, but at the same time he does not let things merely happen. He listens to what is emerging from himself, to the course of being in the world; not in order to be supported by it, but in order to bring it to reality as it desires, in its needs of him, to be brought—with human spirit and deed, human life and death. I said he believes, but that really means he meets." See 81–82. Note the similarity here to the "non-action" of Tao.

68. Buber, "Religion as Presence Lectures," 37 [64].

69. Buber, *Between Man and Man*, 74–75.

70. Ibid., 78–79.

71. Buber, "Religion as Presence Lectures," 38 [65].

72. Ibid., 39 [66].

73. Buber, *Hasidism and Modern Man*, 20.

74. Ibid., 19.

75. Buber, *I and Thou*, 72–73.

76. Buber, "Religion as Presence Lectures," 45 [72]. See *I and Thou*, 106–9, where Buber includes this critique in an altered form.

77. On the "errors" in Schleiermacher's theory, see Scheler's summary in *On the Eternal in Man*, 285–90. See, for example, his comment: "Schleiermacher thought himself entitled to trace religion back to isolated 'intuitions,' 'visions,' and 'emotional experiences' in the 'pious,' without regard for the essentially collective and communal character of religious experience." Ibid., 286.

78. Buber, "Religion as Presence Lectures," 47 [74].

79. Ibid., 48 [75].

80. Ibid., 50 [77].

81. Martin Buber, "What is Man?" in *Between Man and Man*, 184. See also Harold Bershady's "Introduction" to *Max Scheler on Feeling, Knowing, and Valuing: Selected Writings* (Chicago: The University of Chicago Press, 1992), 16.

82. Max Scheler, *Zur Phänomenologie der Sympathiegefühle und von Liebe and Hass: mit einem Anhang über den Grund zur Annahme der Existenz des fremden Ich* (Halle: Verlag Max Niemayer, 1913). As the title indicates, Scheler's argument on the question that interests us was originally

contained in an appendix. In the second edition, 1922, this appendix was included and extended in part three of the book.

83. See letter to Arnold Zweig, 28 January 1914. Subsequently, Scheler wrote an essay and then a book titled, *The Genius of War*. Bershady comments that the attitude Scheler expressed in his essay estranged him from his Berlin friends, including Buber. Buber's views on the war have been shown to be less pacifist than those of some other members of this circle, such as Landauer.

84. Buber is here referring to the section of Scheler's book, *Vom Ewigen im Menschen* [On the Eternal in Man], titled, "The Religious Act." This book was originally published in 1921, the year before Buber gave the "Religion as Presence" lectures. See Max Scheler, *On The Eternal in Man*, trans. B. Noble (London: SCM Press Ltd., 1960), 246.

85. See Buber's critique of Scheler in *I and Thou*, 134–36. Despite their differences, there remains a remarkable similarity between Scheler's radical solution of the originally undifferentiated psychic stream and the a priori of relation posited by Buber.

86. Buber, "Religion as Presence Lectures," 52 [78–79].

87. Ibid., 53 [79–80].

88. Ibid., 57–58 [84].

89. Ibid., 59 [85–86].

90. Ibid., 73 [98–99].

91. Ibid., 77 [103].

92. Ibid., 83 [108–9].

93. Buber, *I and Thou*, 43.

94. Ibid., 37.

95. Buber, "Religion as Presence Lectures," 113–14 [138]. See *I and Thou*, 139–42.

96. Ibid., 115–116 [140]. See *I and Thou*, 140–42.

97. Buber, "God and the Soul," in *The Origin and Meaning of Hasidism*, 196.

98. Buber, *I and Thou*, 102.

Bibliography

Aristotle. *Physics*. Books. 5–8. Loeb Classical Library Series. Translated by P. H. Wicksteed and F. M. Cornford. Cambridge, Mass.: Harvard University Press: 1934. Reprint, 1995.

Balthasar, H. U. von, *The Glory of The Lord: A Theological Aesthetics*. Vol. 4: *The Realm of Metaphysics in Antiquity*. Translated by B. McNeil, C.R.V., A. Louth, J. Saward, R. Williams, and O. Davies. Edited by J. Riches. Edinburgh: T. & T. Clark, 1989.

Benz, E. *Les sources mystiques de la philosophie romantique allemande*. Paris: J. Vrin, 1968.

Bergman, H. "Martin Buber and Mysticism." In *The Philosophy of Martin Buber*. Vol. 12 of The Library of Living Philosophers. Edited by P. A. Schilpp and M. Friedman. La Salle, Ill.: Open Court, 1967.

Bershady, H. *Max Scheler on Feeling, Knowing, and Valuing: Selected Writings*. Chicago: The University of Chicago Press, 1992.

Boehme, J. *The Clavis or Key or an Exposition of some principal Matters, and Words in the Writings of Jacob Boehme, also called Teutonicus Philosophus*.1647. Reprint, Whitefish, Mont.: Kessinger, 2000.

———. *Mysterium Magnum or An Exposition of the First Book of Moses called Genesis*. 2 vols. Translated by John Sparrow. 1623. Reprint, Montana: Kessinger, 2000.

Buber, M. "Alte und neue Gemeinschaft." Unpublished manuscript (1900): 1–10. Martin Buber Archive, Jerusalem, Ms. 47/b.

———. "Autobiographical Fragments." In *The Philosophy of Martin Buber*. Vol. 12 of The Library of Living Philosophers. Edited by P. A. Schilpp and M. Friedman. La Salle, Ill.: Open Court, 1967.

———. *Begegnung: Autobiographische Fragmente*. Stuttgart: W. Kohlhammer Verlag, 1960.

———. *A Believing Humanism: My Testament 1902–1965*. Credo Perspectives Series. Translated by M. Friedman. New York: Simon and Schuster, 1967.

————. *Between Man and Man*. With an Afterword by the author on "The History of the Dialogical Principle." Introduced by M. Friedman. Translated by R. Gregor Smith. New York: Collier Books, 1965.

————. *Briefwechsel aus sieben Jahrzehnten, Band I: 1897–1918*. Edited by Grete Schaeder. Heidelberg: Verlag Lambert Schneider, 1972.

————. "Ein Wort über Nietzsche und die Lebenswerte." *Die Kunst im Leben* 1, no. 2 (December 1900): 9.

————. *Daniel: Dialogues on Realization*. Translated with introduction by M. Friedman. New York: Holt, Rinehart and Winston, 1964.

————. *Daniel: Gespräche von der Verwirklichung*. 2 ed. Leipzig: Insel Verlag, 1919.

————. *Eclipse of God: Studies in the Relation between Religion and Philosophy*. Introduced by R. M. Seltzer. Atlantic Highlands, N.J.: Humanities Press, 1996. Reprint, New York: Humanity Books, 1999.

————. *Ecstatic Confessions: The Heart of Mysticism*. Collected and Introduced by Martin Buber. Edited by P. Mendes-Flohr. Translated by E. Cameron. San Francisco: Harper & Row, 1985. Reprint, New York: Syracuse University Press, 1996.

————. *For the Sake of Heaven*. Translated by L. Lewisohn. New York: Harper & Row, 1966.

————. *Hasidism and Modern Man*. Edited and translated by M. Friedman. New York: Horizon Press, 1958. Reprint, Atlantic Highlands, N.J.: Humanities Press, 1988.

————. *I and Thou*. 2 rev. ed. Translated by R. G. Smith. Edinburgh: T. & T. Clark, 1987.

————. *I and Thou*. Translated by W. Kaufmann. New York: Charles Scribner's Sons, 1970. Reprint, New York: Simon & Schuster, 1996.

————. *Ich und Du*. In *Martin Buber: Das dialogische Prinzip*. Heidelberg: Verlag Schneider, 1962. Reprint, Heidelberg: Lambert Schneider, 1997.

————. *Israel and the World: Essays in a Time of Crisis*. 2 ed. New York: Schocken Books, 1963. Reprint, Syracuse University Press, 1997.

————. *The Knowledge of Man: Selected Essays*. Edited with an Introductory essay by M. Friedman. Translated by M. Friedman and R. G. Smith. London: Allen & Unwin, 1965. Reprint, New Jersey: Humanities Press, 1992.

————. *The Legend of the Baal-Shem*. Translated by M. Friedman. San Francisco: Harper & Row, 1955. Reprint, Princeton, N.J.: Princeton University Press, 1995.

————. *The Letters of Martin Buber: A Life of Dialogue*. Edited by N. N. Glatzer and P. Mendes-Flohr. Translated by R. Winston, C. Winston, and H. Zohn. New York: Schocken Books, 1991. Reprint, Syracuse University Press, 1996.

————. *Meetings*. Edited by M. Friedman. La Salle, Ill.: Open Court, 1973.

————. *On Judaism*. Edited by N. N. Glatzer. "The Early Addresses." Translated by E. Jospe. New York: Schocken Books, 1967. Reprint, 1995.

————. *On the Bible: Eighteen Studies by Martin Buber*. Edited by N. N. Glatzer. Introduced by H. Bloom. New York: Syracuse University Press, 2000.

————. *The Origin and Meaning of Hasidism*. Edited and translated by M. Friedman. New York: Horizon Press, 1960. Reprint, Atlantic Highlands, N.J.: Humanities Press, 1996.

————. *Pointing the Way: Collected Essays.* Edited and translated by M. Friedman. New York: Harper & Bros., 1957. Reprint, New York: Humanity Books, 1999.

————. *Die Rede, die Lehre und das Lied.* Leipzig: Insel-Verlag, 1917.

————. "Religion als Gegenwart" Lectures. In R. Horwitz, *Buber's Way to I and Thou: An Historical Analysis and the First Publication of Martin Buber's Lectures "Religion als Gegenwart."* Heidelberg: Verlag Lambert Schneider, 1978.

————. "Religion as Presence" Lectures. In R. Horwitz, *Buber's Way to "I and Thou": The Development of Martin Buber's Thought and His "Religion as Presence" Lectures.* Translation of "Religion als Gegenwart" by E. Cameron. Philadelphia: The Jewish Publication Society, 1988.

————. "Replies to my Critics." In *The Philosophy of Martin Buber.* Vol. 12 of The Library of Living Philosophers. Edited by P. A. Schilpp and M. Friedman. La Salle, Ill.: Open Court, 1967.

————. "Über Jakob Boehme." *Wiener Rundschau* 5, no. 12 (15 June 1901): 251–53.

————. "Zur Geschichte des Individuationsproblems (Nicolaus von Cues und Jakob Böhme)." Unpublished PhD. dissertation (1904): 1–38. Martin Buber Archive, Jerusalem, Ms. 350/2–1c.

Copleston, F., S..J. *A History of Philosophy.* Vols. 2 and 3. Tunbridge Wells, U.K.: Paulist Press, 1950.

Derrida, J. *Of Grammatology.* Translated by G. C. Spivak. Baltimore: John Hopkins University Press, 1976.

————. *Writing and Difference.* Translated, with introduction and additional notes, by Alan Bass. London: Routledge & Kegan Paul, 1978. Reprint, 1993.

Dilthey W. *W. Dilthey: Selected Writings.* Edited, translated, and with introduction by H. P. Rickman. Cambridge: Cambridge University Press, 1976.

Eckhart, Meister. *Meister Eckhart: Selected Writings.* Selected and translated and with introduction by O. Davies. London: Penguin Books, 1994.

Fackenheim, E. L. *God's Presence in History: Jewish Affirmations and Philosophical Reflections.* New York: New York University Press, 1970. Reprint, Northvale, N.J.: Jason Aronson, 1997.

————. "Martin Buber's Concept of Revelation." In *The Philosophy of Martin Buber.* Vol. 12 of The Library of Living Philosophers. Edited by P. A. Schilpp and M. Friedman. La Salle, Ill.: Open Court, 1967.

Feuerbach, L. *The Essence of Christianity.* Translated by M. Evans. London: Trubner, 1881. Reprint, New York: Harper & Bros., 1957.

————. *Principles of the Philosophy of the Future.* Translated by M. H. Vogel. Indianapolis: Bobbs-Merrill, 1966. Reprint, Hackett, 1986.

Friedman, M., editor. *Martin Buber and the Human Sciences.* New York: State University of New York Press, 1996.

————. *Martin Buber: The Life of Dialogue.* Chicago: University of Chicago Press, 1956.

————. *Martin Buber's Life and Work.* 3 vols. Detroit: Wayne State University Press, 1988.

Frings, M. S. *Max Scheler: A Concise Introduction into the World of a Great Thinker.* Pittsburgh: Duquesne University Press, 1965.

Gadamer, H.-G. *Truth and Method*. 2 rev. ed. Translation revised by J. Weins-
heimer and D. G. Marshall. London: Sheed and Ward, 1989. Reprint,
1993.

Gardiner, P. *Schopenhauer*. Harmondsworth, U.K.: Penguin, 1967.

Gilson, E. *Being and Some Philosophers*. 2 ed. Toronto: Pontifical Institute
of Mediaeval Studies, 1952. Reprint, 1961.

Gordon, H. *The Other Martin Buber: Recollections of his Contemporaries*.
Ohio: Ohio University Press, 1988.

Gordon, H. and J. Bloch, eds. *Martin Buber: A Centenary Volume*. Jersey
City, N.J.: KTAV, 1984.

Gregson, V. *Lonergan, Spirituality and the Meeting of Religions*. College
Theology Society Studies in Religion: 2. Lanham, Md.: University Press
of America, 1985.

Guthrie, W. K. C. *A History of Greek Philosophy*. Vol. 6. Cambridge: Cambridge University Press, 1981. Reprint, 1990.

Harper, R. *On Presence: Variations and Reflections*. Philadelphia: Trinity
Press Int., 1991.

Herman, Jonathan. *Martin Buber and the Human Sciences*. State University
of New York Press, 1996.

Hodes, A. *Encounter with Martin Buber*. London: Penguin Press, 1972.

Horwitz, R. *Buber's Way to I and Thou, An Historical Analysis and the First
Publication of Martin Buber's Lectures "Religion als Gegenwart."* Heidelberg: Verlag Lambert Schneider, 1978.

————. *Buber's Way to "I and Thou," The Development of Martin Buber's
Thought and His "Religion as Presence" Lectures*. Translation of "Religion als Gegenwart" by E. Cameron. Philadelphia: The Jewish Publication Society, 1988.

Husserl, Edmund. *Cartesian Meditations: An Introduction to Phenomenology*. Translated by D. Cairns. The Hague: Martinus Nijhoff, 1960.

John of the Cross. *The Collected Works of St. John of the Cross*. Translated
by K. Kavanaugh, O.C.D., and O. Rodriguez, O.C.D. Washington, D.C.:
ICS Publications, 1991.

Kant, I. *Critique of Pure Reason*. Translated by N.-K. Smith. London: Macmillan, 1929; reprint, 1964.

————. *Groundwork of the Metaphysic of Morals*. Translated by H. J. Paton.
London: Routledge, 1993.

————. *Lectures on Philosophical Theology*. Translated by A. W. Wood and
G. M. Clark. London: Cornell University Press, 1978.

————. *Prolegomena to Any Future Metaphysics That Will Be Able to Present Itself As a Science: With Two Early Reviews of "The Critique of Pure
Reason."* Edited by Günter Zöller; translated by Peter G. Lucas and Günter Zöller. Oxford: Oxford University Press, 2004.

Kepnes, S. *The Text as Thou: Martin Buber's Dialogical Hermeneutics and
Narrative Theology*. Bloomington: Indiana University Press, 1992.

Kirk, G. S., J. E. Raven, and M. Schofield. *The Presocratic Philosophers: A
Critical History with a Selection of Texts*. 2nd ed. Cambridge: Cambridge
University Press, 1957. Reprint, 1991.

Kohn, H. *Martin Buber: Sein Werk und Seine Zeit*. Cologne: Joseph Melzer
Verlag, 1961.

Levinas, E. "Martin Buber and the Theory of Knowledge." In *The Philosophy of Martin Buber*. Vol. 12 of The Library of Living Philosophers. Edited by P. A. Schilpp and M. Friedman. La Salle, Ill.: Open Court, 1967.

———. *Outside the Subject.* Translated by M. B. Smith. London: Athlone Press, 1993.

Lonergan, B., S.J. *Method in Theology.* London: Darton, Longman & Todd, 1972.

Maréchal, J., S.J. *Studies in the Psychology of the Mystics.* Translated, with an Introductory Foreword, by A. Thorold. London: Burns Oates & Washbourne, 1927.

Martensen, H. *Jacob Boehme (1574–1624): Studies in his Life and Teaching.* Translated by T. Rhys Evans. New revised edition. London: Rockliff, 1949.

Mauthner, F. *Wörterbuch der Philosophie, neue Beiträge zu einer Kritik der Sprache.* 2nd ed. Munich and Leipzig: 1920. Quoted in P. Mendes-Flohr, editor's introduction, in *Ecstatic Confessions: The Heart of Mysticism.* Translated by E. Cameron. San Francisco: Harper & Row, 1985. Reprint, Syracuse University Press, 1996.

Mendes-Flohr, P. *From Mysticism to Dialogue: Martin Buber's Transformation of German Social Thought.* Detroit: Wayne State University Press, 1989.

Moore, D. J. *Martin Buber: Prophet of Religious Secularism.* 2nd ed. New York: Fordham University Press, 1996.

Morelli, E. M. "Oversight of Insight and the Critique of the Metaphysics of Presence." *Method: Journal of Lonergan Studies* 18, no.1 (Spring 2000): 1–15.

Mullen, J. D. *Kierkegaard's Philosophy: Self-Deception and Cowardice in the Present Age.* Lanham, Md.: University Press of America, 1995.

Munk, G. *Die unechten Kinder Adams,* Leipzig: Insel-Verlag, 1912.

Murphy, D. *Martin Buber's Philosophy of Education.* Dublin: Irish Academic Press, 1988.

Nietzsche, F. *The Gay Science: With a Prelude in German Rhymes and an Appendix of Songs.* Edited by B. Williams. Translated by J. Nauckhoff; poems translated by A. Del Caro. Cambridge: Cambridge University Press, 2001.

———. *Thus Spoke Zarathustra,* London: Penguin, 1969.

Owens, T. J. *Phenomenology and Intersubjectivity: Contemporary Interpretations of the Interpersonal Situation.* The Hague: Martinus Nijhoff, 1970.

Plato, *The Republic.* Translated by G. M. A. Grube. Indianapolis: Hackett, 1974.

Pilardi, Jo-Ann. *Simone de Beauvoir Writing the Self: Philosophy becomes Autobiography.* Westport, Ct.: Praeger, 1999.

Progroff, Ira. *The Star/Cross: An Entrance Meditation.* New York: Dialogue House Library, 1981.

Rickman, H. P. *Wilhelm Dilthey: Pioneer of the Human Studies.* London: Paul Elek, 1979. Reprint, Berkeley: University of California Press, 1979.

Rome, S., and Rome, B. *Philosophical Interrogations.* Edited, with introduction, by S. and B. Rome. New York: Holt, Rinehart and Winston, 1964.

Rosenzweig, F. "Aus Bubers Dissertation." In *Aus Unbekannten Schriften. Festgabe für Martin Buber zum 50. Geburtstag.* Berlin: Verlag Lambert Schneider, 1928.

Rotenstreich, N. *Immediacy and its Limits: A Study in Martin Buber's Thought.* Chur, Switzerland: Harwood Academic Publishers, 1991.

Safranski, R. *Martin Heidegger: Between Good and Evil.* Translated by E. Osers. Cambridge, Mass.: Harvard University Press, 1998.

Schaeder, G. *The Hebrew Humanism of Martin Buber.* Translated by N. J. Jacobs. Detroit: Wayne State University Press, 1973.

———. "Martin Buber: A Biographical Sketch." In *The Letters of Martin Buber: A Life of Dialogue.* Edited by N. N. Glatzer and P. Mendes-Flohr. New York: Schocken Books, 1991. Reprint, Syracuse University Press, 1996.

Scheler, M. *The Nature of Sympathy.* Translated by P. Heath. London: Routledge & Kegan Paul, 1954.

———. *On the Eternal in Man.* Translated by B. Noble. London: SCM Press, 1960.

Scholem, G. *Major Trends in Jewish Mysticism.* New York: Schocken Books, 1974.

Schopenhauer, A. *The World as Will and Representation.* 2 vols. Translated by E. F. J. Payne. Colorado: The Falcon's Wing Press, 1958. Reprint, New York: Dover, 1969.

Schorske, C. *Fin-de-Siècle Vienna: Politics and Culture.* New York: Knopf, 1980. Quoted in S. Kepnes, *The Text as Thou, Martin Buber's Dialogical Hermeneutics and Narrative Theology.* Bloomington: Indiana University Press, 1992.

Schutz, A. *Alfred Schutz: Collected Papers. Vol. 1: The Problem of Social Reality.* Edited and Introduced by M. Natanson. The Hague: Martinus Nijhoff, 1973.

Smith, R. G. *Martin Buber.* London: The Carey Kingsgate Press, 1966.

St. Amour, P. "Presence and Differentiation: A Response to Elizabeth Morelli's 'Oversight of Insight' and the Critique of the Metaphysics of Presence." *Method: Journal of Lonergan Studies* 18, no. 1 (Spring 2000): 17–26.

Steiner, G. *Real Presences.* Chicago: University of Chicago Press, 1989. Paperback edition, 1991.

Tallon, A. "Intentionality, Intersubjectivity, and the Between: Buber and Levinas on Affectivity and the Dialogical Principle." *Thought* 53, no.210 (September 1978): 292–309.

———. "Person and Community. Buber's Category of the Between." *Philosophy Today,* Spring 1973: 62–76.

Trainor, P. "Autobiography as Philosophical Argument: Socrates, Descartes, and Collingwood." *Thought* 63, no. 251 (December 1988): 378–96.

Ueberweg, F. *A History of Philosophy, From Thales to the Present Time. Vol. 1: History of the Ancient and Mediaeval Philosophy.* 2nd ed. Translated from the fourth German edition by G. S. Morris with additions by N. Porter. London: Hodder & Stoughton, 1875.

Underhill, E. *Mysticism: A Study in the Nature and Development of Man's Spiritual Consciousness.* London: Methuen, 1949.

Voegelin, E. *Anamnesis.* Translated and edited by G. Niemeyer. Columbia: University of Missouri Press, 1990.

———. *The Collected Works of Eric Voegelin.* Vol. 12, *Published Essays 1966–1985,* edited with an introduction by E. Sandoz. Baton Rouge: Louisiana State University Press, 1990.

———. *The Collected Works of Eric Voegelin*. Vol. 28, *What Is History? And Other Late Unpublished Writings*. Edited with an introduction by T. A. Hollweck and P. Carringella. Baton Rouge: Louisiana State University Press, 1990.

———. *Order and History*. Vol. 2, *The World of the Polis*. Baton Rouge: Louisiana State University Press, 1957. Reprint, 1991.

———. *Order and History*. Vol. 5, *In Search of Order*. Baton Rouge: Louisiana State University Press, 1987.

———. *Plato*. Baton Rouge: Louisiana State University Press, 1966. Reprint, 1981.

Walsh, D. *The Mysticism Of Innerworldly Fulfillment: A Study of Jacob Boehme*. Gainesville: University Presses of Florida, 1983.

Windelband, W. *A History of Philosophy with Especial Reference to The Formation and Development of its Problems and Conceptions*. Translated by J. H. Tufts. 2nd ed., rev. and enlarged. London: Macmillan & Co. 1910.

Winkler, P. "Betrachtungen einer Philozionistin." *Die Welt* (Vienna) no. 36, 6 September 1901, 4–6.

Wittgenstein, L. *Tractus Logico-Philosophicus*. Translated by D. F. Pears and B. F. McGuinness. London: Routledge & Kegan Paul, 1974. Reprint, 1994.

Wood, R. E., *Martin Buber's Ontology*. Northwestern University Studies in Phenomenology and Existential Philosophy, ed., J. Wild. Evanston: Northwestern University Press, 1969.

Index